The Piikani Blackfeet

A CULTURE UNDER SIEGE

John C. Jackson

MOUNTAIN PRESS PUBLISHING COMPANY
Missoula, Montana
2000

© 2000 *John C. Jackson*

*Library of Congress
Cataloging-in-Publication Data*

Jackson, John C., 1931–
    The Piikani Blackfeet : a culture under siege / John C. Jackson.
        p.   cm.
    Includes bibliographical references and index.
    ISBN 0-87842-386-9 (alk. paper) — ISBN 0-87842-385-0 (alk. paper)
    1. Piegan Indians—History. 2. Piegan Indians—Ethnic identity. I. Title.
E99.P58 J33 2000
978.004'973—dc21   00-027023

Mountain Press Publishing Company
P.O. Box 2399 • Missoula, MT 59806
(406) 728-1900

This book is for
Alvin and Betty.

CONTENTS

Preface

The old ones are only shadows now, silhouettes moving silently in the soft dawn toward another camp and dancing around the glow of a buffalo-chip fire. Sometimes, in the sunset, a feathered horseman casts a long shadow across the hillside; too often, the image recedes and vanishes. Like a child trying to capture a shadow by tracing it in the sand, this book attempts to outline figures that have stepped away from definition.

For the brief span of a century and a half, the horse people shimmered in the dazzling light of the northern plains. Then, like the buffalo, they were gone. Their lives merit careful attention that goes beyond stereotyping, sketchy images caught by a fur trader's pen, or cold scientific re-examination. Yet this is not another book about injustices, laden with unresolved guilt and smothering sympathy.

The absence of references to Piikani spiritualism in this work is deliberate. "Sacred" appears to be a borrowed word, and the dreams and beliefs of tribal faith seem to have been idealized to satisfy popular appetites. The honorable past of a changed people stands beyond generalizations and fantasy, and unbiased examination reveals astonishing depths of personal and public commitment.

Their country stretched from the Red Deer River to the springs of the Missouri. Depending on the season, the undulating landscape may seem lush and green, or dry and dusty. A casual traveler might find it puzzling that people survived here. But the short-grass prairie nourished immense herds of buffalo.

In this place, in the late eighteenth century, the Piikani were struggling to rebound after a third or perhaps half of them had been swept away by smallpox. Pitted survivors taught the new generation the rules of the hunt. To the fledgling majority, who never knew a world without horses, the expanding world belonged to them. There must have been a moment when the recovering population peaked, when there were more horse Indians than there would ever be again. An inconceivable concept, it would not be recorded in the winter counts. But the People did recognize the year when the buffalo herds failed to return and there was no more real meat.

Most often, it was white traders who recorded the momentous changes imposed on the Piikani. As outsiders, unable to grasp alternative views of the earth as more than real estate, they missed the critical implications these changes had on this place and its inhabitants. Later, well-meaning missionaries would exploit native innocence by imposing a puzzling burden of Old World guilt upon Naapi's people.

Sometimes the darkness of the past is illuminated by a sign as simple as falling stars painted on a hide, or by a stranger's letter, journal entry, or treaty composed by candlelight. Sometimes we glimpse a family silhouetted inside a tipi, or warriors frozen in the strobe of muzzle flashes. More often, invisible speakers murmur in the shadows.

The lives of the old ones cannot be fully revealed by deductions drawn from recovered artifacts and old documents. Staying closer to individuals through select clues seems a better way to recapture a lost humanity, and what follows are scraps from many bowls.

Those who kindly guided my rambling research include Dan Greer, Jim Keyser, David Miller, Edward and Mary Black-Rogers, Tom Thiessen, Dale Russell, and Ray Wood. Donald G. Frantz provided the standard for a consistent vocabulary in his *Blackfoot Dictionary*. Shirlee Anne Smith is a loyal friend and unrewarded critic. Judith Hudson Beattie keeps the marvelous resources of the Hudson's Bay archives with generosity and good humor. In an eleventh-hour reading, Bill Farr provided insightful suggestions, as well as helping to secure use of the cover painting. Editor Gwen McKenna tended the book through the witching hour with consummate skill.

My appreciation of the humanity, strength, and love in today's Piikani community flows from a kinswoman, Nettie Connell, and her son Tom. I am also inspired by the example of Alvin M. Josephy Jr., who set a lasting standard for sensitive consideration of Native Americans and remains their champion.

Synonymy

In names and in naming there is power. It is by names we know ourselves and others know us, by names we gain control of our identity. This selective synonymy is meant to help the reader sort out the various names that have been applied to the people of the northwestern plains.

Fur traders used the terms Gens du Large and Plains (or Meadow) Indians to refer to three related but distinct groups: Siksika, Kainaa, and Piikani.

Siksika, from *siksikauwa* (Black-footed People), became Blackfeet or Blackfoot. The term Blackfeet eventually came to refer to all three bands, and in time this was inflated into the fictive paradigm Blackfoot Confederacy.

Kainaa were also known as Blood (or Bloody) Indians or as Gens du Sang.

Piikani, or Piegan, was variously spelled Peekanow, Pahkee, Pekan, Piedgan, Pikenow, Pekannekoon, Pikaraminiouach, and many other ways. The name comes from *pa'ksikahko*, a muddy place, which in Cree becomes *pikan* or *pikakamiw*, muddy or turbid water. The Piikani were known to the traders as Muddy River Indians. The Cree called them Archithinue, Strangers, Muscotay, Hiatchiritiny, or Slaves. Niitsitapi (the People) was the Piikani's name for themselves. In recent times the Piikani have been called North Piegan. The name of one Piikani band, Inuk'sik, derives from *ikimmata* (poor or pitiful) or *inak ann* (small robes).

Other Niitsitapi neighbors on the northern plains included the Atsiina and the Saahsi.

Atsiina called themselves *aa'nimena* (White Clay People), and their Arapaho relatives called them *hitoune'nan*, or Spongers. Traders knew them as Gros Ventre, or Falls (or Rapid, or Waterfall) Indians.

Saahsi were also called Sarcee (with variations), or Strange Indians.

Two major forces in the Niitsitapi experience were the Asinaa (Cree) and the Assiniboine.

Cree were known to the fur traders as Southern or Southerd Indians. A widely dispersed people, Cree bands included the Pegogamaw or Muddy Water Cree; Sturgeon River Cree; Misshenippee; and Eagle Hill or Upland Cree.

Assiniboine were also called Stone, Stoney, or Plain Stone Indians, and sometimes Paddling Indians. Those who moved west and hunted in the northern forests or the Rocky Mountains were known to the traders as Swampy Ground Stoney, Thickwood (or Strong Wood) Stoney, or Mountain Stoney.

Other peoples who came in contact with the Piikani include the following:

Northern Shoshone, or Snakes
   (*pitsiiksiinaitapi* to the People)
Crow (Mountain Crow and River Crow),
   aka Issapo, Absaroka
Kutenai
Salish, or Flathead
Kalispell, aka Ear Bobs
Coeur d'Alene (Pointed Hearts)
Spokane
Nez Perce (Pierced Noses)

In the tribe of Euro-Americans, the French were *niitsaapiikoan* (literally, original white man); the English were *niita'piaakiikoan* (real white man); and Americans were *omahksisttowyaapiikoan* (long knife), which appears to be a recently borrowed term.

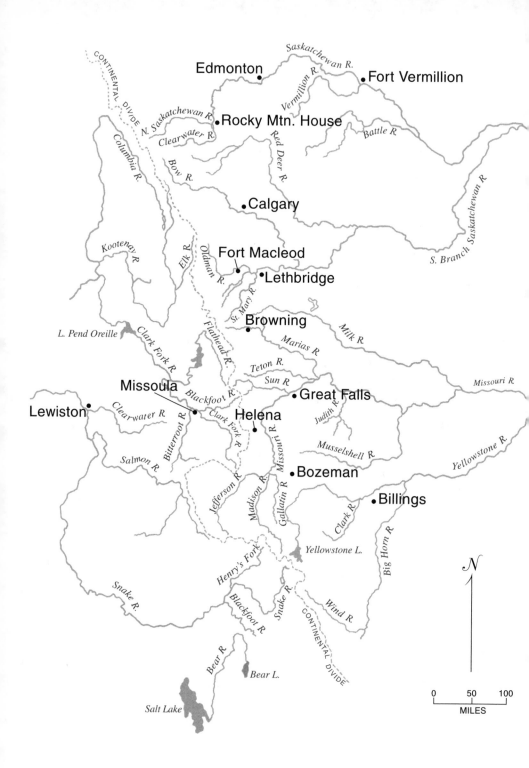

Overview of the ranges of the Piikani

ONE

In the Dog Days

inii! There was a distant, continuous drone, the mingled lowing and bellowing of thousands of animals. Sometimes a low rumble drummed from trampled grass. It was the thunder of stampeding buffalo in numbers beyond comprehension. Those herds conditioned the world of the northwestern plains; the *niitsitapi* (the People) believed that Naapi, the creator, had made them out of mud. More were still under the ground, waiting to come out. The plains herds, broad-horned wood buffalo, roamed the northern regions, while a smaller, darker breed favored the sheltered meadows and valleys of the western foothills. Their migratory patterns ran north and south along the east side of the Rocky Mountains. Buffalo-friendly parklands reached as far south as the Red Deer River, and there were attractive places on the upper Bow. On the open plains, deeply incised river bottoms offered protection from the unrelenting prairie winds, but the buffalo were resolute animals that preferred to face into storms.

Pedestrian hunters and their dogs found the herds in the parklands and piedmont. Those bowmen and spear men were part of an ancient symbiosis, the hunting band and its prey, older than the dreams of Naapi. For centuries the hunters shared in the great communion of real meat, the buffalo. They had worshiped at this woolly altar since the first Americans tentatively sidled down glacier-carved valleys and found giant bison on the sodden plains.

These people who hunted with sticks and stones ate the prehistoric animals into extinction, while smaller, more specifically adapted buffalo inherited the continent and multiplied beyond count. That wonder defied explanation; the buffalo must be extruded through a hole from some endless magma of flesh beneath the ground. Somehow that became connected to the beaver bundle, which contained reminders of all life. The keeper opened it to ask for a successful hunt. Beaver and buffalo, beaver and buffalo.

Early hunters with families to feed were grateful to be left in the dust with a carcass to cut up and carry back to camp. They learned to work together, building corrals of tangled branches where they might corner and slaughter several animals at once. They piled up heaps of buffalo dung or stones to make extended wings that funneled their prey toward the pound. Everyone turned out to haze the nervous grazers into the slaughter yard. If the hunters saw a favorable opportunity, they might incite a herd to stampede over a bluff, where they could kill the injured animals more easily.

In winter, hunters put on snowshoes and allowed their dogs to harry the great beasts into large snowdrifts, where they were immobilized and therefore less dangerous to approach and kill. The half-wolves that traveled with the men could also pull sleds in winter and small drags in summer, but not much more than seventy pounds of meat on a load. Even after gorging on the leftovers, the wolfish creatures were untrustworthy with provisions. Sometimes the men disciplined them cruelly with whips and clubs. During the starving times, the wolf-dogs might go into the cooking basket.

The People were nomads of limited mobility, small bands of extended families that moved as the animals did. They tried to stay within walking distance of the rivers and sheltering woods but ranged onto the grasslands when necessary. When bands came together to construct a pound or make a drive, they could kill enough animals to sustain larger camps.

While those group efforts demanded that individuals work under some kind of temporary authority, the Niitsitapi remained independent-minded. Conservative elders could help temper the rash enthusiasm of the young men, but they really couldn't tell them what to do. The dutiful

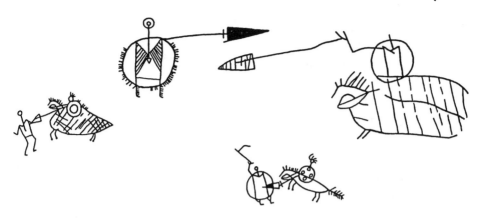

This Indian rendition of a battle scene shows mounted warriors on armored horses. The presence of horse armor, known to have been used only by the Shoshone, could indicate early conflicts between northward-ranging Shoshone and the Piikani before the latter obtained horses.[1] —Courtesy James D. Keyser

women worked hard to maintain the camp, and the respect they earned was not displayed through superficial manners, but dwelled in the hearts of those who depended on them.

They were a bloody people, professional butchers, whose children were raised with the spectacle of a pound strewn with steaming carcasses. Toddlers were taught to take a triumphant hunter's ritual first bite of dripping liver. In the greasy feast that followed, everyone ate to make up for the hungry times. Even the old ones enjoyed a full belly and the promise of another tomorrow. That world was hard and trying, but it was complete and worked quite well.

The People lived in a world without square walls or implied limitations. Home was a cone of gently breathing animal hides. The supple irregularity did not foster abstract thought; the firelight reflecting on the lodgepoles pointed toward the open smoke hole and the great mystery of the stars above. Half-sunken circles of stones that once held down the bottoms of their tents remain on the prairies today. The People were born, grew up, lived, and died within the elbow-close intimacy of the lodge. The leather walls were a constant reminder of the debt they owed to the buffalo. Practical habits of camp life, hunting, and war were entwined with matters of the spirit in their being. They expressed these mysteries through rituals rich in prerogative and taboo.

Out of respect, believers blew smoke to the four cardinal directions, to the earth, and to the sky.

Their answer to the inevitable question of creation was that in a time long ago, Old Man and Old Woman made the world out of mud from beneath the water. Like all couples, the two did not always agree. When it came to deciding how people should live, Old Man (Naapi) claimed the right of the first say. "Let people have eyes and mouths in their faces lined up and down."

But Old Woman, who had settled for speaking second, said no, "let eyes and mouth be set crossways."

"Well then, people should have ten fingers on each hand."

No again, "too many, just four fingers and a thumb."

"The organs to make children should be at the navel."

"Too easy. If bearing children is too easy children may be neglected."

Old Man was beginning to see that he had made a bad bargain giving his wife the final word on creation. But there was one final matter: How long should people live? He proposed to throw a buffalo chip into the water, and if it floated, people would die for only four days before living again.

But Old Woman told him to use a stone. "If it sinks, people will die forever and we will know how to feel sorry for each other."[1]

TWO

Names for the People

he streams of the northwestern plains run cloudy with the powdery residue of the continental backbone. The Rocky Mountains are a craggy wall, but in the south they break up into an archipelago of ranges rising from the grasslands. In the high places of the north, during the few weeks of short, intense summers, melting ice and snow begin the reductive process. Droplets of water trickle into tiny cracks in the rock and refreeze during the night. The expanding ice widens the opening until a fragment of rock is levered off and crashes down the cliff. Rockfalls are the echoing thunder of the mountains. Trickles become rivulets and dashing creeks, which turn and grind the fallen rocks against each other. Sand and silt wash down the steep gradient, clouding the rivers of the plains.

On the South Branch of the Saskatchewan, the roiling water is yellowish brown. The term for a muddy place in the Blackfoot language is *pa'ksikahko*, close to the Cree term *pikan* or *pikakamiw*, which also means muddy or turbid water.[2] Later, downstream traders distorted the Cree term *pegogamaw*, describing their own "muddy water" people, into a fog of spellings describing the Piikani, which translated as Muddy River Indians.[3]

The People came into the historical record through the perceptions of others. Their *asinaa* (Cree) trading partners presumed to call them *iyagihi-inninew* (Slave Indians), a sly allusion to their dependence on goods that the Cree obtained from the strangers at the bay. Those European traders wrote the name as "Archithinue." However, the Niitsitapi knew themselves as the real people and divided themselves into three groups of like speakers, the *piikani,* the *kainaa,* and the *siksika.*[4] The Kainaa became known as the Bloods, and the Siksika entered the record as the Black Foot Indians.[5] Closely associated, but speaking different tongues, were two migrant peoples: the *atsiina,* of southern origin, and the *saahsi,* who drifted down from the north.[6]

Names are how others know you. A case in point were the *aa'nimena,* or White Clay People. Early traders associated them with the rapids of the South Branch of the Saskatchewan River and called them the Falls, or Rapid, Indians. They tried the hospitality of their Piikani neighbors, who called them *atsiina,* the Gut People. Earlier, these people's demanding nature led French traders to disparage them as the *Gros Ventre,* or Big Belly Indians. Even their Arapaho relatives knew them as *hitoune'nan,* meaning Spongers.

How outsiders thought of the Niitsitapi made little difference to individuals, who understood who they were and felt free to change personal names to mark significant events in their lives. Groups were more concerned with identifying outsiders. When they came together in larger camps, those group names were often the teasing, slightly derogatory designations of neighbors. Later, the writings of poorly informed Europeans froze individual identities and group names into simplistic translations of these attributed names.

Cree and Assiniboine intermediaries first brought the Archithinue into the historical record. French traders from the distant St. Lawrence River and English traders from Hudson's Bay heard muddled accounts of Eagle Indians. This probably referred to the Eagle Hills, where young men dug pits to catch the great birds. As inland travelers pushed up the Saskatchewan River, their open-ended itineraries allowed for adding knowledge to a gradually improving understanding. But those adventurers were fur traders, not social scientists, and their observations were colored by expectation, exasperation, and ever-present apprehension.

To men carrying the obsolete baggage of the Old World, the Archithinue were not easy to comprehend. They seemed to be organized into families, bands, or groups of bands or camps, but they lacked the overriding social organization that Europeans recognized. Their odd habits of changing names and taking several wives created a genealogical maze more baffling than the lineages of Old World royalty. The mixing and churning of groups through intermarriage, capture, or individual whim was beyond the grasp of the strangers. The natives' names and vocabularies twisted the tongues of English, French, and Gaelic speakers and defied the spelling skills of trading-company clerks.

Content to be who they were, the People were too distant to sense the earthquake tremors when the *aapamiaapiikoaiksi* (Across the Ocean People) first stepped ashore. The Cree, living closer to the great salt bay, were the first to experience the wonders of the *naapiikoaiksi* (white people). As the European gospel of commerce took root, the Cree and their Assiniboine neighbors soon learned the advantages of carrying iron and brass and cloth up the Saskatchewan River to distant peoples.

The lakes and rivers of the Canadian shield were the home of the water-bound Cree. To a canoe people discomforted by the expanses opening above the riverbanks, the grasslands must have seemed like a great lake surging in the unrelenting winds. The Cree preferred to hunt in meadows broken by islands of birch and pine trees, where pools of wapiti eddied in the tidal ebb and flow of immense buffalo herds. Anyone who pressed up the Saskatchewan paddled against the spring freshet from the mountains. The ones who reached the muddy western waters became known as Pegogamaw Cree.[7] The people they met there were also called the Muddy River People.

The long return voyage to the bay required experienced paddlers to run those challenging waters. But the pedestrian hunters of the Niitsitapi were unfamiliar with the two- or three-man Cree canoes, and a clumsy passenger who couldn't pull his paddle could be dangerous. Only a few westerners were taken down to impress the Englishmen. Sitting all day in cold water, terrified by the raging rapids, was not a pleasant experience. During the half century that Cree and Assiniboine middlemen brought metal tools, utensils, and iron arrowheads to the parklands and prairies, only a few adventuresome plainsmen ever tasted the bitter water. In the end, the white men's log lodges sagging in the bayside mud were not that impressive, so few heroes who completed the mythological journey cared to repeat it.

How did the Niitsitapi feel about the strangers? Rumors surely passed from group to group describing men who were remarkably different in their dress, speech, actions, and possessions. Around the lodge fire the People speculated on the bits of worn-out metal, knives that had been resharpened down to steel slivers, brass pots too often put to the fire, and odd tatters of faded cloth that were traded from Cree middlemen. Although the innocence of natives is an imported conceit, knowing strangers from a long distance is not the same as understanding them. The speculation about the Naapiikoaiksi must have ranged from mystical visions to alien fantasies.

It was curious how the Cree valued beaver pelts and wolf skins. Those who went to York Factory on the bay saw the Cree trade twelve prime beaver skins for a gun that they would use for a year and then pass on to the People for thirty-six kit-fox skins or half as many wolf skins. For one skin, the middlemen bought a pound of powder or four pounds of shot, then turned around and sold the same for whatever the traffic would bear. But in a world without banks or the concept of capital, prices did not mean that much. Still, there was an implied insult in being cheated, and the People must have welcomed the French traders who appeared on the Saskatchewan. After 1733 the "Mithcoo Ethenue," or Bloody Indians, stopped going to the bay.

The vast northern plains that intimidated the riverbound Cree were no buffer against intruders from the south. Buffalo herds moving north from overgrazed summer pastures in search of winter-resistant northern fescue were followed by hunters who competed with the northern people. The parkland-hunting Piikani called the intruders *pitsiiksiinaitapi*, likening them to snakes crawling out of the grasslands. In early days the name Snake probably included others along with the Shoshone.

The northern loop of *kinuk sisakta* (the Milk River) was a natural boundary that those daring Snakes crossed. They incised an intriguing record of their passage in the sandstone cliffs of the area. At Writing-on-Stone Provincial Park, petroglyphs and pictographs record a prehistoric invasion. Graven records of martial contests feature shield-bearing and pointed-shoulder men from a time almost beyond recall.

Unwelcome competition for sometimes limited meat resources demanded definition of territorial prerogatives. But people who depended on the hunt could not afford to sacrifice their young men to principle.

Hostile encounters were limited to opportunities to demonstrate courage, give and get honorable scars, and affirm the integrity of the band. Behind their shield walls, combatants were essentially protected from arrows and spears. This limited warfare was, in light of atrocities that followed, humane.

But the Snakes came in ever greater numbers. They audaciously planted a large camp on the plains of the Eagle Hill, between the two branches of the great river. When the concerned Niitsitapi appealed to their Cree friends for help, the Cree could foresee disruption of their lucrative trade. The entrepreneurs responded by sending twenty of their young men armed with bows and lances. They needed their guns to defend their own camps, and powder was too precious to waste defending customers.

The combined war party that assembled on the north side of the Saskatchewan may have numbered around 350.[8] After crossing over to the Snake camp in canoes and on rafts, the warriors crouched behind tough hide shields, facing about the same number of enemies. Fought at far arrow range, the battle ended in a standoff that satisfied the need for a martial display without producing serious casualties.

During the confrontation, the Snake warriors shouted that they rode on wonderful creatures that were too precious to risk in war. But later, when the Snake herds increased, leather-armored Snakes rode upon scattered Plains hunting bands without mercy. Mounted warriors charged through the shield walls and knocked down footmen with their war clubs.[9] When the plainsmen requested help from their trading partners, only three Cree and seven Assiniboine responded to the call. But this time they brought their guns. Armed with thirty balls in the shot pouch and a load of powder clutched in their sweaty palms, the ten gunmen rose to blast the intruders' shield line. The body count was probably exaggerated in later war stories, but the shock wave spread like a prairie fire.[10]

As guns became more prevalent the People used them to kill buffalo. But the sound was likely to stampede a grazing herd and the guns' real value would remain as a war weapon. By the end of the summer, northern plainsmen had ranged far enough south to kill one of these strange new creatures. Lacking a name for the animal, the People called it *ponokaomitaa*, elk-dog.[11]

THREE
Horses

everal myths assert that the first horses came out of the water. West of the mountains, the plateau tribes spoke of *ikiusi*, the strange creature that came out of the marshes and induced a Yakima woman to leave her husband and go away with it. The next year, when she was seen again, the woman had grown hairy and tossed long, manelike hair. When she returned a second time, she was a mare trailing a colt.[12]

Nez Perce horse traders also told the Niitsitapi that the animals originally came out of the water.[13] Perhaps that was why the Piikani believed that horses first appeared in southern Alberta near Pakowki Lake. Or did they associate horses with water because they first saw the animals coming across the Missouri and Milk Rivers? Their Atsiina neighbors had links to the horse-wealthy Arapaho and Comanche of the central and southern plains.

One petroglyph at Writing-on-Stone is an awkwardly drawn horse. The image suggests that the artist had never actually seen the creature or was drawing a vision from a spirit dream. Later glyphs depict the animals more realistically, some even wearing the leather horse armor peculiar to the Shoshone. In time, the recorders developed a shorthand way of showing herds. Some engravings record hostile encounters between mounted and unmounted warriors. Although archaeological evidence suggests that the Snakes continued coming to the Milk River until around 1750, there is no way of dating when the first horses crossed the river.[14]

Horses arrived on the northern plains well before the winter of 1754/55, when the perambulating Hudson's Bay Company traveler Anthony Hendey walked into the open country with some Pegogamaw Cree. Hendey bought a horse from his hosts and saw other wild horses running free on the prairies. In the Archithinue camp he admired their fine, tractable animals, which were about fourteen hands high, lively, and cleanly made.

Some favorite horses were kept tethered, but others were hobbled and turned out to graze. Archithinue horse gear included hair halters and buffalo-skin reins, saddle pads, and stirrups. Hendey's description of four asses raises the tantalizing question of whether they were actually mules of a southern, Spanish origin. That point would be critical in determining whether the Archithinue had traveled far enough south to steal them, had traded them from middlemen, or had learned to breed them. There is little question that by mid-century the people of the northern plains already had large herds of fine animals and were fully committed to the horse culture.[15] They had become the *Gens du Large*—the People of the Plains.

The primary source for the history of horses among the Piikani is a buckskin Boswell named Saukamappee. He was the son of a former Cree middleman trader and professed to have lived with the Muddy River Indians since the introduction of guns and horses. During the winter of 1787/88, Saukamappee entertained David Thompson, then a Hudson's Bay Company traveler, and recited the memory of obtaining horses.

Saukamappee described the moment when the Piikani abandoned their pedestrian ways and began a long romance with the marvelous elk-dogs. After besting the Snakes with guns, the Piikani boldly traveled south to the Snake frontier and by autumn had killed one of the strange creatures with an arrow. Saukamappee did not specify how they acquired live animals. Speculation holds that trading was more likely than capture because the Piikani still had a lot to learn about handling the sensitive animals.[16]

Before the Piikani could metamorphose into equestrians, they had to become horsemen and herdsmen. Building up a herd in an environment not particularly suited for horses took time. It required learning the unfamiliar fundamentals of herding, training, and breeding. Pregnant mares needed to be sheltered and fed during the hard winters if they were to foal in the spring. Colts needed to develop for several years before they could be mounted and broken. Before entering the glorious race on a trained buffalo runner, the People had to learn the mundane details of packing and leading. Saukamappee gave Thompson no tidy date for when the horse culture began, but by the 1750s the People were riding.[17]

Horses changed everything. They gave hunters greater ability to follow the buffalo herds and made it easier to carry meat back to camp. Horses virtually assured ample food supplies, easing the threat of starvation. A running hunt left mountains of slain flesh scattered across the killing field.

To harvest the meat, hunters began by heaving a fallen beast on its belly with the forelegs doubled under or spraddled for stability. The hunter whose arrow made the kill claimed the tongue. Lacking the means to hang up the carcass, the butchers mined it from the top. Unless there was reason to preserve a complete hide, the butcher made the entry by an incision along the backbone, then peeled down and spread the skin to reap the bounty.

In order of preference, the cuts of meat were the boss, the hump, the hump ribs, the fleece or backstrap with its three-inch-thick covering of fat, the side ribs, and the belly fat. Swimming in the bloody cavity were the choice organs. Liver and kidneys might be eaten raw. Other delicacies included the heart, the soft nose gristle, and the intestines. The diners cracked the bones for marrow, and conspicuously consumed bull testicles for vigor and virility. In the spring, unborn calves might be a tender surprise found inside. The butchers made no attempt to bleed the fallen animals, and they cut the meat with the grain to retain the juices.

The hunters took only choice parts in a light butchering, just what one horse could carry back to camp. Two pack animals were necessary for the four hundred pounds or so of a more complete harvest; one carried the quarters and the other hauled the slabs of meat, backfat, ribs, and flanks, which were bundled into the fresh hide.[18]

The Piikani's was a sacrament of real meat, the gift of the buffalo duly honored and honorably eaten. The People mined the depths of the bloody chalice, and what they didn't know about animal anatomy wasn't worth knowing. In an odd, almost inhuman way, the same understanding also applied to themselves. Being flesh eaters, they were close to the flesh; mutilating the bodies of slain enemies became just another kind of butchering. In Naapi's world, they were all animals, and in the true way of it, they consumed one another.

Feasts were the best of times, when bellies were filled and apprehensions muffled. Taking a seared strip of buffalo backstrap firmly between his teeth, the diner sliced off a bite just clear of his nose with the same blade that had recently severed the meat from the steaming carcass. The feasters fished out chunks of boiled meat from the pot with a buffalo-horn ladle. With their knives they sliced off slabs of slow-roasted meat glistening with melted fat and seasoned with smoke. Naapi's world was bountiful. Forget the bad times when all there was to eat was dried meat as hard and juiceless as a parfleche. Forget the times when the women had to scrape old hides to make thin broths. The Gens du Large were true hunters, heirs of past generations that had known both feast and famine as normal life.

With horses the Niitsitapii found spare time for honing new customs, beliefs, and arts. Gifted with new mobility, young men ranged out on the open country. Those exuberant young men rode into a vast expanse of geographically unfixed, overlapping tribal perimeters, figuratively scent-marking their ranges like wolves. The constant vigilance necessary to protect a shifting range fostered a martial tradition. Having known guns before they knew horses, the People relied on them for defense. But the true cost of that security was dependence on outsiders who were still fixed to the rivers. Guns became a fatal linkage that plainsmen could never outrun.

Having horses meant more than just getting around. In the dog days, a family walked about the same distance in a day that it later covered with horses, so keeping up with the buffalo wasn't the problem. The difficulty was getting fresh meat back to camp before it spoiled. Horses could carry heavier loads of meat than dogs could. Unlike dogs that consumed their share of flesh, horses grazed on readily available grass.

When winter closed in, providing grazing and shelter for the horses became an important consideration. After the winter hunt, the nomads left the open country and found shelter for themselves and their animals in the piedmont woods or river valleys. When the buffalo also crowded into the tree line, dogs were useful for winter hunting on snowshoes.

Every sentimental and loving thing that one hears about horses is true. But the counter reality is that horses stomp, bite, and kick. Assertions about the positive impact of horses on the pedestrian world of the northern plains must be tempered by ordinary details. Before enjoying the romantic horseback jaunts through an endless sea of grass, the Piikani learned the grandness and grossness of animal husbandry; the glory of the gallop and the modifying reality of horse turds. Initiate horsemen probably studied the example of their experienced southern or western neighbors. But they also got their fair share of the bruises that accompany trial and error.

The value of horses was apparent from the first. Careful men kept a favorite buffalo runner tethered near the lodge door, where thieves could not slip it away. Mornings began when the men and boys went out with the grazing herd. While younger men worked with select animals, breaking them to a rider or pack saddle, older ones crafted gear or braided ropes. Children played under the hooves of spirited animals.

The last generation of the dog days had about fifty years to devise the techniques for keeping horses in an unfriendly environment. In his lifetime, a man might have gone from a pedestrian child, to a boy learning the

Indian on Horseback *by Karl Bodmer (the Indian in the foreground is probably Mikotsotskina, The Red Horn)*[2] —Courtesy Arthur H. Clark

responsibilities of herding and training, to a mature horseman breeding up a respectable herd. The children who survived the terrible smallpox epidemic of 1781 were also the first who had never known life without horses. Careless with their history, they left tribal memory to a few pockmarked old people. The few keepers of a rapidly fading past sang as they unwrapped the sacred bundles. Feathers, bits of bone, or scraps of hide became increasingly obscure symbols of a bygone relationship with the world.

The new generation belonged completely to the horse culture. Perhaps they outran the sorrow of smallpox with the exuberance of being ahorse. Now they were as dependent on those big-headed ponies as they were on the buffalo. Tribal days were herd days. Placement of summer camps was determined by the availability of good feed and fresh water; winter camps, by the proximity to shelter and to the cottonwoods and willows whose bark fed animals unable to paw through the snow. Babies began life rocking in cradleboards slung across a trusted mare's neck. Boys dreamed of herds of their own and, when they were old enough, went afar to steal horses. Men measured themselves against each other by counting horses. Single women counted the number of ponies their suitors tied before their fathers' lodges; wives determined one another's status by the number of household pack animals they had. Old men who could no longer ride dismounted and died beside the trail.

Calling in, feeding, and stroking a receptive horse is one of life's finest rewards; bridling and saddling without getting kicked or bitten can be a contest that verifies a partnership. On the long trail, every rock and stick and insect is a mutual experience. Listening to your pony sucking water or ripping up grass is a unique pleasure, and it is a mark of honor to smell like your animal. At night men and women settled into their sleeping robes with the comforting sound of a picketed favorite pony munching just outside.

Horsemen have an appreciation of animal personality. Sometimes a treacherous pony is only reciprocating its owner's distrust. Others are just perverse. Dealing with raw animals is dangerous work, but the number of Gens du Large accidentally killed or maimed by horses is not a readily available historical statistic. Casualties and scars were as much a part of tribal life as they were of cowboy life. Yet Indian mothers, through some commonality of motherhood and marehood, confidently trusted their babies under the bellies of horses.

While horses may have made the Gens du Large into an unrooted people who lived for the moment, nomadic tribalism demands a highly cooperative state. Breaking camp required a good deal of coordination. The wives of the camp chief took down all the poles of his lodge except for the main tripod, its heavy cover still sagging and fluttering in the wind. Responding to the signal, the other families packed and began breaking down. When most of the lodges trembled like a grove of mountain aspens, the chief's tent was dropped and the others followed. After a flurry of final packing and loading, the community was on the move.

The People had perfected the demanding art of packing. The high-horned saddles of the women were convenient pack frames. From them were suspended parfleches, the large folded rawhide envelopes that held loose items. Distinctive surface decorations helped identify matching parfleches, which were used in pairs to balance a load. No tricky diamond hitches for these women. They used a simple belly strap tied tight to the horse with what is still called a squaw hitch. Having plenty of animals kept packs light but increased the chore of catching and loading the ponies.

The size of lodges increased with the advent of horses. An average lodge of twelve to fourteen buffalo skins weighed about one hundred pounds. Working in pairs, women lifted the roll of skins across a pack frame on one horse and tied the eighteen- to twenty-two-foot-long tent poles to other animals. In later times, the large lodges of important leaders might require as many as fifteen horses to transport cover and poles.[19] Packhorses were usually driven rather than led, but a travois horse required the attention of a rider. Bands could move easily across open country but had to take care on mountain trails to avoid dead ends and impassable cutbanks.[20]

The northern Rocky Mountains seem a formidable barrier. However, valleys had trails leading to easy passes, and high places were cut by horse trails only a foot or so wide. Narrow tracks crossed shale slides and traced switchbacks up steep grades. Some places in that country were more accessible in the time of the horse than they are today. Bones found in the canyons nowadays are probably those of unlucky Forest Service packhorses, but the Indians also considered their stock expendable. Camps moving under pressure sometimes left a trail of exhausted and injured animals.

As the Piikani increased their wealth in horses, they elevated their status. In 1830 they averaged about 10 horses per lodge, while for their

Kainaa and Siksika neighbors the norm was only 5.[21] Perhaps this statistic reflected the difficulty of wintering animals on the exposed prairies or river bottoms instead of in the sheltered foothills. Twenty years later, the Piikani ratio had dropped to 8.6, about 1 per person. After a series of epidemics and killing winters, in 1874 the Montana herds were reduced to 1 horse for every two persons. Twenty years later, the numbers were up to 3.8 per person, and at the turn of the twentieth century they stood at 10.5. That was a figure any real horse lover would not find unreasonable—but the end of the prosperity was at hand.[22]

Those who lived by following the buffalo could not be bound to collecting traditional valuables, so they fixed their wealth in horses. Having a large herd showed that a man was either a very successful breeder or a very daring horse raider. Horses became heavily laden symbols of power, prestige, and sexual prowess. Like the cycle of the seasons, the magnitude of the plains, and the depth of the night sky, horses were intrinsic to the Piikani world.

Of a quiet summer evening, horsemen strolled away from the camp circle to watch the grazing herd in the twilight and exchange comments about their animals. They might be concerned about a limping animal, a recent saddle sore, or when a particular mare would foal. Often it was just an excuse to see the horses at ease one more time before dark.

Horses could be obtained through gifts or trading, but capturing other people's horses became a Gens du Large addiction. Those who failed to look after their stock were likely to count fewer heads in the morning. Expeditions went to the Snake River valley as far west as the Boise River to steal Shoshone and Bannock horses. Other adventurers crossed the Rocky Mountains, sometimes in winter, to be in position to take Kutenai and Salish ponies in the spring. Branded animals were lifted from the Crows and Arapaho, and some quests went as far as New Mexican corrals. Homebodies could always make do with handy Gros Ventre, Cree, or Assiniboine animals, and the herds of the Sioux were welcome when their owners were not. The attention was reciprocated; the Blackfoot wealth in horses continued to attract raiders until the mid-1880s, when they passed from a mobile buffalo-hunting economy to sedentary reservation life.[23]

Horse capturers confidently hiked great distances in the expectation of riding home in style. They risked being overtaken in the open, run to the ground, and slaughtered. Often they braved these appalling hazards to get animals they really didn't need. In the heart-pounding darkness, daring rustlers slipped between the sleeping lodges to cut out the best buffalo runners. Others lassoed broncs from the grazing herd and threw themselves on the startled animals to get away. An excited rider might be thrown at the most inopportune moment. One old horseman recalled the experience of a young would-be rustler that was just short of disaster. Bucked off his first horse, the inept young man failed to mount two others that his cohorts had caught for him. Disgusted, his companions finally rode off, leaving him to his own devices. However, conscience made them return to rescue him before the pursuing owners caught him.[24]

Horse stealing was not as vicious as warfare, but taking someone else's animals was sure to bring retaliation. One challenge to the concept of a Blackfoot confederacy was the Siksika and Kainaa practice of setting up their Piikani brothers. Using a protective screen of relatively uninvolved Piikani, the raiders ran off with the booty, leaving their supposed friends to endure the inevitable retaliation.

To the Gens du Large, horses were too magnificent to be seen as part of the European intrusion. This blinding love would prove another factor in the unbalancing of the Niitsitapi world.

FOUR

Getting to Know the Archithinue

On the other side of the equation were the English traders along the shores of Hudson's Bay. They were putting together what they could about the inland peoples. Most of their information about the Piikani came through the filter of Cree middlemen, who bragged that their landlocked customers were slaves. The brush-bound and soggy English accepted whatever the Cree and Assiniboine told them about the inland spaces. In the Cree language, *muskatao* means plain or prairie, but to the white traders the word suggested a place as exotic as the steppes of Russia.[25] As long as there were intermediaries to bring furs out to them, there was no reason to risk traversing the Muscotay Plains and meeting up with the wild men roaming there.

In 1690, just nine years after the Company of Adventurers Trading into Hudson's Bay established its first post, a boy with an affinity for Indians left York Factory. Henry Kelsey traveled west of Lake Winnipeg to the edge of the parklands. He returned so impressed by what he had seen that a dry report seemed inadequate. Putting his experiences down in rhyme, Kelsey made a kind of song out of the western mystery.[26]

In the summer of 1715, the occupants of 172 canoes came to trade at York Factory. The fleet was paddled by a conglomeration of Misshenippee, Sturgeon, Stone, Upland, Mountain, Muscotay, and Strange Indians. Fixed on the idea of establishing peace for "a thousand miles round," the factor James Knight was concerned that the Assiniboine suffered "a great deal of bloodshed . . . along the southwestern frontiers." Foreshadowing things to come, the Assiniboine had adopted the use of guns and lost the skill of the bow. When their access to ammunition was interrupted, they were vulnerable to their enemies.

The Cree emissaries that Knight sent back to the Plains Indians returned and reported that they had "made a peace wth 4 Nations that lyes between the S.W. and the W, they are a people as never has any trade or Commerce wth any Europeans."[27] But in the annual letter from Fort Churchill in 1738, the "Atchue-thinnies" were described "as a people bordering near the Western Ocean who are great enemies to our inland trading Indians." The general term Archithinue may have included the hostile Snakes.[28] In 1743, a slave brought down from the plains by the "Southwd Indians" (Cree) reminded York factor James Isham of an "Earchethinune."[29] Drawing on ten years' prior experience, Isham could only say that their language was different from others he was familiar with, and they had never before been seen at the fort.[30]

By that time, French traders from Quebec and Montreal were coming inland via the difficult route through the Great Lakes. Those voyageurs heard the Lake of the Woods Cree using the name "Hiatchiritiny" to describe western native peoples. The numerous "Pikaraminiouach" Indians in the area took their tents with them, as the Assiniboine did.[31] They lacked firearms but had obtained axes, knives, and cloth from traders on the lower part of the river where they dwelt. Sometime after August 1737, the French entrepreneur Pierre Gaultier de Varennes et de La Verendrye drew a *carte de l'Ouest* and lettered the name Pikaraminiouach into the vaguely defined area of the northwestern plains.[32]

In the spring of 1751, La Verendrye's successors built Fort Jonquierre above Lac Bourbon near the mouth of the Saskatchewan River. The next year, Sieur Drouet de Richardville took a load of trade goods, including brandy, up the Saskatchewan to a post that he called Tete-de-Boeuf.[33] Later, Jean-Louis de Lacorne, Sieur de Chapt, decided to set up a trading post a few miles below the union of the two main branches of the

Saskatchewan. The location was perfect for intercepting trading Indians. The place known as Fort St. Louis, or Fort Lacorne, was the first of many *Forts des Prairies*. In 1754, when their companions returned to the resupply point on the north shore of Lake Superior, only four Frenchmen remained lower on the river as a summer complement. By then, New France and New England were beginning another war, so there was no certainty that any supplies would be available.

Faced with countering French intrusion into the Hudson's Bay Company's chartered domain of Rupert's Land, York factor James Isham sent a delegate to encourage the distant Indians to come to trade. The laborer and net-maker whom Isham selected, Anthony Henday, had past experience as a smuggler, which suggests that he was an adventurer at heart.[34] In July 1754, Henday started inland with a flotilla of twenty-six "Keschachewan and pegsgoma" canoes. Equipped with a compass, a fishing line, paper, and a full measure of audacity, Henday's ace in the hole was the Cree guide Attickasish (Little Bear), who had "lived long with thee Earthithinues."[35]

On 14 October, the party was hiking along the Battle River in what is now Alberta when they were approached by forty mounted Indians. Topping a rise, Henday saw a camp of more than two hundred Indian tents pitched in two rows. At the far end of the camp was a large lodge where the old men were seated around their head chief. The trader boldly went down to meet them.

After a ceremonial smoke, Henday was presented with the best gift his hosts had to offer, twenty boiled buffalo tongues. In discussions over the next two days, Henday suggested that their people might learn to hunt beaver and foxes, which were highly valued at the bayside. After Henday's Cree guides went off on a raid toward the southwest, the remaining Cree scattered to hunt beaver. Although the Cree family that Henday traveled with during the winter was nervous about being alone, they did not hesitate to hunt in the Archithinue territory.[36]

In the spring, the Cree reassembled on the North Branch of the Saskatchewan River to prepare canoes for their return to York Factory. On 12 May 1755, about a hundred tents of Archithinue arrived at the rendezvous, bringing wolf skins. Henday admired their fine horses, but he was disappointed to learn that the proud equestrians refused to go to the bay. Their leader insinuated that if the Bayman didn't like it, the Indians could always trade with the French instead. Those traders were within an easy ride.

As long as the Cree or Canadian traders brought goods to them, the Gens du Large saw no reason to change. But then the Frenchmen went away to war with the English, and Canadian supplies dried up. Two years after Henday's visit, the anxious Archithinue gave in and came to the bay. The Bloody Indians reappeared there for the first time in twenty-five years. Unfortunately, they had to live off the land as they traveled, and some of them starved to death on the journey home.

Four years passed before Henday was able to return to the Saskatchewan. By then, New France had fallen to the growing British empire. All Canadians were now British subjects, but they were still competitors to the Hudson's Bay Company. To answer the challenge this presented, travelers from the bay went inland in the years 1763, 1766, 1767, 1768, 1769, 1772, 1773, and 1774. Those who kept journals often recorded tidbits of information about the Gens du Large.[37]

Henday's companion on the 1759 trip, Joseph Smith, accompanied some Cree west of the forks of the Saskatchewan in 1763/64. His hosts were hesitant to kill buffalo on the barren ground for "feer of the earsheaddenys."[38] Smith returned with a more confident guide in 1764/65. The same reputable Cree, Mousinnickissack, later took William Pink to winter on the grasslands.

By 1765, Canadian pedlars were aggressively shouldering into the Saskatchewan trade. Sent to assess the intrusion, the Hudson's Bay Company's Matthew Cocking convinced some plainsmen to come down to the bay and speak with factor James Graham. Fearing that the outside world would doubt his statements about the equestrian Indians, Graham authenticated his observations with scholarly references to published but inaccurate hearsay.[39]

William Pink's reports for the years 1766 through 1770 suggest that disturbances on the northern plains were souring the relationships among the Cree, Assiniboine, and Archithinue. The reason for this might have had something to do with what an Archithinue saw when he came to York Factory in 1766. Surprised to learn the actual standard of trade, the observer realized that the Cree had been taking advantage of their friends. Not only were they getting more for furs, they were also marking up the goods that they retraded to the plainsmen.[40]

In December 1769, Pink encouraged the Blood and "Black Footed" Indians to snare wolves. Raiders returning from the south in the spring reported that the Snakes had acquired guns, "But they Cannot Shote well yet." A Snake invasion wasn't much of a threat because the camp that assembled at the canoe rendezvous numbered as many as nine hundred to eleven hundred people.[41] By December 1772, British competitors from Montreal had also become a serious threat to the Hudson's Bay Company's Saskatchewan operations.

Cree names had been used to identify the western tribes, but in about 1772 Matthew Cocking assigned them English names. Differences among the tribes were still unclear to the traders, but at least the western geography was beginning to fall into place. The Cree knew the South Branch of the Saskatchewan as *askoueseepee*, while the Piikani called it *namakaysissata*, or the Bow Hills River.[42]

During the last seventeen years, white traders had made most contacts with the Archithinue in the region between the North and South Branches of the Saskatchewan. Cocking's Pegogamaw Cree companions came there to trade for horses and buffalo-skin garments, but Cocking himself was looking for wolf skins and other furs. After failing to connect with the Archithinue, Cocking wrote, "I shall be sorry if I do not see the Equestrian Natives who are certainly a brave people, & far superior to any tribes that visit our Forts: they have dealings with no Europeans, but live in a state of nature to the S. W. Westerly: draw towards the N. E. in March to meet our Natives who traffick with them." At the end of November, the traders were joined by twenty-one tents of Atsiina who understood the Assiniboine language.[43]

With more competition entering the market, the plainsmen became shrewd shoppers. At York Factory the Hudson's Bay Company charged fourteen beaver skins for a three-and-a-half-foot gun. During the winter of 1772/73, a Canadian trader at Nipiwi on the Saskatchewan was willing to sell a similar gun for twelve skins. However, the best price was offered by Thomas Corry, the pedlar at the Pas, on the lower Saskatchewan. He asked only eight beaver for a gun and was generous with good tobacco.

By now, the English from the bay were trailing Montreal-based pedlars. The New Jersey–born, Montreal trader Alexander Henry obligingly wrote a memoir that helps explain developments. To improve his understanding of a rapidly developing competition, during the winter of

1775/76 Henry made a tour of the prairies. Traveling south from the Forts des Prairies, he visited the Assiniboine winter camp of the leader known as The Great Road. A war chief who bragged of raiding as far west as the mountains had lost his brother and son there but captured a female slave. The Great Road described both the Snakes and Archithinue as troublesome neighbors. In an attempt to discourage Henry from visiting the mountains and expanding trade, the chief described a trip of many days over plains without firewood for winter travel and lacking water for summer treks. How would the white man enjoy broiling his meat over a fire of dry buffalo dung?[44]

In 1774 the Hudson's Bay Company finally established its first inland trading post, Cumberland House, above the mouth of the Saskatchewan River. By the following October, the inland-traveled Matthew Cocking was keeping the Cumberland House journal. In it, he noted that ten canoes of Pegogamaw Cree had come from the Saskatchewan in the vicinity of the Eagle Hills. After being treated to tobacco and brandy, they agreed to take Robert Longmore and Charles Isham back to their camp to winter with them. Although the plainsmen continued to use the arms and ammunition they obtained from the Canadians mostly for war, the more productive Pegogamaw promised the traders that they would hunt beaver toward the Stoney Mountains.[45] The following spring, Longmore and Isham returned, riding among the packs of wolf and bear skins provided by the dependable Cree.

In 1777, Robert Longmore came to *mekisew-wacky* (the Eagle Hills), where he recognized Pegogamaw and Sturgeon River Cree and their Assiniboine associates.[46] The Pegogamaw had to travel sixteen days on the river ice to trade at Cumberland House—about the time it took to come from the Sturgeon River. That fall, Longmore and his party built Upper Hudson House, which operated as a canoe factory as well as a trading post, about forty miles above the Sturgeon River.[47]

But the audacious entrepreneurs from Montreal were not to be denied. The Canadians soon leapfrogged the Baymen with an establishment at the Eagle Hills. Unfortunately, the injudicious use of liquor at the post soon caused problems, which the traders countered in one instance by slipping an obnoxious Indian some laudanum—he died from the overdose. By spring, the situation had deteriorated until interpreter John Cole was killed in a firefight. Leaving bribes to slow the Indians' pursuit, the

Canadians fled in terror. They returned in the autumn, but the cowards refused to go beyond the Sturgeon River, leaving the Baymen free to establish themselves fifteen miles farther upriver.

The eighteen Cree men and women whom the Baymen welcomed on 29 November took Charles Isham and James Spence away with them. The two soon returned, however, because their hosts had started to act "saucy."[48] When the same Indians who had killed Cole then drunkenly threatened Lower Hudson House on 4 March 1781, the redoubtable Longmore simply disarmed them and locked them up in the house.

It was apparent that, as the stores moved to the customers, the dominant role of the Cree and Assiniboine middlemen was falling apart. The change might have proved troublesome for them, but a greater disaster intervened. In the fall of 1781, William Walker returned to Hudson House, where he was soon visited by twelve tents of Pegogamaw Cree. Within ten days the horrified Walker recognized the pustules of smallpox on the Indians.[49] Because the Cree had come from the plains, the trader immediately attributed the infection to their hostile summer contacts with the Snake Indians. In the past, the Saskatchewan Indians had gone to war with the Snakes about one year out of three. Now, with competition between traders providing them with excess ammunition, they could fight every year. To Walker's way of thinking, the Cree were suffering the consequence of that unproductive belligerence.[50]

Northern ranges of the Piikani

FIVE

Inside the Piikani World

Traveling Indian families usually moved at a leisurely pace, maybe 10 or 15 miles a day. But those who fled the Hidatsa villages on the Missouri River after mid-April 1781 knew they had death at their heels, so in the ten or twelve days before smallpox erupted, they may have gone 150 to 200 miles.[51] Those doomed fugitives could have been the Snakes who had menaced the Hidatsa villages. If so, it would fit the Piikani recollection that they found smallpox victims in an abandoned Snake camp on the Stag (Red Deer) River, perhaps as early as midsummer.[52]

The old Cree Saukamappee recalled that Piikani observers on a hill overlooking the Snake camp thought it was strange that there was no activity. There were no hunters afield, only a few horses, and buffalo were grazing unconcerned near the silent lodges. Gathering courage in the face of an uncertain situation, the Piikani attacked at dawn. After slashing the lodge covers, they recoiled at the sight of the dead and the dying, ghastly masses of corruption. "We did not touch them, but left the tents, and held a council on what was to be done. We all thought the Bad Spirit had made himself master of the camp and destroyed them. It was agreed to take some of the best of the tents, and any other plunder that was clean and good, which we did, and also took away the few horses they had, and returned to our camp."[53] David Thompson's account goes a bit awry in that he recalls that the disease broke out among the Piikani on the second day and quickly spread from tent to tent.[54]

By fall, infected Pegogamaw Cree were staggering through the ashes of a recent prairie fire to Hudson House with foul pustules bubbling under their hot skin. The Orkney Islander Michel Oman set off to investigate 150 miles upriver to the Eagle Hills. He later described to young Thompson his horrible recollections of what he found there: "We saw the first camp and some of the people sitting on the beach to cool themselves, when we came to them, to our surprise they had marks of the small pox, were weak and just recovering."

Oman and his companions did not grasp the full horror until they went up the bank and looked into the tents where rotting bodies lay unburied. "Those that remained had pitched their tents about 200 yards from them and were too weak to move away entirely, which they soon intended to do; they were in such a state of despair and despondence that they could hardly converse with us, a few of them had gained strength to hunt which kept them alive." Three-fifths of the people had died, and from what the survivors knew, all the rest of the Gens du Large were in the same dreadful state.[55]

A notable lone pine tree known as *netuckis* stood in a patch of aspen about a hundred miles north of the Bow River. That unusual growth marked the end of the parklands and the beginning of the open plains. A band of Piikani were camped nearby when the disease overtook them. All that the desperate father of one infected family could think to do was to appeal to the spirit power of the mythic tree. After watching the disease destroy his family, the sorrowing father recovered enough strength to climb and top the pine tree, cutting what the voyageurs called a lob stick, as a monument to his sorrow. Burdened by his own survival, he never took another wife but lived alone. During battles, he would place himself in the front without a shield, as if he wished to die. In a final irony, enemy arrows always missed him.[56]

Grim reminders of the disaster were still visible eighteen years later. At the place along the Saskatchewan's South Branch where the parklands give way to the open plains was another attractive camping place. The whitened skulls of seven "upgrown people" and a child of about eight, fragments of wooden and buffalo-horn dishes, a woman's rusty knife, and remains of a fire circle suggested that five tents had endured the lonely horror and perished there.[57]

Some bands that had scattered on the plains for the summer hunt may have been quarantined by distance. The mortality was heaviest among the men who tried to cool their fever with sweats followed by fatal dips in glacial waters. Because they were camped by a stream too small to throw themselves into, only one-third of Saukamappee's band died. Deaths in other bands ran as high as half the community. Vulnerable old people took many of their traditions with them to the grave. The Pegogamaw Cree disappeared from the historical record during the epidemic.[58]

Some recovered. Still the disaster was not complete. Saukamappee's version continues:

> When at length it left us, and we moved about to find our people, it was no longer with the song and the dance; but with tears, shrieks, and howlings of despair for those who would never return to us. War was no longer thought of, and we had enough to do to hunt and make provisions for our families, for in our sickness we had consumed all our dried provisions; but the Bisons and Red Deer were also gone, we did not see one half of what was before, whither they had gone we could not tell, we believed the Good Spirit had forsaken us, and allowed the Bad Spirit to become our master. What little we could spare we offered to the Bad Spirit to let us alone and go to our enemies. To the Good Spirit we offered feathers, branches of trees, and sweet smelling grass. Our hearts were low and dejected, and we shall never be again the same people.

The prairie fire of disease left the People charred in their hearts. Now they understood the full meaning of Old Woman's decision that the dead were dead forever, and the living should know the feeling of sorrow. Mourning in the old way by cutting off a finger would have required them to cripple their hands, but the survivors needed to pull bowstrings and wield skinning knives. They hunted beaver, wolves, and foxes with a new dedication, to have something to trade for necessities. They ignored enemy scouts who wandered in the empty land.

Meanwhile, another disaster caught their friends from the bay. York Factory was attacked and destroyed by a French fleet. When the inland traders returned from the coast without goods to trade, the greedy pedlars from Montreal exploited the lack of competition. At a time when the

Piikani had their backs to the wall, liquor flowed freely on the upper river. On 7 March 1782, Bayman Robert Davey intercepted fourteen Blackfoot men on the burned plains. They had recovered from smallpox and were going to the French house to trade.[59]

Pockmarked young men hunted for wives. The scarred young women would carry the future of the nation in their bellies. It should have been a time of rejuvenation, but the old enmities persisted. For a few years after the shock of the smallpox epidemic, the Piikani camps were too stunned to worry about their enemies. In the autumn of the third year, five Piikani families went to hunt sheep in the mountains. When they did not return before the first snow, thirty warriors set off to find them. Two days' march brought them to a destroyed camp. The raiders had left sticks painted with the marks of snake heads there to proclaim their evil deed. Wolves and dogs had been eating the scalped bodies of men, women, and children.[60]

The outraged tribesmen raised the war tent and allowed the women to flatter them into taking revenge. But the elders, concerned about their already seriously eroded male population, cautioned against wasting more lives. When that counsel was disregarded, the elders suggested that raiders at least spare any Snake women or children who might be adopted to increase the Piikani population.

The length of time that Piikani contacts with traders had been filtered through Pegogamaw Cree middlemen could not have been reckoned on a painted buffalo skin of winter counts. Saukamappee was a living example of that old symbiosis, but now the intermediaries were gone. The rendezvous with the Cree near the forks of the Saskatchewan was replaced by annual or semiannual visits to the trading houses. Need had created dependence. The old guns the Piikani had traded from the Cree for exorbitant prices still required powder and shot.

Piikani elders came to dread those excursions. The traders used liquor as the catalyst for their dealings, and all too often trading ended in drunken brawls or humiliation by jealous men from other tribes. Hunters unwilling to make the long trip entrusted their pelts to friends to trade, but they worried whether their proxies would be seduced by *naapiaohkii* (white man's water). The Siksika and Kainaa learned to time their visits to coincide with the return of the boats, which gave them first chance at the most desirable goods. Unhandy as beaver hunters, the Siksika and

Kainaa made themselves obnoxious by rifling through Piikani packs, often appropriating beaver pelts as passage tolls. Going to the store was not a pleasant experience for the Piikani.

Three winters after the terrible death, seven Baymen came to the Piikani winter camps near the mountains. James Gaddy and his companions left Hudson House, trailing or being trailed by Canadians from William Holmes's Battle River plantation.[61] Sending excess personnel to winter with the hunting bands was a tactic that transferred the cost of supporting the engagees from the trading companies to their Indian clients. During their time with the Indians, winterers could also encourage beaver hunting and show their hosts how to prepare the pelts properly.

The Saskatchewan superintendent, William Tomison, advanced six skins' worth of goods to Gaddy and each of his companions but made them furnish their own horses, one to ride and one to pack their outfit. Items useful to the Piikani would buy their keep and leave something extra to be traded for furs. The guests paid their hosts with knives, awls, and fire steels while using attractive iron arrowheads or ammunition to bargain for as many pelts as possible. They expected to make a gain of about one-third of the profits for their initiative.[62]

James Gaddy was an Orkney Island lad who had come to the northwest four years earlier. The twenty-five-year-old workman had a rapport with the Indians who came to the house, but that was not quite the same as being totally immersed at the winter lodge. Still, the life of a Hudson's Bay Company servant in Rupert's Land was not so different from life with the Indians. Trading-house workers existed as close to starvation as the natives did. In either case, life at the subsistence level was pretty much a matter of getting out, no matter how cold the weather, to find meat for the pot.

The seven Baymen traveled about 450 miles across the northwestern prairie to the Muddy River Indian winter camps nestled in the shadow of the Rocky Mountains near the head of the Bow River. A wooded draw sheltered the Piikani camp from the cold winds that swept the plains during that winter of 1785/86. The guests lodged with willing families who welcomed the extra powder and ball they'd brought.

Only three years after the smallpox outbreak, mothers had not forgotten how their children died sweating and writhing in their arms. Pockmarked fathers tried to put the cruel memories out of mind, and young people still mourned lost parents. Because more men than women died, the camps on the upper Bow River had an excess of widows and young girls, which created a sexual paradise for the strangers. Very likely the next generation of Piikani included some of their guests' Viking genes.

The visitors spoke enough Cree to communicate on a basic level, and they pestered their hosts to teach them Blackfoot words. According to his pleased superintendent, in two winters Gaddy learned enough Blackfoot to be as fluent as a Canadian. In his hunts with the Piikani, Gaddy traveled about a hundred miles along the mountains and reported that he saw no end to them. When the Baymen left, about the last week of March, they were leading eight horses loaded with enough furs to justify sending them back again next winter.

For Gaddy and his associates, an understanding of the logic of band habits grew from daily familiarity. But these traders couldn't write, and their gentlemanly London employers were not so interested in learning the details of their men's experiences. Because they left no written record, Gaddy's kind have been consigned to the footnotes of documented history.

In the fall of 1784, a Bayman noticed that a former associate was now working for the pedlars. After being disappointed in the Hudson's Bay Company's reward for his loyalty, Edward Umfreville had returned to Rupert's Land as a clerk for the North West Company. He was sent to assist the rough William Holmes at the reestablished Battle River plantation.[63]

Umfreville soon perceived the distinction between the Siksika and Kainaa, who were associated with the North Branch of the Saskatchewan River, and the Piikani and Atsiina, who ranged on the South Branch. All these bands raided the Snakes for horses and for women to sell to the Canadians. Horses branded with roman letters and other Spanish trophies suggested how far they went on those quests.

Umfreville found the Siksika and Kainaa generally friendly to wintering traders and attributed their good behavior to a moderate use of liquor. They took the pelts of the predators that followed the buffalo herds and exchanged the wolf skins for weapons and domestic items. Echoing his frustrated employers, Umfreville lamented that the equestrians failed to take beaver pelts. Given their pride as horsemen, it was unlikely that they would step down to set a trap. The supply of beaver pelts depended on the Cree, Assiniboine, and Piikani.

By Umfreville's estimate, the smallpox epidemic of four years earlier had claimed at least half of the native population.[64] When Umfreville inquired about missing fingertips on the hands of some of the Indians, the Englishman was appalled to learn that cutting off the joint of a finger was a mourning ritual. Umfreville saw the mutilation only on the men because the tribes tried to keep their women at a safe distance from the temptations of the trading houses.

Two years later, Umfreville was sent to establish an outpost in the vicinity of present-day Frenchman Butte. He was there to counter the activities of a bothersome independent trader not inappropriately known as "Mad Donald" Mackay. By a curious coincidence, Mackay had been at the Mandan villages on the Missouri River in spring 1781, just before the smallpox epidemic broke out. His return as an independent trader and the push up the Saskatchewan to Pine Island forced a general realignment of posts.

The pugnacious Mackay wrote a memoir of the years 1785 to 1787 on the Saskatchewan. He traded with the beaver-trapping Cree and Swampy Ground Assiniboine who hunted on the wooded north side of the river. Although Mackay failed to mention the Blackfeet in his memoir, a map that he later inspired located the Bloods on the upper Battle River. The Piikani were also missing from Mad Donald's writings. However, his errant clerk, James Mackay, may have met them on his travels or gleaned information from the Hudson's Bay Company's James Gaddy that he later promoted as his own experience.[65]

Donald Mackay's neighbor on Pine Island was the Hudson's Bay Company master William Tomison. The stiff-backed old Orkneyman hated the behavior of his competitors. He believed that they used Indian women immorally and destroyed the men with liquor. Gaddy's report to the Manchester House master had convinced Tomison that the "Peekaenow" and Blood Indians were the quietest of those who came to trade. That condition would continue "until the Canadians got amongst them which is the ruin of every Nation by debauching the women and destroying themselves [*sic*] with poisonous rum."[66] In the spring, Tomison wrote to the British commander in chief in Canada that "it grieves us to see a Body of Indians destroyed by a set of men merely for self-interest, doing all in their power to destroy posterity."[67] Tomison's warnings would go unheeded, however, and seven Canadians went out to trade with the western Indians in 1787/88.

On Gaddy's third trip, in 1787/88, he was accompanied by six men, including William Flett and the young clerk David Thompson.[68] Another group of six Baymen wintered with the Bloods. Thompson and Flett were lodged with a tall, erect old man named Saukamappee, who admitted to being Cree. The correct spelling of his Blackfoot name is Saahkomaapi, which means boy. Five years later, another wintering Bayman set Saukamappee's age at about fifty-five rather than Thompson's guesses of seventy-five, eighty, or even ninety.[69] The old expatriate Cree had been living with the "Pekannekoon" for somewhere between twenty-five and fifty years. He seemed to be a living record of the changes that had taken place on the northwestern plains.[70]

Thompson also saw the great warrior Kootenae-appe (Kotonaa'ninaa, or Kutenai Man) returning from a two-month-long raid in the south. He was six-foot-six, all bone and sinew, and impressively upright in his bearing. An aquiline nose set off his manly countenance. Kootenae-appe's contribution to the restoration of the Piikani population counted a family by five wives of twenty-two sons—some almost as impressive as their father—and four daughters.

Kootenae-appe usually acted like a medieval march lord by keeping his large band a full days' travel toward the Snake country. His proven military tactics included organizing large war parties, encouraging lesser leaders, and conducting careful retreats. In the war leader's supervision of operations in 1787 he sent three parties of scouts to view the country. When the scouts found no enemies within a five-day ride, Kootenae-appe sent out a fifty-man war party. After riding south for six days, the party found a large enemy camp and managed to bring in thirty-five horses and fifteen mules without a fight.

Kootenae-appe claimed a fine brown mule equipped with a Spanish saddle and bridle, which he presented to Saukamappee.[71] The bridle had an awkwardly made, heavy iron bit. Somehow the animal and its gear had passed intact through several capturings. Having killed thirteen Snakes and acquired considerable loot, the raiders were ready to go again by the next summer.[72]

David Thompson, the seventeen-year-old former London Charity School student and apprentice fur trader, may have heard stories from oral tradition rather than direct experience. As a new generation grew up after the smallpox epidemic, the mourning songs of dazed survivors were already yielding to the voices of children. These would grow into bright young men and women looking forward to a new world. By 1790 the traders estimated that the buffalo-skin lodges of the Piikani housed 150 families. Three years later there were 190. Within nineteen years the population had swelled to an estimated 350 lodges, including 700 warriors—almost 3,000 persons in total.[73] There were still three men for every five women, but that imbalance might eventually be corrected since more boys than girls were born.

There were disadvantages to growing up in a world of young people. The boys missed having experienced horsemen to teach them. They came perhaps a little too early to adult responsibility, and that at a time when they were being forced to respond to rapidly changing outside pressures.

Tomison complained that the "Pekenows" who came to Manchester House on 25 March 1788 were "poorly gooded." They delivered only 1,200 wolf skins, 2 foxes, and 50 parchment beaver as well as 80 pounds of provisions. Gaddy's men also brought 170 skins of different sorts. As far as the trader was concerned, it was bad news that Piikani war parties intended to go against the Snakes in the spring. War games disrupted production.

The trouble at Battle River that spring involved the Cree and Atsiina. Ten tents of Southerd (Cree) Indians killed and viciously mutilated an Atsiina man. After appropriating his untraded furs, they fled toward the south. Tension apparently spread; by fall the South Branch trader complained that his business was off because the Blood and "Pee Kee No" Indians were no longer coming in together.[74]

James Gaddy and four men returned from wintering with the "Pegogomy" Indians on 2 April 1791. They were accompanied by one Piikani family from the Rocky Mountains, and over the next week other Muddy River Indians straggled in. They delivered nearly eight hundred "made beaver" (an accounting term representing the value of a prime beaver skin, but it could also be applied to other furs), of which three hundred were whole or parchment beaver. The usually parsimonious Tomison was so encouraged by the Piikani dedication to taking beaver that he gave them free ice chisels and files so they could break open winter dens.[75]

The large band of Muddy River Indians who visited the recently established Buckingham House in late October 1792 were disappointed that their old friend James Gaddy was not there but had been put in charge of the bypassed Manchester House. Young Thompson had been sent north. When Tomison's stingy trading left the Piikani displeased and sullen, most of the Hudson's Bay Company servants were unwilling to winter with the Indians. The only Baymen prepared to risk it were Peter Fidler and John Ward. Tomison rationalized that the promising Fidler could "make some observations at the Rocky Mountains." The two adventurers, each riding one horse and leading another, left on 8 November 1792 under the protection of a Piikani leader named Sakatoo.

Sakatoo had been a great warrior in his youth, but at the advanced age of forty-five he was no longer active enough for that demanding role. He had grown up during the great changes of the horse culture and helped push the Snakes south until no enemy lodges remained within five hundred miles. Sakatoo had been a mature man when the smallpox epidemic hit.

Three days from the post they overtook a Southerd leader named The White Owl who was going to hunt buffalo near the mountains.[76] As *omackcowatchemook* (Swan's Bill, the present-day Devil's Head) rose to the southwest, they were nearing the places favored for Piikani winter camps. At the crossing of *namakaysissata* (the Bow River), Fidler learned that the Cree called it *askoue seepee*. After a month on the trail, they came to *oo oose spitcheyee* (a branch of the present-day Highwood River), where 150 skin lodges were surrounded by a large herd of grazing horses.[77]

On 10 January 1793, Fidler described the composition of the winter camp:

> They are now all together of this nation being 190 Tents. There are here also 13 Tents of Black feet, 5 of Southern Indians & 12 of Sessews, in all 220 Tents altogether, having amongst them upwards of two thousand Horses, that feed in a fine level, near the Tents, a very fine sight. The Indians particularly the Slave Indians very careful of them. The Southern Indians pay very little attention to them & frequently they have none.

The camp was alert to rumors of lurking Flatheads (Salish), but the political situation was promising. In June a tentative peace had been arranged with the Snakes. Fidler's hosts were still on the trail when they were informed that four Snake emissaries had come back with gifts to confirm the agreement. Sakatoo insisted that the whites put on their best clothes to impress the visitors. He and most of the Piikani welcomed the peace overture, but some doubters suspected that the visit was just a pretense to spy out the country.

One of the Snake delegates turned out to be a young man of about twenty-five who was dressed very much like his hosts except for his outrageously long hair. His leggings were about a foot longer than his leg and bunched up over his moccasins. After exchanging presents, the four Shoshone set off on a return journey of ten sleeps (perhaps 250 to 300 miles) to their home. Meanwhile a sixteen-year-old Flathead boy had been apprehended trying to steal horses. The White Owl and other militants wanted to kill him, but the majority opinion prevailed and he was apparently sent back with the four Snakes. Seventeen Bloods also accompanied the Snake delegation on the return trip, hoping to stir up some joint venture with the Snakes against the Crows.

In Sakatoo's large, thirty-hide tipi, Fidler learned that the forty-five-year-old civil chief was actually the son of the still-presiding seventy-three-year-old civil chief, also named Sakatoo. Known as The Orator, the old man collected information from travelers between the scattered camps. Just after sunset each day he strode around announcing the news and broadcasting his comments, to which few seemed inclined to attend. The old man's emblem of office was two otter skins covered with mother-of-pearl, which he wore around his neck and draped across his breast. When his son acted for him, the younger man wore the vestment, strengthening his claim to inherit his father's role.

In the complexity of camp politics, the junior Sakatoo had demonstrated his commitment to peace by honoring the Snake delegation and magnanimously releasing the Flathead boy. But his hope for a lasting diplomatic achievement was in jeopardy because the Bloods were keeping the southern marches in uproar. The June peace overture failed to deflect a Kainaa raid on the Snake herds. Not long after the agreement was confirmed, they returned with twenty-five horses.

The seventeen Bloods who had ridden off with the Snake warriors, however, returned at the end of January with their faces painted black to celebrate a victory. Cooperating with the Snakes, they had crossed the Missouri River and attacked an unwary party of thirty-five Mountain Crows. The loot included Spanish guns, twenty swords, several painted shields, bows, arrows, clothing, and thirty-two fresh scalps.

The returning raiders found a party of Cottonahew (Kutenai) Indians tenting at *naw pew ooch e tey cots* (the Oldman River), hoping to barter horses. Back at the Piikani camp, word of the opportunity led to a scramble to collect old kettles, hatchets, cloth, beads, knives, and tobacco, which a well-armed party of thirty men took to trade. Some of them walked, in expectation of riding home on a fine western pony. The old chief tried to discourage Fidler from riding along, but the trader insisted on seeing the country.

The seven Kutenai tents were nested in the surrounding mountains at a place the Indians knew as the Old Man's Playground. Myth held that an old white man built it ages ago so that the different nations would have a place to meet each year and bury their animosities. Trails across the mountains led to the Elk River and the favored Kutenai pastures that would later become known as the Tobacco Plains.

While the bargains were being made, Fidler recognized that the Muddy River Indians enjoyed the catbird seat in their relationship with the tramontane Kutenai. The western hunters had beaver pelts and desperately wanted to visit the Saskatchewan trading houses. But the Muddy River, Blood, Blackfoot, and Southerd Indians monopolized the merchandise and bought ten skins for a price the Kutenai would have received at the store for each one. Later a party went on to the trading houses to cash in the pelts.

Soon after the trading party returned, the main camp broke up and Fidler got to see the winter hunt. By the end of December in 1792, it was cold enough for fresh meat to keep. Hunting techniques included stampeding small herds of buffalo over rimrock jumps called *pisskan*, edging them into brush and wood pounds, or pursuing them on horseback to bring down desirable cows with metal-pointed arrows. In two weeks the wide-ranging drovers and hunters had killed over two hundred animals.

Driving animals into the pounds between wings of piled brush or heaps of dried buffalo dung was not always a successful tactic. Band members of all ages laying flat behind the "dead men" piles risked being trampled if a running herd turned at the last moment. Women and children who were butchering the slaughtered animals in a pound sometimes had to run for their lives when excited drovers unexpectedly ran in more animals. Risks excepted, it was a joyful time for a meat-dependent people.

The wolves that picked over the leavings from the butchering became so bloated that they could be run down on horseback and killed with arrows. Those pelts made up a large part of the packs that the Piikani brought to the traders, though that easy commodity was less desirable than beaver.

As a perambulating businessman, Fidler faulted Piikani attitudes toward beaver hunting. Most of the furs they took were obtained by shooting animals during the spring, summer, and fall, when the streams were open—not the best time to take a prime pelt. Some Piikani considered the animals almost as taboo as fish and avoided touching beaver or even allowing a pelt in the lodge. They superstitiously refused to eat the flesh, which their Cree associates relished.

For at least half a century, the Cree who lived with the Piikani had demonstrated effective methods of taking beaver. The Cree would block the entrance to a winter den and then break it open to slaughter whole colonies at a time. It was a labor-intensive process with some danger. One old Cree, who may have been Thompson's Saukamappee, was presently suffering from a beaver bite and made a poor example for Fidler's proselytizing. The wounded Cree seemed secondary in influence to Sakatoo

Methods of hunting buffalo; drawing by Father Nicolas Point —Courtesy Jesuit Missouri Province Archives

but may have represented an older relationship between the two peoples.[78] The beaver bite would claim the old man's life in June 1793. Some entrepreneurial-minded Cree simply traded Piikani out of their catches and obtained as many as two or three hundred pelts, enough to repay their debts to the traders without real effort.

It is curious that Fidler never mentioned the war chief Kootenae-appe in his journals. Perhaps that omission reflected what Thompson had noticed earlier: the war leader lacked regard for Sakatoo and rarely camped with him.

The Indians who escorted Fidler and Ward back to Buckingham House in the spring of 1793 rode into a darkening cloud. Coming to repay their debt from the previous fall was not a pleasant experience. The Piikani's sense that their old trader friends no longer cared about them was emphasized when they saw beaver hunters from the northern woods received with greater deference. The northerners got generous welcomes and better prices for beaver pelts than the plainsmen received for their wolf skins, pounded meat, and fat. To the traders, even the Piikani's wonderful horses were just another commodity.

The Piikani were great warriors who galloped over the bodies of fallen Snake and Crow enemies, who chased the Flatheads back across the mountains and cowed the Kutenai. But in the trading house, the Piikani were just ordinary customers, their packs received with ill-concealed frowns by men who wanted only beaver. After almost a century of coming to the fountain of imported wealth, the Plains tribes saw it drying up for them. Now the traders shifted their houses to pander to beaver hunters. Every time those places moved to a better location, the plainsmen had a longer trip from the upper Bow. And getting to the store meant running the gauntlet of jealous Siksika and Kainaa, ready to pick a quarrel. Meanwhile, the Assiniboine prowled both sides of the river, stealing horses from the trading house herds and from anyone foolish enough to leave an animal untethered. With their Atsiina neighbors on the lower Bow River simmering in resentment for the Piikani's Cree partners, going to market was not much fun for anyone.

SIX

Expansion and Riposte

hat happened when the skin games that were played on the upper Saskatchewan River began to pit trading and trapping Indians against each other? Would the Niitsitapi fall underfoot as the pedlars and Baymen chased a business increasingly focused on beaver peltry? The mercantile thrust was sorting out its friends according to their productive value. There is good reason to believe that the Cree usage of "Slaves" to refer to the Piikani no longer applied. The faction known to the traders as Southerd Indians continued to get along with the Muddy River Indians because they shared old habits, similarities of language, and a common interest in beaver hunting.

But other well-armed, beaver-hunting Cree were coming on the plains to hunt buffalo. The Piikani and Southerd Cree were also colliding with the Siksika and Kainaa over the appropriation of peltry. The Siksika ranged south of the Saskatchewan as far as the Red Deer River and west toward the Rocky Mountains. Next to them were the Kainaa, with their reputation for ill temper. Beyond the Red Deer ranged the largest tribal entity, known to the traders as the Piegan, Peekanow, or Muddy River Indians. They shared those ranges with a group who spoke a different language, the Sarcees. The Piikani knew them as *sa sasi,* "not good."

This petroglyph from Writing-on-Stone Provincial Park shows a panoramic battle scene. The degree of detail suggests that this depicts an actual incident. —Courtesy James D. Keyser

Their Atsiina neighbors along the South Branch of the Saskatchewan were called Gros Ventre by the French and Falls or Rapid Indians by the English. After attacking trading houses at the mouth of the South Branch, they moved southwestward.[79] David Thompson recalled a band of seventy Atsiina tents who were led by a chief of such bad character that he and his followers had to leave their country and wander along the Missouri River. Due to these wanderings on the plains the traders sometimes described them as the Flying Big Bellies. The Atsiina also liked to make visits to the like-speaking Arapaho on the southern plains.

As if their relatively friendly neighbors weren't troublesome enough, the Piikani were also ringed by enemies. East along the Missouri River lived the Hidatsa, who sometimes raided into the plains. On the Yellowstone were the Crows, who enjoyed a trading relationship with the Hidatsa and the Salish, and a raiding relationship with the Gens du Large. The Piikani had worn down the once-terrible Snakes, but the Salish and Sahaptan from across the mountains persisted in coming over to hunt buffalo and show off their herds of fine horses.

That fluid, ever-dangerous universe made the Piikani into frontiersmen. They had fallen into the role of turf patrolers to inhibit intrusions and discourage competitors for buffalo. Piikani raiders harried Shoshone in the distant valleys of the Wind, Green, and upper Snake Rivers, and struck the River Crows along the Yellowstone. They guarded the Rocky Mountain passes against the regular appearance of Salish and other western buffalo hunters and carefully monitored Kutenai attempts to bring beaver pelts to the Saskatchewan houses.

The traders had completed the exploration of the navigable North Saskatchewan in 1790, when New Jersey-born trader Peter Pangman reached a point just above the mouth of the Clearwater River. Trading with the Piegans was nothing new, so Pangman must have been looking for more productive beaver hunters. His main accomplishment amounted to carving his name and the date on a tree a mile or so above the forks. That was within reasonable distance of the Piikani winter camps on the upper Bow, but the North West Company wasn't ready to make that move.

Trading had developed a certain formality. Heralds rode ahead of an Indian trading party to announce their approach and carry back welcoming gifts of tobacco or liquor. Used with caution, liquor created an amiable trading atmosphere, but it was risky to cheat inebriated customers and jeopardize a long-term relationship. After the visitors repaid their advances and obtained new outfits, they were free to spend the rest of their credit on Canadian rum or English brandy. Until the Indian drinkers built up tolerance to alcohol, the stuff could be substantially diluted with water. But liquor trading furthered the erosion of mutual respect.

Until the summer of 1791, the Hudson's Bay Company servants enjoyed a good relationship with most their Indian trading partners. Then the experienced inland traveler Isaac Batt made the mistake of going on the barren ground (plains) with two Indians who were attached to pedlar rivals. Apparently murdered for his outfit, Batt earned the distinction of becoming the first Englishman killed by Indians. This showed that Hudson's Bay Company men were just as vulnerable as the Canadians.[80] The Siksika and Kainaa who brought wolf and fox skins to Buckingham House in 1791/92 were at war with the Cree by the following March. The fifty-four Muddy River and Falls (Atsiina) Indians who arrived after the first of the year seemed so sullen that Baymen were reluctant to risk wintering with them.

In the summer of 1793 the pot finally boiled over. Cree went to the South Branch of the Saskatchewan and massacred sixteen lodges of Falls Indians. Fearing to pursue the Cree into the woods, the survivors vented their rage on the trading houses that provided munitions to the transgressors.[81] Siksika opportunists, goaded by the Atsiina, ran off a number of horses from Fort George on the North Branch. Allied Kainaa also discouraged the Cree and Assiniboine from visiting the South Branch houses during the winter of 1793/94. After the transport brigades departed in the spring, about a hundred Falls Indians pillaged the Pine Island houses. A year later, the same number of Atsiina descended on the South Branch houses, killed most of the Hudson's Bay Company summer complement, and drove the neighboring white traders back to the forks.[82]

Shaken by their own audacity and rightfully fearing revenge, the Atsiina split into two factions. The most guilt-ridden went to the recently amiable Snakes, creating the Snake legend that the Snakes had helped the Gros Ventre in their time of trial. The other Atsiina faction retreated up the Bow River. That summer, apprehensive Plains tribes waited to see how the abused traders would react. If they didn't return, the Indians' supply of powder and balls would dry up and their guns would soon be useless. The balance of power on the northwestern plains teetered in ways too dismal for the worried elders to contemplate.

After an unusually long winter, seven nations appeared at the houses in the spring. Sarcee, Cree, Piegan, and Bloods—who had all traveled far—encountered one another in an unpleasant atmosphere of sour temper and simmering apprehension. Three kegs of the Nor'westers' diluted rum didn't help the situation. Although Southerd Cree failed to hunt beaver during the winter and wasted their time with the Piikani, the Hudson's Bay Company gave them generous advances to make a summer hunt. But the Piikani, who faithfully delivered their returns to Buckingham House, received little and went away vowing never to return.[83]

In fact, the Piikani were only blowing smoke. Access to the traders had become a necessity. Piikani women needed iron axes to gather firewood more easily. Sharpening butchering knives on stones soon ground them down to slivers so they had to be replaced. While the men might still use bows to kill buffalo, powder and shot were indispensable for sniping beaver and shooting raiders. To satisfy the yearly requirements of his family, a hunter needed about a hundred skins to trade. About two-thirds of that credit went for ammunition, metal tools, and cloth. The rest was spent on what the Baymen called luxuries: tobacco, ornaments, and liquor. Those weak-willed individuals who squandered precious credits on a binge condemned their families to poverty through the long year ahead. Although the Indians' revolving accounts sometimes showed a surplus, which the traders let them carry over for the next visit, savings plans were not encouraged.

Meanwhile, the Indians' winter hospitality to the traders had taken on a new dimension. The Canadians returning from the plains in spring 1795 were freemen, and some had married among the Indians. Those marriages allowed the traders to hunt beaver with their new relatives, and one steel trapper's harvest could clean out a wide area.

Newcomers were also adding to the pressure on the animals. Indians wishing to escape United States expansion in the Great Lakes region were now moving into the Northwest. Moreover, competing Canadian firms tried to increase beaver production by enlisting nonresident Ottawa and Ojibwa trappers. After the 1795 collapse of the western Indian confederation at Fallen Timbers, Canadian hiring agents also exploited disillusioned Iroquois. Using the new steel traps baited with castoreum, the strangers could clean out an entire beaver stream in one swoop. In their greed to scoop up rapidly declining beaver resources, the Canadians were recklessly destroying the formerly symbiotic relationship between trader and native hunter.

Competition for declining resources was forcing the Cree and Strong Wood Assiniboine to hunt ever higher on the Saskatchewan. With the weaponry obtained from trading, they pressed south for access to buffalo, in turn forcing the Siksika and Kainaa to crowd the Piikani ranges. The earth seemed to be shifting under the horses' hooves of the Gens du Large.

North West Company trader Duncan McGillivray documented the events of 1794/95 at Fort George on the Saskatchewan. McGillivray and his mentor, Angus Shaw, returned to the post to find the summer complement expecting an attack by the Gens du Large. But the rumor never materialized, and it was a considerable relief to learn that at least half of the troublesome Atsiina hoped to restore an amiable relationship with the Nor'westers. Blackfoot elders had also appeared during the summer to make amends for their excesses at Pine Island. But when they came to trade in the fall, they were intercepted and pillaged by Cree who were trying to control access to the posts.[84]

The first small band of Piikani, which arrived on 12 October, traded quickly and left before the Strong Wood and Grand River Assiniboine appeared. A month later, four Piikani chiefs and twenty young Piikani men came accompanied by three Sarcees. Most of the party went to the Hudson's Bay Company, but some traded with the Nor'westers, one chief because he was related to a woman at their fort. Another Piegan, who had never visited a fort before, was so dazzled that he presented the Nor'westers with a favorite horse and a war bonnet.[85] Although two Piikani leaders and seven young men traded with the Nor'westers on 16 November, twice as many went to the English, "owing to some old connections."[86] McGillivray rationalized that his partnership got two-thirds of the trade of other Indians, but it is clear that the North West Company lacked influence among the Piikani. Apparently quite a few men from both companies were sent to winter with the tribes that year.

The Nor'westers considered the trade over by mid-December, but Blackfeet, Piegan, and Bloods continued to straggle in through the winter with wolf skins and some meat. McGillivray picked up gossip that the Kutenai who lived west of the mountains were determined to force a passage to the trading posts. They hoped to bribe the blocking nations with horses and even had a passport—a parchment roll written by Spanish authorities to the traders in the north.[87]

On 9 April 1795, ten Blackfeet and thirty Bloods, whose horses had not yet recovered from the winter, struggled in over the softening snow with dog trains. A few Sarcee and Piegan came a few days later, and by mid-month the rendezvous had grown to about two hundred men representing seven different nations. After repaying debts, they got a last drink before the well dried up. Conspicuously absent was the Siksika leader Gros Blanc, who was still smarting from an insult by McGillivray the previous fall. The wintering Canadian men also returned with two thousand beaver skins, which were probably taken north of the Saskatchewan. McGillivray was not forthcoming about their returns, but the Hudson's Bay Company took in furs totaling 16,417 MB (made beaver). That included a large percentage of the less-desirable wolf skins taken on the barren ground.[88]

As the trade shifted away from the river, horses commanded greater attention. The traders needed to move outfits around and bring provisions from the distant hunting camps. Voyageurs and Baymen were no better horsemen than the Indians had been in the beginning. Canadian canoemen were more familiar with plodding pullers of carts and plows, and the highland ponies the Baymen knew were not quite the same as prairie mustangs. Much of what the traders knew about horses they had learned from their customers.

After Duncan McGillivray lost a horse that bolted after a herd of elk, he wrote,

> Most of these horses are trained from their youth to the exercise of hunting, their education indeed is not regular but practice makes them perfect. The Horse of this country tho' not large is bold and intrepid: he delights in the pleasures of the chace, and is so animated at sight of a Band of animals that he can scarcely be restrained from pursuing them. The operation of gelding is seldom performed by the Indians as it generally diminishes the strength and vigour of the Horse, he is therefore full of fire and can with ease outrun most of the large animals on which we depend for subsistence.[89]

In 1795 a Bayman paid goods worth 45 MB for a horse; four years later, another horse was traded for 30 MB. That was nothing compared to the vanity of a gentleman trader visiting the Mandans on the middle Missouri River. There, a horse was usually equal in price to a gun, and the discriminating horseman Alexander Henry paid 100 MB for a good buffalo runner.[90] Upper Saskatchewan masters fell into the bad habit of allowing engagees to retain horses of their own. Dealings with Indians inevitably led to the problems of horse trading: the "sharp deal" later regretted, the clinker slipped to a sucker. Private arrangements could turn into disputes or even killings.

The northern plains were not a hospitable environment for horses. Unlike the relatively winter-resistant buffalo, horses might die during difficult times in large numbers. One mixed-blood man riding with the Inuk'sik Piikani during the winter of 1829/30 reported that they lost six hundred horses.

The exchanges with the Kutenai that Peter Fidler had observed in 1792 continued. By December 1830, the Rocky Mountain House trader was complaining that the Piegan had traded their beaver to Kutenai Indians in exchange for horses.[91] Two years later, a Hudson's Bay Company party returning from the Missouri River traded lean horses for fat from some entrepreneurial Kutenai near the Old Man's meeting place.[92]

The traders were gradually climbing up the long northern curve of the Saskatchewan on a ladder of outposts. The idea was to keep rival tribes apart during the trading, but the moves tended to favor the beaver-hunting Cree and Strong Woods Assiniboine. When beaver became trapped out in an area, the posts were packed up and moved. But that instability was a disadvantage to the wolf- and fox-skin commerce of the Gens du Large, and they resented it.

After the North West Company built Fort Augustus, 130 miles higher up the river, in October 1795, the Hudson's Bay Company's William Tomison countered with Edmonton House. The stores were meant to claim the trade of the beaver-trapping Southerd Cree and Swampy Ground Assiniboine. But within two weeks, Sarcee and Muddy River Indians were also arriving with beaver pelts, and by late November a few Bloods had come in to keep abreast of developments.[93]

Eighty-three Muddy River and Blood men, accompanied by three hundred women and children, arrived at Fort Augustus and Edmonton House in early March 1798. Two Kutenais were also allowed a glimpse of the new store.[94] But a year later the Hudson's Bay Company spring returns amounted to only 1,511 made beaver, and Tomison had to go to London to drum up better logistical support. In the meantime, Tomison's protégé, James Bird, assumed supervision of the upper Saskatchewan posts, along with the problems of a business that had finally butted up against the Continental Divide.

During the summer of 1798, the Canadians attempted to steal a march by building a new post near the mouth of the Clearwater River. The crew ran into problems getting provisions and had to retreat, but when the proprietor returned he made them try again.

When Muddy River Indians came to Edmonton House on 11 September, Bird was already putting together an outfit to take farther upriver in response to the Canadians' move. After clearing the idea with his enthusiastic customers, Bird rode to the new location accompanied by three Indian hunters. A band of Muddy River Indians on their way to Edmonton House met the party on 18 September and fell in with them toward the new house instead. Two days later, Bird saw his first "most grand and romantic view" of the Stoney Mountains from an open place appropriately named Pikenow (Piegan) Plain.

The overland party was a week ahead of the outfit coming by water, but the Bloods, Sarcee, and Piegan hung around to watch the construction of both the Hudson's Bay Company's Acton House and the North West Company's Rocky Mountain House. Convinced that the Canadians intended to open trade with the Kutenai, Bird gave an unidentified Piikani chief presents to induce the westerners to bring their furs to the Baymen. The establishment of Acton House and Rocky Mountain House shortened the trip from the Muddy River winter camps on the upper Bow River to a mere fifteen or twenty sleeps. The investment paid off, as the next spring the Hudson's Bay Company was pleased to receive forty-six packs of beaver and eight bags of pemmican.[95]

The century turned on the upper Saskatchewan with nothing worth noting in the winter counts. Tension mounted, however, as increasing layers of tribal middlemen strained to prevent their western and southern neighbors from gaining direct access to the upper Saskatchewan traders— reliable suppliers of guns and ammunition. The fur trade threatened to upset the balance of power along the Rocky Mountains.

SEVEN

Action at Acton House

The North West Company partner John McDonald of Garth initiated the construction of Rocky Mountain House during the summer of 1799 and then went to the annual rendezvous at Grand Portage. Returning to Fort Augustus, McDonald dropped the surveyor David Thompson off to winter at Fort George. The next spring, Thompson made a horseback and boat survey of the upper Saskatchewan as far as Rocky Mountain House and reported his findings to the assembled partners. When Thompson returned in the fall of 1800, he was trailed by the real force behind westward expansion, Duncan McGillivray.[96]

Word of the new establishment soon reached interested Indians. That autumn a Kutenai party of twenty-seven men and seven women crossed the eastern mountains hoping to reach the new trading house with bear skins, wolverine and fisher pelts, and over a hundred beaver skins. The journey was another test of Kutenai determination to have a direct connection with the traders, which had been largely frustrated for the past eight years. Four Kutenai elders made the difficult journey to ensure that things did not get out of hand. But even before the party reached the mountain pass, opportunistic young Piikani were picking over their pony herd.[97]

Piikani were camped where the Red Deer River came out of the mountains, and five lodges were planted between the Red Deer and the

Clearwater. Some families may have been hunting in the hills, others catching eagles, but they were also waiting to intercept the Kutenai and levy a passage toll. One camp was that of Old Bear, who went to the new post and proposed to direct David Thompson to the Kutenai. By the time the two parties met on 14 October, the Kutenai were already huddled with their backs to high cliffs, trying to hold on to their last eleven horses.

The Kutenai journey was more a trial for them than a risk of outright hostility. Thompson recognized that the Piikani were jealous of the new connection and meant to discourage it, but he wisely sidestepped a confrontation with three bullies. To his credit, an indignant Piikani chief lectured his young men on their rude reception of the strangers. Another elder invited the visitors to feast at his camp. But the gambling that developed afterward put the peace in jeopardy, especially when the westerners won.

After a trying week, the Kutenai were down to two horses, and Thompson had to send ahead for remounts just to bring the Indians to the post.[98] Two days after Thompson finished trading with the Kutenais and arranged for two of his men to winter with them, Duncan McGillivray and their Hudson's Bay Company opponent James Bird arrived. Bird regretted missing the opportunity to send one of his men with the Kutenai, but he had his hands full maintaining the trade of the Slave nations.[99]

In mid-November, McGillivray and Thompson rode south to the Piikani winter camps along the upper Bow River. In the first camp, they met the principal chief Sacotowtow (Fidler's Sakatoo), who complained that the guns they were trading with the Kutenai eventually ended up in the hands of his Salish enemies. The traders reminded him that the Piikani themselves had already introduced guns to the Kutenai through their own trading.

Among the horse-oriented Gens du Large, it was the Piikani that brought in the most beaver and understood the value of that commodity. When the two traders revealed the agenda for their visit, the elders had a new problem to consider. McGillivray wanted to know their feelings about introducing Iroquois contract hunters to the South Branch of the Saskatchewan.

At that moment, the two negotiators had no way of knowing that the similar experiment of sending Iroquois to trap beaver in the lakes at the head of the Qu'Appelle River had failed. But McGillivray understood that North West Company agents around Montreal were authorized to arrange contracts for approximately three hundred Iroquois, who were to be introduced into the Northwest next year. Using the malleable Old Bear as a conduit, Duncan assured the Piikani that imported Iroquois trappers would live peacefully "in the woody Hills at the foot of the Mountain and serve as a Barrier between them and their Enemies." According to Thompson's recollection, "Upon those Terms they gave us permission to bring them up as soon as we pleased. Cut a Pipe of Tobacco to each Man & gave them a few pints of Mixed Rum to drink."[100]

Thompson's explanation seems a bit facile. While Iroquois beaver trapping on the South Branch would be more of a problem for the Atsiina than for the Piikani, having unwelcome neighbors in the foothills would mean competition for meat and horse pasturage. When seventy-five Ojibwa and "Eroquee Indians" came to the Red Deer two years before, their gambling with the Atsiina resulted in a quarrel in which a third of the visitors were killed.[101] Supercilious Iroquois were not the sort of neighbors that the Piikani would welcome.

Nor were the attentive Piikani reassured when McGillivray and Thompson used the return trip to explore up the Bow River toward the mountains, looking for a trail to the Kutenai country. That was odd, as Thompson had seen the east end of the Kutenai road only a month before. Later in December, McGillivray and the Hudson's Bay Company neighbor made another exploration, up the Brazeau River. In the spring, Thompson and James Hughes made a third investigation, of the Ram River. Both branches of the upper Saskatchewan appeared to be dead ends as far as the transport of goods was concerned. The Piikani understood that the Nor'westers were looking for a passage across the mountains as the next step in their practice of building posts for the convenience of the Piikani's potential enemies.

The record of events for Acton House and Rocky Mountain House during summer 1801 is missing. The Bayman Alexander Flett observed that in June the Nor'westers Thompson and Hughes failed to locate a passage across the mountains. This was in spite of the fact that the two freemen who had wintered with the Kutenai returned in time to have shown them the way. Piikani who came to trade with Thompson found his generosity a bit lacking. By fall, twenty-one tents of Piikani and a like number of Kainaa were camped on the upper Bow River, about seven sleeps from the new trading houses on the South Branch.

The Piikani's old friend Peter Fidler brought the Hudson's Bay Company outfit of 1800/1801 to the mouth of the Red Deer, where he built Chesterfield House, opposed by two Canadian parties. Falls Indians, Blackfeet, and Bloods flocked there with a trade of mostly fox and 250 ill-prepared wolf pelts. Although for the Piikani it was only half as far to Chesterfield House as to Acton House, the only Muddy River Indian Fidler saw that winter was one who came with Bloods in the spring. Perhaps they were distracted. Fidler had heard nothing of the Nor'wester's visit to the Piikani. On 20 December, some Blackfeet told Fidler that the Snakes had taken 120 Muddy River Indian horses. Two months later he learned that the pursuit of the thieves cost the lives of six Bloods and five Piikani.

In spring 1801, Cree from the upper Assiniboine River raided the Atsiina, taking scalps and slaves, having "made a great slaughter." When Fidler returned to Chesterfield House in September, he heard about the raid from waiting Bloods. A combination of Cree and Assiniboine had struck the Falls Indians about a month before, killing fourteen men and sixty women and children at the Cypress Hills and on the Oldman River, right in the Piikani's backyard. The Atsiina were also suffering from smallpox that had come to them from the south, which claimed about a hundred lives, mostly children. They must have caught it from their Arapaho connection. Fortunately it did not spread to the neighboring tribes.[102]

The developments of the past year showed that the Nor'westers were pandering to enemies of the beleaguered Falls Indians and planned to overrun their country with imported trappers. The Piikani could remain indifferent to matters affecting the Atsiina, but they now had good reason to doubt the trustworthiness of the Nor'westers. The four Piikani and six Kainaa who came to Chesterfield House on 27 October 1801 were overshadowed by the arrival of the Cold and Feather bands of Siksika, who dominated events around the South Branch houses for the rest of the winter. Gros Blanc's troublemakers wasted no time in killing a family of visiting Arapaho and setting the Atsiina on edge.

Fidler sent the visiting Piikani and Kainaa back with a gift of tobacco for "Cooten a haw se" [Kutenapi?] to distribute among the Muddy River Indians.[103] The five Muddy River Indians who appeared on 10 November expressed displeasure with the hard bargaining at Rocky

Mountain House and Acton House, but they'd brought very little to trade. The lone Piikani who appeared on 29 December was familiar with the customs of the traders and with their calendar, so it was no coincidence that he arrived just in time to get in on the New Year's revels.

Chesterfield's competitors had returned to the mouth of the Red Deer, but the Nor'westers were conspicuously absent. They had put McGillivray's proposal into operation. As the Iroquois trapped up the South Branch on their way to the Cypress Hills, the Atsiina intercepted them. Fourteen Iroquois and two Canadian trappers were killed and mutilated. The murders represented an emphatic rejection of "direct" trapping by freelancers.

It would be useful as a positive image of the Piikani to suggest that the party of twenty-two Piikani chiefs, one Kainaa, and fourteen Siksika who arrived at Chesterfield House on 19 March 1802 came in response to Fidler's terror.[104] But that party had been on the trail for twenty sleeps and had no way of knowing about the killings when they set out. They were fulfilling a Kainaa promise to come in February that had been delayed by cold weather. Nor did they hang around after their trading was done—they were on their way home the next day. This confirmed their lack of regard for McGillivray's proposal; they were just as indifferent to the slaughter of Iroquois.

Fidler's list of the twenty-two visiting Piikani included one man familiarly identified as Toby, who carried messages between Chesterfield House and Edmonton House. The Siksika appropriated the role of functionaries around the South Branch houses. In addition to keeping the diverse groups in line, their leader Akamoki (The Feathers) provided some very interesting information about western geography. But he could not restore the confidence of the shaken traders, who were relieved to get away from the awful place on 21 April 1802. When Fidler connected with the Edmonton brigade he learned that the Nor'westers had seduced colleague Alex Flett with an offer of sixty pounds per annum and perks.[105] By now Baymen could not be bribed to return to the upper Saskatchewan, or to the South Branch, with the next outfit. The Gens du Large who wanted to trade would have to make the long journey to Fort Augustus and Edmonton House.

There are questions concerning the accuracy of the recollections of John McDonald of Garth, but other sources show that he reestablished the North West Company outfit of 1804/05 on the South Branch about a hundred miles above the forks. That could still intercept the trade of the Cree, Assiniboine, Ojibwa, and Muskagoes without getting too close to the deadly Atsiina.[106] McDonald recalled that the house was soon visited by Indians from the Missouri River. They were at war with the five hundred Siksika camped nearby, but they vowed to fight through to the trading house. By noon of the following day, the Blackfeet had attacked and driven them off.

After convincing the Siksika that the Cree and Assiniboine planned to attack them, McDonald slipped the brigade away in the spring. During a night attack on the traders' camp the interpreter was killed.[107] As it turned out, the culprits were Hidatsa, who were ranging rather far afield from their homes on the Missouri River. In June, two North West Company traders to the Mandan villages saw Hidatsa women dancing over a Blackfoot scalp.[108] Adventuresome Hidatsa also attacked four or five tents of Salish buffalo hunters in the fall of 1804. The next year, one of the captured women from that raid was redeemed when three hundred tents of Crows came to trade at the Knife River villages. Such brief glimpses of tribal interactions show that hostilities were virtually universal on the northwestern plains.

Keeping the Northwest Company's South Branch post in August 1806, Daniel Harmon heard that eighty lodges of Cree and Assiniboine had joined about as many Blackfeet to attack the Atsiina. But a quarrel over a horse at the end of July broke up the army—twenty Siksika and three Assiniboine were killed.[109] James Bird learned that the dispute also involved four hundred Blackfeet and a like number of Southerd Indians. When the Siksika threatened indiscriminate slaughter, the Cree retreated into the woods, where plainsmen feared to ride.[110]

Upon his arrival at Edmonton, Bird was told that a party of Southerd Indians had been coming from the Muddy River Indian country to trade at Acton House. Unaware of the quarrel, they were intercepted and butchered about a hundred miles to the south. The bloody-handed Siksika who then came to the reopened Acton House coerced a resupply of ammunition from the intimidated Hudson's Bay clerk John Peter Pruden.[111]

In spring 1805, two Nor'westers, Charles McKenzie and Francois-Antoine Larocque, were hanging around the Mandan villages on the Missouri and watching a new development. When the American Corps of Discovery passed up the Missouri River, Larocque shadowed them by traveling with Indians along the parallel Yellowstone River. The Americans spent nine days exploring around the mouth of the Marias River (Bear River to the Piikani) and two weeks portaging the Great Falls. Captain Meriwether Lewis and Lieutenant William Clark went on toward the Three Forks without contacting any of the Gens du Large. Perhaps the Piikani were distracted by the Siksika and Cree war.

After wintering at the mouth of the Columbia River, the Corps of Discovery returned to the vicinity of present-day Missoula, Montana. Lewis and three others of the returning party followed the Salish Road to the Buffalo back to the Great Falls, and then set off overland to determine the upper reaches of the Marias. Keeping watch for the terrible "Pawkees" who terrorized the Shoshone and Salish, the four men rode over plains that seemed like an undulating ocean of grass. Along what would be later known as Cut Bank Creek, they discovered a ten-day-old camp of eleven lodges. Rainy weather over the next few days prevented Lewis from making the crucial calculation of location (48 degrees 40 minutes north). The explorers started back to the Missouri on 26 June.

The eight Piikani Indians who appeared along the Two Medicine Lodges River were probably buffalo hunters, because half of the thirty horses they drove were saddled. Displaying the American flag, Lewis made a cautious contact. After he gave a medal, a flag, and a handkerchief to the three leading men, everyone descended the 250-foot bluffs to the Two Medicine Lodges River, where the parties camped together about four miles below the mouth of Badger Creek.

During the evening, Lewis gleaned that the Indians' camp was a half-day march to the west, on a main branch of the Marias River at the foot of the mountains. From that camp it was a six-day march to the Bow River branch of the Saskatchewan. There was a white man with those Piikani. Another band of their people were hunting buffalo in the Broken Hills farther to the north, but they were expected at the mouth of the Bear in a few days.[112]

The next morning the Americans woke to find the Piikani trying to slip away with their guns. These hunters had no reason to instigate an incident, and they were not so politically astute as to instantly recognize the threat of American trade with their western enemies. (A later development suggests that the Muddy River Indians actually welcomed an alternative southern trade.) On hearing that the country was crawling with terrible "Pawkees," Lewis and his three men may have unintentionally telegraphed their apprehension to the eight hunters. The Indians may have feared that the strangers would leave without visiting their elders.

Reuben Field and Joseph Field pursued the Indian who grabbed their guns and, struggling to recover them, fatally stabbed the boy in the heart. Drawing his pistol, Lewis chased two others into a gulch. When one turned and fired at thirty paces, the captain shot him in the belly. The panting explorers recovered four of their six horses and nine Indian ponies. Abandoning the poorest animals and taking four of the Indian's ponies, they started for the mouth of the Marias before the unhorsed Piikanis could get reinforcements. Lewis repossessed the flag but left a medal around the neck of the dead man so that tribe "might be informed who we were"—not exactly an auspicious beginning.[113]

The Piikani reaction to the incident was not as bad as the fleeing Americans supposed. By 23 December, James Bird noted that "A party of Americans were seen last Summer where the Missoury enters the rocky Mountains & tis reported by the Muddy or Missoury River Indians that four of them set off with an intention to come here but that they kiled one and the rest returned."[114] This suggests that the gut-shot man actually survived. Contrary to historical speculation, the Piikani had not taken the incident very seriously. It was just another unpleasant episode in the ongoing horse-capturing contests and war games.

EIGHT

Over the Stoney Mountains

By 1845, when David Thompson was devising his *Narrative*, the former trader needed to malign the "Peeagans." The Oregon boundary settlement was looming and the old trader wanted to convince British officials that he had crossed the mountains in 1801. But "an overwhelming force of the eastern Indians obliged me to retreat a most desperate retreat of six days, for they dreaded the western Indians being furnished with Arms and Ammunition."[115] That fabrication fitted in nicely with prevailing ideas of the Blackfoot barrier.

Thompson's field journals and other contemporary evidence do not support his statement that the Piikani were distracted by the Meriwether Lewis incident and were drawn south looking for revenge. They had hunted along the Marias and Two Medicine Lodge Rivers for many years. For the past year, the Muddy River Indians had been watching some very obvious North West Company preparations for crossing the mountains, a business extension that would spoil their domination of the Kutenai. But the tribe had taken no steps to prevent it.

In the spring of 1807, the big distraction on the northwestern plains was some Cree children that were being held by the Bloods. The previous year several Cree families had been murdered. The Cree, supported by the Assiniboine, were looking for revenge, to the neglect of their beaver hunting. Those who came to Acton House in April 1807 brought a poor trade but hung around drinking with the Piegans. Caught in a difficult middle ground, the Piikani refused to smoke the pipe of peace until the Cree and Blackfeet settled their differences. With some difficulty, the Acton House trader Peter Pruden induced his Muddy River customers to hunt beaver in the Rocky Mountains instead of hunting men on the plains.

At Edmonton House, the only thing that factor James Bird could promise the Piikani was a more convenient trading post, and that promise was made just to counter potential American inroads into the Piikani trade. The truth was that Bird had no hope of building a new trade house with the limited resources available to him.

In May, the ever-difficult Atsiina compounded an already tense situation by reappearing at Edmonton. For the past two years they had been away near the Spanish settlements with their Arapaho kinsmen. Returning through the Bighorn country, they had managed to offend the Crows, who threatened an invasion. Now the Atsiina clamored for arms and ammunition to defend themselves.

David Thompson left Rocky Mountain House with his men and a pack train on 10 May 1807. He intended to follow the Saskatchewan upriver and cross the mountains on the Kutenai trail to set up a new post. Since the previous summer, Jacco Finlay and Nicholas Montour had been working to improve that road to accommodate packhorses. Several times during the winter, parties had carried goods to caches nearer the divide.[116] Unfortunately, the trail improvements were not up to Thompson's expectations and it took fifty-two days to make the crossing.[117] Clattering down the rocky streambed of the Blaeberry River, the party came to the Columbia River. After building canoes, the Nor'westers paddled upstream to the large lake near the headwaters.

Thompson had not forgotten Sakatowtow's objection to arming the Salish. Not long after his men began building Kootenae House, small bands of Piegans showed up and hung around. Guarded social exchanges between the two tribes were not unusual and the visitors made no overt demonstrations of hostility. Thompson worried while the Indians watched the building, much as the Siksika had done during the establishment of the South Branch houses. Apprehension was as thick as autumn leaves around Kootenae House, but the Piikani seemed to accept the new post as an accomplished fact. Astute Piikani elders like Old Swan did not want to give the Nor'westers grounds to cut off their trade.

Until mid-August Thompson fretted about why the main body of the Kutenai Indians remained at a distance. He was finally informed that they had been with the Salish, participating in a peace council with the Piegans. Did that mean that the latter were trying to placate their western enemies in order to neutralize his new post?

The peace council convened on the horse plains south of Salish Lake at the end of July. During a week of discussion, ceremony, and gambling, the elders arrived at an agreement. But the Siksika and Kainaa, who observed the negotiations, had little interest in a truce that threatened to inhibit their horse raiding. As the gathering was breaking up, one of their young warriors attempted to appropriate a Salish horse and got himself killed. In the ensuing melee, fourteen Piikani and four Salish were also cut down and the peace delegates forced to flee for their lives.

In his brief field notes, Thompson does not seem very disappointed by the collapse of the agreement. He also swept another arresting development under the table: when the Kutenai finally came in, they reported counting forty-two men in an American party located just south of the Salish camps. Thompson was handed a long letter from the commanding officer. That disconcerting document clearly stated United States territorial claims, not only to upper Louisiana but to the Columbia River drainage as well. It set up regulations for governing and taxing British operations.[118] Thompson could only believe that the United States had foreseen what he was up to and was warning him off.

If the Piikani had gone south looking for Americans in the summer of 1807, they would not have been disappointed. The letter suggested that the Americans had been on the upper Yellowstone in July and had since moved into Salish country. Perhaps they'd had a hand in promoting the peace council.

It had taken only a month for that outrageous statement of national sovereignty to travel the moccasin telegraph. The Americans must have been in contact with the Piegans very soon after Thompson left Rocky

Mountain House. If the Piikani now had an alternate source of supply, they had no reason to fear offending the Nor'westers.

The North West Company management needed to be informed of the developments, and soon Thompson sent the letter, his journal, and some papers across the mountains to catch the winter express. His couriers returned with more appalling proof of American intentions. It was a purloined copy of one of the first reports that Meriwether Lewis wrote after returning from the Pacific. By 11 December, Thompson was copying a full outline of the American exploration into his own discovery journal. Lewis's account disturbed Thompson: it suggested that the Americans meant to counter, perhaps even absorb, the British interior trade.[119]

Precisely a week later, five Piikani men crossed the winter-locked mountains in another attempt to find peace. Through some prior arrangement, a Salish delegation and the old Kutenai chief came to Kootenae House to meet them. The trail-worn Piikani confirmed that Cree were assembling to strike all the Plains Indians (except the Piikani), but no one had any intention of making war on the western peoples. Emboldened

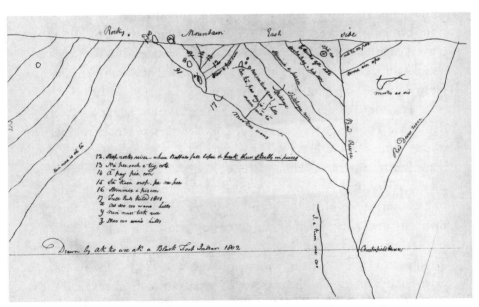

Map drawn by the Blackfoot Ak-ko-wee-ak, 1802. The map reflects his understanding of the country near the Red Deer River, the Oldman River, the South Branch of the Saskatchewan, and as far south as the Milk River (eastern Montana and southern Alberta). Note the description of the pisskan: "steep rocks river where Buffalo fall before & break their skulls in pieces."[3] — Courtesy Hudson's Bay Company Archives

by their guns and reliable ammunition supply at Kootenae House, the western Indians were unresponsive. After some convivial drinking and dancing over Christmas, the Piikani left the next day carrying Thompson's unenthusiastic gift of tobacco to encourage the peace initiative.

The Salish delegation also brought another letter from the American officer. By 29 September the audacious fellow had moved west to the lake of the Poltito Palton (Lake Pend d'Oreille), which seemed to block Thompson's plans for extending trade southward. The letter was so testy and threatening that Thompson felt obliged to answer. Careful to avoid committing his partnership to international incident, he wrote only the minimum.[120]

The Piikani who hung around Kootenae House were more interested in Kutenai horses than the inhibition of commerce. At the end of March 1808, Thompson sent two of his men to the Kutenai camp to encourage the Indians to work beaver. Passing where the Elk River came into the Tobacco Plains, the pair fell in with forty-seven Piikani, who accompanied them to the ten lodges of the old Kutenai chief. Before long, there was a fight in which three Piikani were killed and the old chief wounded.

After losing thirty-five horses, the Kutenai were too upset to make a spring hunt. When Thompson wrote that high water prevented the Salish from bringing any furs to the Nor'westers, which was true, given the normal condition of that country, he must have wondered if the Americans had also had a hand in it. The good news was that the Americans had returned to the east side of the mountains.[121]

That and a couple of carefully veiled references to earlier events are all that David Thompson recorded about a development of remarkable portent to the North West Company. Three years later, when another dark cloud hung over his enterprise, Thompson mentioned some deaths in a letter to a friend in Montreal. An American officer and eight men had been killed by Indians sometime after the eventful winter of 1807/8.[122] By then the British trader believed that he had come quite close to a similar fate.

After exploring the Kootenai River as far as the Flat Bow Indians, Thompson returned east to receive a new outfit. He needed to test the partnership's reaction to the unexpected appearance of Americans. At the Rainy Lake depot in July 1808, Thompson questioned whether it was advisable to extend trade south of the generally accepted dividing line of forty-nine degrees north latitude.[123] Sent back to consolidate the Salish trade and forgetting for the present the idea of establishing a British presence on the lower Columbia, David Thompson had no need to be a strong supporter of Piikani peace initiatives.

Trading posts now ringed the northwestern plains. The British encirclement started at New Chesterfield House and South Branch House and continued up the North Branch of the Saskatchewan to include the shifting locations of Fort Vermillion and Buckingham House, Fort Augustus and Edmonton House, and several lesser outposts. That thrust was grounded at Acton House and Rocky Mountain House, which became the bases for western development. From the initial Kootenae House, Thompson followed up in 1809 with two additional establishments: Kullyspell House on Lake Pend d'Oreille and Saleesh House in the heart of the Flathead country.

Fixed on developing the Salish trade, the Nor'westers ignored the Piikani. Although the Hudson's Bay Company's James Bird continued to promise a post more convenient to the upper Bow River winter camps, he was unable to take that short step. By 1807, American traders had moved in to claim the Crow trade. The Lisa-Drouillard adventure, which later became the St. Louis Missouri Fur Company, came up the Yellowstone and built a post at the mouth of the Bighorn. In addition to servicing the productive Crows, founder Manuel Lisa meant to attract Snakes, Salish, and Nez Perce. His Fort Remon also became the staging point for trapping parties that moved up to the Three Forks area to take beaver. Those hunters merged with the forty-two Americans who had returned from Salish country.

The intrusive American trappers underlined something that had been developing on the upper Saskatchewan since the turn of the century. It was the insidious development of "direct" trapping. Fur company engagees had always been released to winter with the Indians, but after the mergers of rival Canadian operations in 1800 and 1804, a number of excess engagees were turned loose in the country. The term "freeman" came to mean an independent trapper who could take advantage of his native consort's tribal connections while working in his own self-interest. With families to support, these professional trappers competed with Indian hunters for the declining beaver resources.

Contract trappers from dispersed eastern Indian nations were also resented, particularly the Iroquois, who continued to conduct themselves as if the defunct League of Six Nations meant something on the plains.

The Cree, who understood how beaver pelts translated into power through powder and ball, were moving on to the plains as buffalo hunters. With the outsiders' noose tightening on their natural resources, the Gens du Large had to react.

The Atsiina, Siksika, and Kainaa that made the first documented attacks on American traders in 1808 were probably opportunists. James Bird at Edmonton and Alexander Henry at Fort Vermillion heard reports of those attacks but failed to record any Piikani involvement. Piikani continued their contradictory policy of peace gestures and horse raids directed at the western tribes, but there is no direct evidence that they menaced the Americans. After all, if the Americans built a trading house at the Bear (Marias) River, that would spare the Piikani the long, difficult journey to the Saskatchewan houses.

Although other Plains Indians killed the active young Hudson's Bay Company mixed-blood William Walker on the South Branch, the Muddy River Indians traded peacefully at Edmonton House in November. After the first of the year in 1808, James Bird learned that some Gens du Large had been in contact with Americans on the Missouri the previous fall. The newcomers were willing to sell guns for 5 MB but denied having liquor. Lacking the goods or manpower to undertake a post toward the Missouri, Bird consoled himself that the rival Nor'westers would need to commit at least forty men to undertake it.

During that winter, the St. Louis Missouri Fur Company had sent travelers in several directions from Fort Remon to invite Indians to the new store. George Drouillard and John Colter were former members of the Corps of Discovery with a reasonable understanding of basic western geography. Drouillard provided the first information on the upper Bighorn, and Colter made a swing through the Wind River valley.

By spring 1808, Colter was in contact with the Salish and Nez Perce on their winter buffalo hunt and was leading a delegation toward the Missouri Fur Company fort. Just east of the Three Forks, a considerable body of Plains Indians intercepted them. It is unlikely that the fight could have involved fifteen hundred Blackfeet against five hundred Flatheads and three hundred Crows, as the inflated yarns later said. But this was an early glimpse of a developing confrontational attitude.[124] If its purpose was a preventive strike to discourage the arming of western Indians, that represented an astonishing leap in tribal perception and combined strategic reaction. It is more likely that Colter and his new friends were just unlucky enough to bump into some of the Atsiina and their allies on a preemptive strike against the threatened Crow invasion.

The fight was another encounter in the ongoing buffalo wars. The Piikani had managed to overlook the unfortunate incident with Meriwether Lewis, but Colter's participation on the part of his new associates disproved American neutrality. The violent mythology of the mountain men began without close distinctions among the Gens du Large; it was the Atsiina who brought evidence of two slain Americans to Edmonton in October 1808.[125] Undaunted by his experience, Colter, along with John Potts, another veteran of the Corps of Discovery, returned to the Three Forks to trap the next year. Confronted by the Atsiina, Potts was killed when he resisted, but Colter was given a sporting chance to race for his life. With that incentive, the naked man outdistanced his tormentors and made it back to Fort Remon.

After Thompson's brush with American competition across the mountains, the North West Company redesigned the supervision of the upper Forts des Prairies. The new proprietor was the experienced Alexander Henry the Younger, previously stationed at Pembina on the upper Red River. After visiting the Mandan villages on the Missouri between the departure and return of the Corps of Discovery, Henry had a unique grasp of the developing international confrontation. At Fort Vermillion the Nor'wester did not hesitate to receive beaver that the Siksika took from Americans on the Missouri.

In his analysis of the department, Henry estimated that the Slave Indians totaled 650 tents. That calculated out to around 1,420 warriors. The 120 lodges of the Painted Feather Siksika band followed Old Swan, Three Bears, the powerful Ermine Tails, and approximately thirty other principal men. The 80 tents of the Siksika Cold band had forty significant men led by the quarrelsome Gros Blanc. The Siksika, intent on dominating the trade, looted the Pine Island posts in 1793 and killed Arapaho near Chesterfield House in 1801.[126]

The Kainaa, who followed Boeuf qui Boit, also traded at Fort Vermillion. They were accompanied by a few Piikani, but the majority of the Muddy River Indians and their Southerd Cree associates took their trade to Fort Augustus and Edmonton House, or the seasonally opened Rocky Mountain House and Acton House.

In the fall of 1808, the alienated Siksika patched up a fragile peace with the Cree, leaving one of their young men as hostage to the agreement. When an impetuous Cree killed him not far from Fort Vermillion, his relatives vowed revenge. Passing Battle River on 7 September, Alexander Henry heard that some Cree had killed three Piikani, whose friends promptly killed four of the transgressors. The surviving Cree saved themselves by retreating into the woods, where horsemen were reluctant to follow. The concerned trader feared that a serious war might result.[127]

During October, James Bird received three hundred beaver at Edmonton House. Bloods had taken the peltry from two small American settlements on a southern branch of the Missouri. The Bloods had also killed one trapper and stripped ten others. From recovered papers, Bird concluded that the victims were Canadians operating under American colors. Even the usually reticent Sarcee got in on the looting, as did the Falls Indians, who arrived on All Hallows' Eve with a curious, heavy, stolen gun. But the Muddy River Indians were not implicated.[128]

Because the Hudson's Bay Company was short of tobacco, the Piikani who came to trade in early November went to the neighboring Fort Augustus. Bird consoled himself that they usually brought upward of four hundred beaver to him through the winter, as well as the greater part of the bear skins shipped from Edmonton House and Fort Augustus. A large band of Muddy River Indians that included forty-five principal men appeared on 21 April 1809. They had been attending to business (by trader's standards) and turned in seventeen hundred wolf skins and a few bear skins, but only fifty beaver.[129] They made no mention of hostile activities against Americans.

Gens du Large piracy on the Missouri was producing almost as many beaver skins as the Piikani took by hunting. However, the Painted Feather band, Cold band, and other opportunists lurking along the Missouri through the summer of 1809 were disappointed in their expectations. When they turned in only a few less-than-desirable wolf skins at Fort Vermillion in the fall, the disgruntled Henry concluded that the trade of the Slave tribes was piddling. Like Duncan McGillivray before him, Henry professed to be unconcerned that his Hudson's Bay Company rival was getting two-thirds of their business. The stupid Baymen were still buying unprofitable wolf and fox pelts at a high price. Beyond beaver, what the Nor'westers wanted was dried meat and pemmican to fuel their canoe brigades to more lucrative beaver grounds.[130]

Not long after Alexander Henry and James Bird rode into Fort Augustus and Edmonton House on 30 October 1809, Boeuf qui Boit and his Blood followers appeared. They came to smooth out the bad feelings caused by their disputes with the Cree. There was also the matter of some inspired rustling from the traders' herds. After amends were made and drinks dispensed, forty of the principal Blood men traded with the Nor'westers while sixty took their business to the Hudson's Bay Company. But the tranquillity was fleeting: a quarrel that winter between the Painted Feather and Cold bands left Gros Blanc simmering.[131]

Most of the tensions between the Assiniboine, Cree, and Blackfeet either derived from or were diverted into horse stealing. Dark rumors from the dangerous South Branch related a plot to kill the Nor'wester Francois Decoigne. There must have been some substance to it, because in February the experienced Nicholas Montour Jr. refused a direct order to go there.

Repeated accounts of tribal disharmony and violence reflected a sickness infecting the northern plains. It grew at least in part from the greedy competition between rival trading and trapping organizations for shares of Indian furs. When hunters brought beaver to the posts, the competitors often resorted to bribes of liquor to acquire their business. Drinking created a dangerous environment.

The journals do not record any suggestion that British traders deliberately encouraged the Gens du Large to harass American trappers. But it cannot be overlooked that they showed little reservation about accepting the loot. Ironically, the munitions the traders pumped into tribal war machines destroyed their customers. The northern plains were turning into a treacherous no-man's-land. As the Piikani sidled away from these boilings, they were forced into new contests with the western buffalo hunters.

In 1792/93, Piikani were running buffalo in the teeming plains and breaks of the Oldman River. Thirteen years later, Meriwether Lewis brushed with scouts in the attractive valleys of the Marias River. There were more than enough buffalo for everyone, but the territorial prerogative required an expression of sovereignty. When Salish and Sahaptans came over the easy mountain trail to the Sun River and spread out to run buffalo there, the Piikani felt obliged to resist them.

The Salish favored a little valley near the east end of *cokalarishket,* the Road to the Buffalo. The place was enclosed to protect grazing horses, and a fortified camp served as a base of operations. When it came to fighting the "Pawkees," the Salish had a couple of worn-out guns that had passed to them through Crow middlemen and whatever powder had been saved. But it wasn't blood or scalps the Piikani wanted from them. The threat to the Flatheads came in the night: a nervous nickering from the ponies, a cry in the dark, and the sound of receding hooves. The valley wasn't so much a battleground as a stock exchange—horses for buffalo.

After delivering the returns of the outfit of 1808/09 to Rocky Mountain House, David Thompson headed west again. He needed a full summer to push the next stage of western operations into the Salish country. As he crossed, Thompson met a Bayman exploring the road. At the risk of alienating their Piikani connection, the Hudson's Bay Company was going to follow the Nor'westers into the Columbia drainage.

Thompson followed the soggy Lake Indian Road to Lake Pend d'Oreille and built his second western post on a defensible peninsula along the north shore. While construction was under way, he scouted for a downstream outlet to the Columbia River but returned disappointed. After Kullyspell House was secure, Thompson trailed up the river known locally as *nemissoolatakoo* (Clark Fork) to a second promising place, close to the favorite Flathead wintering grounds on the horse plains. After building Saleesh House, the North West Company men spent the winter of 1809/10 near those accommodating folk.

But the British traders did not enjoy exclusive control of the area. American freemen were already hunting there. In early 1810, several American trappers arranged outfits from Thompson. They had been working on the upper Missouri for three years. The previous fall, their leader, a Detroit trader and trapper named Charles Courtin, had led them across the mountains to winter with the Flatheads. Courtin had left a number of packs of beaver taken during the winter hunt cached near the Three Forks, and he took the first opportunity to return to that cache. Packing the peltry taken during the winter hunt, he joined the early Salish buffalo hunters. The party got only as far as the ominous defile where the Nemissoolatakoo and Bitterroot Rivers come together. In an ambush, Gens du Large raiders killed Courtin as he struggled to control his pack string. The discouraged Salish buried the body and dutifully collected the scattered property. Courtin's former associates asked Thompson to adjudicate the division of some salvaged property and, since he ran the only store in sight, the Nor'wester was pleased to oblige.

By spring 1810, Thompson had to move out of Saleesh House to make room for the packs that were piling up. Peltry taken by American trappers finally put Thompson's western adventure into the profit column. Leaving his red-bearded assistant Finan McDonald as summer master, Thompson bundled up his family and departed. He planned to take a long-overdue furlough in Montreal.[132]

During the past three years, the Piikani had seemed to tolerate the North West Company expansion. Their young men were more interested in raiding Kutenai and Salish herds or contesting them during the twice-yearly buffalo hunts. But now the Saleesh House trade had put new guns and ammunition into the hands of their enemies. Meanwhile, western hunters persisted in coming great distances to take buffalo that the Piikani considered their own. Worse, the other Gens du Large raided through Piikani ranges to get at the Salish and Kutenai ponies. Those reivers retreated with their loot, leaving the Piikani to bear the inevitable re-taliation. A desire to mitigate that injustice may have been the force behind the 1807 peace initiatives. But three years later the problem was still unresolved, and now the western tribes were armed.

After Thompson was out of the picture at Saleesh House, one of Courtin's former associates, Michael Bourdon, convinced Finan McDonald and Baptiste Buche to accompany the Salish buffalo hunt that summer. The bait was the same that drew Courtin to his death—those twenty packs of beaver pelts still in a cache near the Three Forks.

In July 1810, the chivalrous Piikani marshaled themselves in the usual order of battle for another contest with a Salish hunting camp. The timing was unusual because hunts were generally conducted in late winter or early fall. In the past, their edge in fire power had always favored the Piikani gunmen. As the opposing lines of battle closed in, the Plains warriors were surprised to receive fire from North West Company trade guns. And three of them were being fired, again and again and again, by their Nor'wester friends.[133]

The firefight lasted all day. After the initial shock, the Piikani dug in and returned fire until their ammunition was exhausted. In the end they were reduced to heaving rocks over the hilltop. For warriors whose tactic was always to avoid casualties, the loss of sixteen Piikani was a complete disaster. The reaction spread rapidly, and by mid-August infuriated Piikani had crossed the mountains to block the traders' road to the Salish.[134]

James Bird watched the growing rift between his Piikani friends and the Nor'westers. He drew information from the South Branch houses and Acton House, but the most immediate data came from moles inside the rival organization. Bird's list of informants included the disaffected Jacco Finlay, several other tramontane freemen, and likely his own brother-in-law, Nicholas Montour, a clerk assisting the North West Company expansion.

Bird's "corporate espionage" successfully tracked the western developments and convinced him that he had to follow the opposition. In 1809, he had sent Joseph Howse to explore the road across the mountains. Now, in the summer of 1810, Howse and a substantial party had started for the Salish country with a trading outfit.[135] The expedition was under way before news arrived of the fatal encounter between the Salish and the Piikani. Howse encountered Piikani who were blocking the western trail and was held up for awhile. In the end, he managed to placate them and was allowed to proceed to a wintering place near the lake of the Salish. Undaunted by the experience of his competitors, Howse even accompanied the early Salish buffalo hunters and saw the Road to the Buffalo for himself.[136]

In October another blockade was planted across the mountain portage trail above Acton House and Rocky Mountain House. The three enforcers were Le Borgne (One Eye), Black Bear, and his brother Big Throat, who may have been an orator or herald. Too small for a direct confrontation, the party was more symbolic than actually threatening, but it was enough to turn back four laden canoes and scare David Thompson.[137]

The next spring, the Muddy River chiefs assured the concerned James Bird that they would not molest Howse's returning party. But Bird wrote that they "declared that if they again met with a white man going to supply their Enemies they would not only plunder & kill, but they would make dry meat of his body."[138] Bird believed it, because he knew that they had made three attacks on an American settlement in the south and "killed most of the men, roasted the body of the principal American and ate it with the most savage Exultation."

Later he learned that Atsiina and Kainaa had made those attacks on the Missouri Fur Company trapping party at the Three Forks. The loot and brags brought to Edmonton House confirmed the killing of

George Drouillard, one of the men with Meriwether Lewis at the fatal encounter with the Piikani in 1806. The Piikani confined their activities to pursuing Crow horse raiders across the Missouri, where they saw an American fort that must have been Fort Remon at the mouth of the Bighorn. Directing their attentions to the Crows, those raiders were home by May.

Although the Salish returns were good, Howse returned to Edmonton convinced that their trade was not worth the risks. Accepting that evaluation, Bird took a new tack. When the Piikani trading party headed home, he sent young James Whitway with them. The boy would try to repair the damaged relationship while learning to speak their language.[139]

NINE

Blowing the Piegan Connection

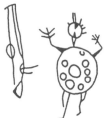

On 26 September 1810, Alexander Henry intended to go upstream and fulfill the promise made in the spring to reopen Rocky Mountain House. While David Thompson was away on furlough, a proprietor was needed to back up the less-experienced clerks left in charge of the North West Company's western operation. But before Henry got under way, Thompson returned from the Rainy River inland depot. The news from the Fort William summer rendezvous was that an American was sending sea and land expeditions to the mouth of the Columbia River.

Their new opponent was the substantial New York entrepreneur John Jacob Astor and his Pacific Fur Company. At the moment, the Nor'westers' western enterprise was just beginning to show a profit. More competition could ruin expectations. Resigning themselves to an uncharacteristic compromise, the North West partners who had wintered inland decided to accept an offer of one-third interest in Astor's venture. Thompson was sent back to descend the Columbia River and work out a cooperative agreement with Astor's people.[140] The pragmatic businessmen were not overly concerned about weakening the British Empire's claims to the Pacific Northwest. It was the Indian trade and an outlet to the Pacific that they cared about.

When Thompson arrived at the Rainy River resupply depot on 22 July 1810, the inbound wintering partners he met did not let him off the hook. He would have to return west. Convinced of his own canard about the menacing Piegans, Thompson proposed a new supply route that would cross the mountains well north of their territory. But those tough men rejected the suggestion—no Indians were going to dictate their plans.

Black Bear, Big Throat, and Le Borgne had planted their lodges along the upper Saskatchewan to prevent the Nor'westers from hauling arms or ammunition to the Salish. Their presence was enough to discourage the canoes preceding Thompson; those men were found cowering around Rocky Mountain House when Henry arrived on 5 October. But where was Thompson?

Coming up the river by a land trail, Thompson also learned of the blockage. Just the suspicion of Piegans was enough to turn back Thompson and his overland party. The shaken trader also retreated downstream and had gone into hiding without checking to find out what had become of his boats. He cowered in a state of indecision until the exasperated Alexander Henry located him. Whatever transpired between the two proprietors was discreetly left unrecorded in Henry's journal. But the outfit got started on the alternate northern route. The route was so difficult that the party became stranded in the mountains until the following spring.

During the winter of 1810/11, Henry learned that the traders Thompson left in the west were living with the Indians. That seemed to confirm that Finan McDonald had abandoned Saleesh House. Henry's intention of placating the Piegan at Rocky Mountain House was also frustrated by the blockade. It was small consolation that the Piikani had made a momentary check on the Hudson's Bay Company party the summer before, eventually allowing the Baymen to proceed. That outfit surely dominated the Salish trade this winter.

Henry found the chiefs Big Throat and Le Borgne friendly enough, though secretive. But it was obvious that both trading houses were being watched from the lodges pitched nearby. Black Bear (Sikohkiaayo) was

Henry's shadow while White Buffalo Robe watched William Flett at Acton House.

Generally, it was business as usual at Rocky Mountain House. Small parties or individuals came to trade, and most of Henry's problems were from the drunks that he helped create. The Indians were two-faced as well: after lecturing unruly young men on the benefits of temperance, Black Bear and his brother got drunk and made trouble. To divert problems, Henry told the thirteen Bloods who appeared in mid-October that they must trade downstream at Terre Blanche in the future. Rocky Mountain House was reserved for the Piegan, Falls Indians, and Sarcee.

On 7 November, the last Piikani left for their winter camps. The loss of sixteen warriors had not deterred the Piikani and Atsiina from raiding western herds and driving away sixty Flathead horses. Other Piikani joined an Atsiina expedition against the Crows. During shouted exchanges somewhere south of the Missouri River, the Crows boasted that they intended to invade the Atsiina country with the assistance of their American friends.[141]

That winter at Rocky Mountain House, Henry was a frustrated commercial strategist convinced that Thompson was dragging his heels. He even made a trip to the top of the mountain to assess the actual difficulty of the mountain portage that the Piegans had blocked and that Thompson was ready to abandon. Fully conscious of Piegan sensitivity, he lied to them about his intentions. Back at the post, Henry indulged himself by writing an essay on the geographical and ethnographical aspects of his surroundings. He had not seen the Flat Bow (or Lake) Indians, the Salish, the Kullyspell (or Ear Bobs), the Sheetshue (or Pointed Hearts), the Spokane, the Simpoil, or the Sapetans, so his data came from those who had. He must have taken his specimens of the Salish language from Thompson's vocabulary.

Not long after Henry's return from his winter hike to the pass, the Cree wife of a Piikani came with a warning. The Falls Indians had bad hearts toward the Nor'westers because of the treatment they had been getting at Fort Augustus. The traders' refusing their wolf skins meant that the Indians could not trade for ammunition. Crow enemies on the Yellowstone were bragging of the support they were receiving from the Americans and were threatening an invasion. If the Falls Indians could not obtain powder in trade, they would be forced to seize it from the traders. Based on that warning, Henry decided to forgo his planned visit to the Piikani winter camps on the upper Bow River.[142]

Henry's former warden, White Buffalo Robe, also confirmed the plot but assured Henry that the Piikani were committed to defending their friends. The old man was not going to let the excesses of others disrupt his own trade. Nevertheless, Henry set his men to repairing the bastion and cutting loopholes in the walls. He discovered a renewed appreciation of the Piegans. Although he might have preferred dealing with people of less pride, Henry recognized the Piegans' difficult position. Penned in along the mountains, they were surrounded by enemies who could "have just as much war as they chose." Henry rationalized that the Piikani "were too busy in this way, and in providing for their families to have leisure to indulge in greater vices."[143]

That was just as well, as the Rocky Mountain House journalist estimated that there were 350 Piikani lodges, up from 150 some twenty years earlier. Over half that population must have been under the age of twenty, with a fading memory of the smallpox epidemic and no grasp at all of a world without horses. Now they were part of the social and cultural tensions of a baby-boom generation. During the dangerous summer raiding season, the Piikani congregated in camps of one or two hundred. In winter, when there was less risk of raids, they broke up into bands of ten to twenty families. Perhaps there were as many as fifteen to thirty winter bands looking for places to graze their herds.

One group of thirty or forty lodges stood out because they seldom went to the plains but generally stayed in the thick woody country along the foot of the mountains. Because they had beaver to trade, they were better off than their buffalo-running brethren. Henry may have caught an early glimpse of the Inuk'sik band. They would be known as the Small Robes, whose propensity for beaver hunting grew from old relationships with expatriate Cree. In 1792/93, Fidler had met some Cree in the Piikani camps, and two years later, Duncan McGillivray named three Cree chiefs— Gauche, Sitting Badger, and The French Bastard—who were living with the Piegan. The Piikani's wife who warned Henry of the Atsiina plot was also Cree.[144]

Henry saw the Missouri River as the southern boundary of the Piikani ranges without realizing the ambiguity of that description. Actually, the river bent south above the Great Falls, creating a broad corridor between the river and the mountains. That perfect road for horses dragging travois ran south through the Three Forks and up the Jefferson Fork to the Continental Divide. It was part of what was to be known as the Old North Trail.[145] Six years earlier, when Lewis and Clark found the Lemhi Shoshone cowering in the Red Rock country, it was because the far-ranging Piikani had already made the Three Forks very dangerous.

Cokalarishket, the Salish Road to the Buffalo, trailed up the Big Blackfoot River and crossed the mountains to intercept the Old North Trail. Western buffalo hunters emerged on the heights of the Dearborn River or popped over to the Sun River on their way to cross the Missouri. That put the flank of Piikani expeditions against the Shoshone in jeopardy. Until the sixteen young Piikani fell to Flathead guns the previous July, aspiring young warriors had always known exactly where to go to make their reputations.

During the preceding summers of 1808 and 1809, there had been several attacks on American trappers. The Hudson's Bay Company had finally followed the North West Company's example and tightened its acceptance of unprofitable fox and wolf skins. To obtain something worth trading, the horse-fixated Gens du Large learned to rob other Indians or American trappers of beaver pelts. In his journals, Henry mentioned two recent attacks on a disharmonious group who had built a fort at the Three Forks. Watchful Bloods struck them when they scattered to go trapping. The leading man whom the Bloods boasted of roasting and eating was George Droulliard, who had convinced two of his Shawnee kinsmen to return with him to the West. Their oddly tattooed bodies were impressively mutilated.[146]

The two attacks convinced the Missouri Fur Company trappers that the Three Forks was too dangerous, and most of them returned to the Bighorn post. But a few determined men followed the indomitable brigade leader Andrew Henry across the divide to the upper Snake River, where they could winter in Shoshone territory beyond the Blackfeet's interference.

In 1810, James Bird sent young James Whitway to live with the disaffected Piikani, learn their language, and ensure that they brought their beaver to the Hudson's Bay Company.[147] During his Piikani summer, Whitway traveled along the east side of the mountains. He returned to the Bow River winter camps by November and reported that his hosts were still hanging around the Missouri River, hoping to cut off Americans. But the Missouri Fur Company trappers kept well to the south when they returned to Fort Remon in the summer of 1811.[148] As the ragged Andrew Henry descended the Missouri, he met the outward-bound overland expedition of Astor's Pacific Fur Company and advised them to follow a safer route west through the Wind River valley.

The misfortunes of the remarkably inept Astorians created some unintended trouble for the Piikani. The Pacific Fur Company brigade tried to navigate the Snake River in dugout canoes, which swamped at Caldron Linn and had to be abandoned. For lack of transport, part of the outfit was cached. Three men—Andre LaChapelle, Francois Landry, and Jean Baptiste Turcotte—were left to winter with the Shoshone. As soon as the others left, those three scamps led their hosts to the caches and broke out the guns and ammunition.

John Jacob Astor's purloined arms gave the Shoshone a new illusion of spirit power. They aimed to test that by hunting on the Blackfoot-interdicted Jefferson Fork. Somewhere beyond the Red Rocks in the Beaverhead country, they were intercepted and soundly thrashed. Piikani may have mentioned the skirmish when they traded at Acton House on 30 January 1812.[149] They had grown to regard the Snakes as mere old women to be killed with sticks, and it was disturbing to find them firing guns and supported by white men. As the trade west of the mountains turned downriver, goods brought from western depots would be beyond Piikani interference. The American competition might even lower the prices of arms and ammunition for the Salish and their allies.

During the usual summer assembly of Piikani bands, the elders had an opportunity to reconsider this deteriorating situation. To maintain themselves in an increasingly hostile world, they had to have a dependable supply of ammunition and the beaver pelts to buy it. The best places to trap were in the disputed southern marches. But to gain dominance there, they would have to stop the arming of the Salish, which would offend the traders and risk losing the store.

Making peace with the Salish would have to be a unilateral agreement; the other Gens du Large had little interest in making life easier for the Piikani. They preferred to continue raiding for horses and pelts, using the Piikani as a buffer against retaliation. The five Piegan diplomats who traveled to the Salish winter camps on the horse plains in

February 1812 left behind young men who might spoil the peace overture. What they could not foresee was that an old friend was waiting to sabotage that dream.

The Flatheads heard the Piikani delegation out but withheld a response because they wanted to consult the Saleesh House master. But David Thompson was an unlikely source for an impartial opinion. In the spring of 1811, when Thompson finally got back to his western posts, he found that Finan McDonald and Jacco Finlay had built a new house beyond the reach of Piegan retaliation. Spokane House stood on the left flank of the portage connection to the Columbia and might become a base for operations toward the Snake River. Soon he was on his way to the mouth of the river to coordinate with the Astorians.

Alexander Henry reported Thompson's difficulties crossing the mountains to headquarters. The new northern route didn't look that promising. Thompson's pugnacious brother-in-law, John McDonald of Garth, was sent to affirm the right of passage across the old mountain portage, and he was just the man to put the Piegans in their place. But the deal with Astor had fallen through—David Thompson had gone down the Columbia on a wild goose chase.

Accompanied by John George McTavish, McDonald of Garth led a reinforced brigade past Rocky Mountain House. The small party going ahead of the main brigade ran into Piikani still enforcing the blockade. After his point men were stripped and humiliated, McDonald decided to winter at Kootenae House, where he could guard the middle passage. McTavish went on to reconnect with Thompson.

In November, Thompson had already superseded those actions by going up the Columbia to receive his outfit over the northern route. By bringing goods down the Columbia as far as the Fishing Basket Falls (Kettle Falls) and then packing overland to Spokane House, Thompson put operations beyond Piikani interference. McTavish found Thompson at Saleesh House and informed him that there was no deal with the Astorians—bad news. Given what Thompson had seen of the ambitious Americans and how much he had contributed to their understanding of the upper Columbia's geography, he knew they would soon appear in his backyard.

In his discovery book, David Thompson carried a copy of Meriwether Lewis's letter outlining a plan for infiltration of the greater northwest.

It called for using a road that ran through the Salish country, so mediating peace between the tramontane antagonists would be a step toward the Americans' draining off the trade of the northwest and maybe even the northern plains. Having taken the first step of establishing Okenagan House halfway up the Columbia, the Astorians would soon extend their operations into Salish country. But continuing hostilities west of the mountains might discourage further inroads.

Such was Thompson's thinking when in February 1812 the Salish elders asked him to advise them about the latest Piikani peace proposal. The elders were worried that the proposition made by the five "respectable Peeagan men" was not entirely convincing. Thompson reinforced those doubts by pointing out that a unilateral agreement would leave the Blackfeet, Bloods, and Atsiina free to continue their nefarious activities. He advised the elders to hold out for a general agreement with the entire Blackfoot nation and to continue to exercise their right to hunt buffalo east of the mountains. However, they should avoid giving first offense, and watch their herds, camps, and women carefully. Their North West Company friends were prepared to supply their ammunition and other necessities and would be pleased to accept beaver taken during the spring hunt as payment. In the face of the Piikani inability to guarantee that the other Gens du Large would respect a peace, the Flatheads rejected the proposal. Having thrown a stone at the dove, David Thompson closed his part of the western expansion and left the country.

That summer, two western freemen accompanied the Salish buffalo hunt. One was a trusted North West Company engagee, Michael Kinville. The other was the persistent Mich Bourdon, who already carried a Piikani price on his head. Very likely, Mich was willing to risk another foray because Courtin's cache at the Three Forks was still waiting to be claimed.

A fight took place between the hunting party and the Piikani in August 1812. By then Thompson had left the country, so he heard about it secondhand. Years later, when he was reworking his *Narrative* for publication, the old man wrote that both of the freemen were killed, and he went on to describe them as the last of 350 careless American free hunters. But Thompson was wrong. It was another ten years before the Piikani finally ran down and killed Mich Bourdon.[150]

As Thompson had foreseen, by autumn 1812 the Pacific Fur Company was in Salish country. In November, Thomas Farnham and Ross Cox brought an outfit to the horse-plains winter camps, where they saw dejected survivors of the August encounter.[151] The returning Salish buffalo hunters morosely reported that several of their warriors had been killed in a fight with the Piikani and a chief's wife had been captured.[152] They were learning that guns alone were not going to solve their problems with the plainsmen.

Later that year was the first time that Edmonton master James Bird referred to the Piikani as Missouri River Indians. They were not as intimidating as the unpredictable Falls Indians, who continued to circulate threats and behave in a disquieting manner. Whitway, Bird's man with the Piikani, reported that they had resided on the Missouri all summer, hoping to cut off Americans ascending the river, but they had been disappointed. Crossing the burned plains in December, Falls Indians and Bloods slept twenty nights, an indication that their winter camps were still on the Bow River.

Sarcee coming to trade in the spring of 1813 had lost horses to Bloods and Blackfeet. Those two militant groups were seething over the deaths of fifty of their relatives killed by the Flatheads since the previous summer. They were convinced that white men were supplying their enemies with firearms, an estimate of the situation that was also held by the large body of Muddy River Indians who arrived at the beginning of May with a few furs. Confessing to killing a Canadian and two Iroquois near the mountains, the Piikani vowed to kill any white man found west of the Rockies or going there. Deciding that he could take the Muddy River trade less expensively at Edmonton, Bird closed Acton House.

The War of 1812 panicked the Astorians into selling out to the Nor'westers. That left the North West Company in uncontested control of the western trade, with a seaport at the mouth of the Columbia. The war also gave the financially floundering Missouri Fur Company an excuse to withdraw from Fort Remon and the Crow trade. Those distant conflicts allowed the Gens du Large a decade free of intrusive trappers, but at the cost of making them even more dependent on the distant Saskatchewan posts.

American pressure on two fronts had evaporated, but the recently reorganized and suddenly aggressive Hudson's Bay Company now moved to challenge the bully North West Company in the most productive beaver regions. The Northwest wintering partners had to fend off Baymen in Athabasca and find an answer to a strategically threatening colony that was being planted at the forks of the Red and Assiniboine Rivers. To the incompletely informed Piikani, such business conflicts must have seemed like convoluted versions of their own war games.

After making the long winter trek north to the trading posts, the Gens du Large spent the munitions they obtained on martial games, limited little horrors that reflected a tenuous balance of terror. In the autumn of 1813, Blood raiders ranged so far south that they found themselves killing previously unknown Indians. Because they passed three major streams beyond the Marias River, they were probably raiding in the Bear River valley of northern Utah. The four Sarcee who tagged along counted nineteen sleeps, which, calculated at the rate of thirty miles a day, put them 570 miles south of the Marias.[153]

By then there were freemen and Iroquois trapping with the Kutenai and Salish. Some leftover Astorians, inherited by the North West Company, dared to trap along the branches of the Snake River. Bannock Shoshone annihilated the party that John Reed took to the Boise River in January 1814. The only survivors were Madame Dorion and her two children, who met the spring boat brigades on the Columbia River with their chilling report. Tough nuts like John Day refused to be intimidated and returned to those beaver-rich streams.

According to Fort Augustus master James Hughes, the Nor'westers were also considering the recovery of the Piegan trade from their Columbia River base. If those Indians objected, the traders would build a fort in their country to keep them in line. As Hughes talked in his cups about an armed invasion of the Piikani heartland, his bemused audience was James Bird, who knew that was unlikely. Ironically, Bird's own suggestions about southward expansion were lost on a London board of management playing a larger competitive game.[154]

Hughes found it profitable to buy a few buffalo robes. For the price of a yard of tobacco he got robes that he reckoned to be worth twenty shillings. Those came from the Siksika and Kainaa. In March 1815, James Bird also bought thirty robes from the Atsiina and twelve from the Piikani. But the most valuable contribution from the Muddy River and Sarcee Indians was 78 beaver, 1,002 kits, 265 rats, and 60 wolves. Bird was pleased that the Piikani were applying themselves to the hunt, but he was not around to harvest the reward of his seventeen years' careful stewardship of that trade. The next year he was called downstream to clean up the fatal mess that commercial colonialism had created at the Selkirk settlement and in Athabasca. Colonists were massacred and workmen starved to death.

The trader sent to replace him was one of the Irish toughs Hudson's Bay had recruited to brawl with the Nor'westers. Francis Herron found the Muddy River Indians who came to trade at Edmonton House in October 1818 to be a saucy lot. In the spring, after the Slave Indians made peace with the Assiniboine and Cree, Herron assigned a northern Scot named Charles McKay to summer with the Piikani and learn their language.[155] A year later the small party he sent to reopen Acton House included a young Canadian named Hugh Munroe.[156]

Pressure on the Piikani heartland also built up from southern approaches. In 1816, former Astorian Donald McKenzie returned to the Columbia as a Nor'wester with forty men. After dealing with the reluctance of fellow traders, he took Alexander Ross as his clerk and went to the mouth of the Walla Walla River. McKenzie established Fort Nez Perce as a base camp for trading and trapping expeditions into Snake country. By July 1818 he was moving toward those beaver-rich streams with fifty-five men and three hundred traps.

In 1818, Great Britain and the United States tidied up loose ends from the War of 1812 by agreeing to a boundary across the northern plains. The line that followed the forty-ninth parallel of latitude made the Missouri River an American outlet and limited British traders to the southern tributaries of the Bow. But what practical reality did that diplomatic abstraction slicing across their ranges hold for the Gens du Large?

After the experience of the first Snake River hunting brigade, McKenzie was not entirely optimistic when he wrote from the head of the Snake Canyon on 15 April 1819. "I am now about to commence a very doubtful and dangerous undertaking and shall I fear, have to adopt the habits of the owl, roam in the night and skulk in the day, to avoid enemies." Writing to Ross from Black Bear's Lake on 10 September he noted, "We have passed a very anxious and troublesome summer. War parties frequent. In danger often; but still we do not despair." McKenzie planned to winter in the country and return to Fort Nez Perce by the following June.[157]

The nemesis of that large trapping brigade was generalized as Blackfeet. Raiding parties continued to harry the Shoshone, but an attack on a Shoshone camp by eight hundred Piikani raiders in the summer of 1819 was a strategic failure. It cost the lives of thirty warriors. The survivors blamed their defeat on McKenzie's trade with the Snakes and would not soon forget.[158]

The improvement of commerce, rather than humanity, led McKenzie to suggest a peace council between the tribes. At the Shoshone winter camps near the mouth of the Portneuf River, the respected Snake leader Pee-eye-em told McKenzie that "the Blackfeet and the Peigan are our only enemies, a peace with them would be more desirable to us than a peace with the Nez Perces."[159]

When the Snake River brigade returned to Fort Nez Perce on 10 July 1821, McKenzie's five-year contract was up. There were rumors of an impending merger of the rival British companies, which would probably create a surplus of clerks. By the time McKenzie began thinking about his future, the North West Company and the Hudson's Bay Company had already agreed to a coalition of interests.[160]

The new corporation put a promising young businessman in charge of the northern department of the Hudson's Bay Company. George Simpson immediately began to look for new areas to exploit while the beaver reserves of the north recovered from overhunting. The beaver resources of the upper branches of the Missouri River were nearly irresistible, but there were two major drawbacks: the area was in United States territory, and it was in the Piikani heartland.

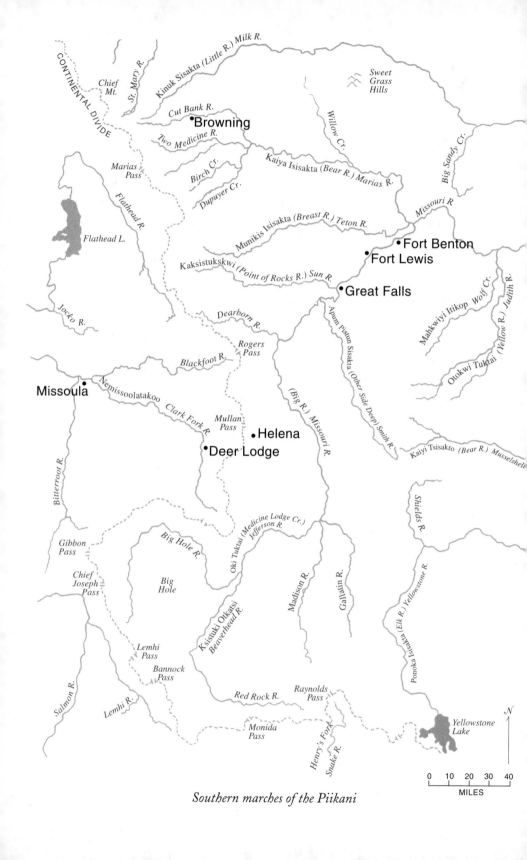

Southern marches of the Piikani

TEN

Drawing the Line

rom the Lone Pine to the divide overlooking Snake country, the land was an undulating buffaloscape of cutbanks, rimrocks, washes, gullies, coulees, and river bottoms, occasionally punctuated by patches of cottonwood, aspen, or isolated evergreens. That part of the northwestern plains was a breathing sea of rolling brown grass, with a distant tide line of forest rooted on the drainage slope of the continental spine. It was a large area for horse people to cover, but the Piikani knew it intimately as they ranged for buffalo and worked the streams for beaver.

Those great spaces were bounded to the west by parallel mountain ranges that made traveling north or south relatively easy for a band. Little Foxes Medicine was a great warrior when the Piikani moved south and asserted themselves beyond the Oldman River. Now known as Tete qui Leve (Rising Head), he agreed to be the guardian of a young trader sent to learn their language.

Of the hundreds of lodges in the camp on Belly River, it was the twenty-skin tepee of Nitowaka the Lone Walker that stood out. Two tame bears guarded the door while as many as eighteen men gathered inside to draw thoughtfully from his big two-hour pipe and discuss where to find buffalo or when to move the camp.[161]

On the morning of a move, nothing else was done until the lodges of the three pipe-stem carriers were taken down. Then the conical community collapsed and everything was hectic as chattering women rolled the lodge covers and secured them on travois. Lone Walker, who maintained sixteen wives, disdained the chore of breaking down his five lodges. He strode away, using his lance as a walking stick, trailed by his bears. Behind him came the three pipe-stem carriers who wore their hair piled high on their foreheads as a sign of their special status. Two hundred mounted warriors fell in. Those societies had the responsibility of defending the band during its vulnerable time on the trail. The walking women and children straggled out, leading or driving ponies laden with the modest possessions of a mobile people.

Dust rolled up from the herd of hundreds of horses. Some had been raised and trained from colts by their owners, but the oddly dappled animals mixed with them were likely stolen from Salish or Sahaptan herds. There were a few mules, wearing Spanish brands. After a mile or so, the pipe-stem carriers spread a robe and sat down to smoke. That gave time for the column to sort itself out and the women to adjust loose packs.[162]

Above the Three Forks, the Piikani knew the western branch of the river as *oki tuktai*, or Medicine Lodge Creek (Jefferson River), so called due to the misfortune of a medicine woman who was thrown from her runaway horse there. Higher up was *ksistuki otkatsi* (Beaverhead River), named for the great rock that resembled that animal. The headwaters almost overlooking the Snake country was *katoyis*, Clot of Blood (the Red Rock). Those names did not match what Lewis and Clark lettered on their maps, but it was the Piikani who were in possession, and that is how they knew the land.[163]

The southern marches opened endless possibilities for taking beaver, Salish horses, or Shoshone scalps. But going there exposed the Piikani to flank attacks by Salish buffalo hunters. After two decades of disappointed overtures, the Piikani were still offering their left hands in peace to Salish and Shoshone neighbors. Other uncaring Gens du Large were spoiling the dream. In winter, horse thieves crossed the mountains on snowshoes as audaciously as they rode through the several notorious passes in summer. Young men found glory at the cost of keeping their bands in jeopardy.

The Piikani were about to be squeezed between British mercantilism from the north and west, and American enterprise from the south and east. This other world was closing in on them as relentlessly as the onset of winter. Elders recognized their precarious relationship with the outsiders and questioned whether moderation would prevail in the inevitable confrontation.

After the merger of British trading interests in 1821, the new corporate management decided to exploit their presence in the Oregon country, which for the time being they jointly occupied with the United States; those beaver preserves would probably be lost when the boundary compromise came up for reconsideration in 1828. Another attractive area for exploitation extended from the Milk River through the Three Forks to the headwaters of the three branches of the Missouri River, which was where the Piikani ranged.

While British traders adjusted previous enmities to accommodate the new union, American entrepreneurs were gathering resources for a return to the upper Missouri. The reorganized Missouri Fur Company got a hunting and trading party into the field by 1821/22, which operated profitably from the old location on the Yellowstone River. The returns from the Bighorn post justified a second venture for the next winter.

News of the alternative market flashed across the mountain west. Piikani visited the new post during the winter and "the Americans gave them to understand that they intended to Establish a Post at Bears River where they intended to trade largely and supply the natives at a lower rate than the European traders."[164]

During the summer of 1822, the Hudson's Bay Snake River brigade came under the tenuous command of Mich Bourdon. The retiring Donald McKenzie couldn't have found a replacement more odious to the Piikani than Bourdon. The brigade included a number of the generally hated Iroquois, and it was no surprise that they had several battles with Indians they reported as Blackfeet (meaning the Piikani) in the upper Snake Valley. In truth it's uncertain who the attackers were. In total, two trappers were killed and two others wounded, but Mich counted the scalps of seven attackers.

Getting killed for company prices was not too appealing to the freemen. At the end of the Snake River, four former Astorians and ten price-minded Iroquois saw an alternative beckoning from the Bighorn post. Balking at running the Piikani gauntlet to Spokane House, the dissidents had promised Bourdon they'd return to Fort Nez Perce. Bourdon lacked animals to carry all the packs up to the Flathead post, so he was obliged to cache seven hundred pelts on the east end of the Snake plain and took what he could to the seasonally opened post. As soon as Bourdon was out of sight, the fourteen rebels headed east to check out American prices. They would winter with the Mountain Crows and go to the American post in the spring.[165]

After leaving most of his remaining men with the Flatheads, Mich Bourdon appeared at Spokane House on 12 September. He brought thirteen hundred pelts as far as Lake Pend d'Oreille in canoes. Bourdon's claim of two thousand beaver in hand, and good prospects for more, led to the re-outfitting of the freemen within a week. Bourdon hurried back to lead the fall hunt toward the Missouri headwaters while his old comrade in arms, Finan McDonald, conducted the Salish trade. McDonald took in 1,669 beaver skins from the Indians and 1,549 from the freemen who were now heading back with Bourdon.

In writing the Spokane District report, Alexander Kennedy recognized that the east boundary of his district was in the Blackfoot country around the North Branch of the Missouri. When Kennedy wrote in spring 1823, Bourdon and the brigade had already returned from an uncontested winter hunt on the Jefferson Fork. Finan McDonald now took charge, keeping Bourdon as his second, and set out to hunt in the Snake country. When the brigade returned in the fall, he would recover those seven hundred cached pelts.

Trader Kennedy was out of the loop—Spokane District was unaware of the corporation's intention to penetrate the Piikani country from the South Branch.[166] The London management had already authorized Governor George Simpson to devote sixty Canadian voyageurs to an expedition that would be augmented by a hundred "Irriquois, Half-breeds and free Canadians" going along as beaver hunters. Fox, beaver, and buffalo hides obtained from the complacent Indians would pay the expenses while profits would come from trapping on the Missouri River. This was American territory, but London seemed unconcerned about that and suggested only that it might be advisable to obtain the permission of the Piegan. John Rowand, who was familiar with the Piikani, would bring servants and freemen from the upper Saskatchewan to meet the York Factory contingent at the forks.

The only man familiar with operating a brigade in the field was Donald McKenzie. He was induced to head the party of 143 that would "trade with the Indians in that part of the country and introduce parties of Iroquois, Half-breeds and Freemen to hunt on the head waters of the Missouri." After building a depot at the mouth of the Red Deer, McKenzie would proceed up the Bow River to the borders of the mountains, moving in a southerly direction. If everything worked out as anticipated, McKenzie might even open a connection with the Snake Indians and "drain the valuable track of country they occupy of it's Riches."

About twelve hundred Indians congregated in the vicinity of the latest version of Chesterfield House. The leading Siksika was Great Bear. The Kainaa and Piikani were soon referring to the newcomers as "white dogs" and boldly trying to climb over the walls of the new trading house. A small cannon had to be fired to discourage them. Drunken Indians made threats and even fired into the traders' tents. When one Siksika miscreant was apprehended and severely beaten, Great Bear growled that the traders despised his people and delivered a gratuitous lecture on false hospitality. When horses previously stolen from Carlton House showed up in one Indian's herd, the confronted culprit turned one animal over to the indignant traders and laughed because he still had so many more.[167]

In that unhappy place it was clear that the Gens du Large were no more receptive to direct trapping now than they had been twenty years before. Donald McKenzie led the first attempt to go to the Missouri River with five clerks and forty men, but they were turned back by belligerent Atsiina. Tough Francis Herron took out a second group but was also discouraged. In November the risky operation fell to clerks John Edward Harriot and William Sinclair, accompanied by twenty-eight trappers and two Blackfoot guides.[168]

They soon found a camp of five hundred Atsiina lodges, where seven hundred men were making up a war party to go against the Crows. Some of them came from the three hundred Siksika lodges planted along the trail to the Cypress Hills. Trailing the war party, Harriot and Sinclair marched thirty-five miles across the Sand Hills and plains to the nearest part of the Cypress Hills. As he trudged on snowshoes breaking trail for the dog train, Harriot tried to convince himself that his display of hardiness and perseverance would impress the Siksika guides.

Skirting the Cypress Hills to avoid the war party, the trappers crossed the breaks of the Milk River to the Sugar Loaves (Sweetgrass Hills). This was Siksika's enemy country, and one of the guides had such a bad dream that he began building defensive enclosures and keeping watch at night. Unimpressed by typical war trail procedure, Harriot and two unnamed mixed-blood men pushed on to the Bear River and into the Piikani paradise. "The view of the Mts. Was magnificent and enough to drive a sportsman into Ecstacies—all over the Mts—now quite white you could see moose—deer—big horn—antelope everywhere and on the open plain herds of buffalo."

The winter excursion of the Atsiina-Siksika war party was a fiasco. Their attack on a Crow camp near the mouth of the Musselshell was defeated at the cost of a good number of warriors. When the Indians returned to the traders' camp on 19 March 1823, the warriors reported seeing six Americans camped near the mouth of the river. That was the first intimation that the Americans had also returned to the skin games. Later, a party of Blackfeet traveled to the mouth of the Yellowstone to investigate rumors of an American settlement there. They found a deserted fort and two graves containing the rotting corpses of the infamous riverman Mike Fink and his good friend and final victim, Carpenter. The bodies were so putrid that the clothes were not worth taking. The Siksika most likely turned up the Missouri, hoping to intercept and rob the six men seen at the mouth of the Musselshell.

By May, the Bow River expedition had broken camp and started back to Fort Carlton. The venture had been an expensive failure, and it must have been a chilly meeting with the disappointed Governor Simpson. Simpson took the York faction back to the bay with him while the Edmonton men turned upstream. On 20 July 1823, chief factor Colin Robertson recorded that the Mountain House, Edmonton House, and Carlton House trade amounted to only 2,591 large and small beaver. The freemen that Governor Simpson discharged carried an additional 550 pelts across the mountains to trade in another department. Robertson estimated that another 1,100 untraded beaver pelts were still floating around the Bow River, where nearly three-fourths of the Indians were drawn by the failed expedition. Because so many Indians were distracted by the new establishment at the Bow, Mountain House was closed and the Muddy River Indians would again have to bring their trade to Edmonton.

Thirty Missouri Fur Company trappers left the Bighorn staging post in spring 1823 "for the purpose of trapping beaver" as well "as to ascertain the prospect of introducing our trade among the Blackfoot Indians, and any other tribes in that country." Michael J. Immell, a veteran of the 1810 harrowing at the Three Forks, was assisted by Robert Jones. In hunting up the Yellowstone to the Three Forks, they were instructed to "use every effort to obtain a friendly interview with the Blackfeet . . . and to impress them with the friendly disposition of American citizens towards them."[169] Forty miles up the Jefferson they found evidence of trapping by Bourdon's Snake River brigade. Having thirty packs already in hand, the Missouri Fur Company men turned around and headed back toward the Three Forks.

The two- or three-man tents of the Americans made a sprawling camp that was not easy to miss. On 17 May, thirty-eight Piikani appeared behind a darkly painted apparition. The figure came forward, displaying a letter headed "God Save the King," and introduced himself as Mexkemauastasn (Iron Shield).[170] The certificate he confidently presented to the traders attested to his good reputation. It had been signed at Mountain House by John Rowand.[171]

Mexkemauastasn (Iron Shield) and Tatsicki-stomick (Middle Bull) as rendered by Karl Bodmer —Courtesy Arthur H. Clark

Mexkemauastasn and his followers were on their way to raid the Snakes, but bumping into the trappers put everything in a different light. The Piikani had been aware of the Bighorn post for a year and also knew of a rival establishment at the mouth of the Yellowstone. Perhaps they could find out more. During an amiable evening together, the Missouri Fur Company brigade leaders proposed establishing a trading post at the Three Forks. Iron Shield suggested that the mouth of the Marias River was a better location. When the groups parted, the traders were so pleased that they gave Mexkemauastasn another certificate of recommendation.[172]

Iron Shield had stumbled onto something the Piikani had desired for the past twenty years—a trading house of their own. This understanding verified what the Piikani had been told when they visited the Bighorn post. Faced with the realization of that dream, Iron Shield demonstrated considerable aplomb. Believing that he had initiated a welcome arrangement, Iron Shield called off the raid and hurried home.[173]

In Piikani camps or on the trail there could be as many opinions as there were individuals. Only tolerant of their leaders at best, those independent-minded and emotionally direct tribesmen were poor material for central government and even poorer prospects for consensus. The elders who gravely pondered Iron Shield's report around their leader's lodge fire could consider the new development with only limited experience. It took someone of considerable ability to translate his own enthusiasm into inspiration for a largely uninterested community.

"Chief" has always been an ambiguous term that grew from basic misconceptions. Indian hunters who did not want to make the long, trying journey to a trading post might consign their peltry to someone who was going. At the posts, the traders wanted to deal with someone in charge and recognized trading "captains" by giving them gaudy uniform coats and control of the liquor gifts. Other Indians might defer to that false hierarchy there, but it did not always reflect the power structure of their own society.

Tribesman recognized a man of substance with respect but not necessarily obedience. In order to exercise direct power, leaders needed favorable circumstances and a good deal of natural presence. Whipping an obvious malfeasant always carried the possibility of later revenge, so men's societies collectively took responsibility. Public ceremonies gave individuals the opportunity to restate their achievements, but the flip side of excessive pride could be ridicule, ostracism, or, in extreme cases, even extrajudicial assassination.

A roaming leader like Iron Shield had to deal with his peers before he had the opportunity to confer with the elders. He relied on instinct and personal initiative, governed by his sense of civic responsibility, to wield influence. While Indian practices did not conform to European expectations of central authority, they provided enough structure for a self-reliant people.

In Blackfoot, *kainaa* seems to mean "many chiefs." When the Bloods learned that whites had been seen near the Three Forks, they raced to intercept the retreating Missouri Fur Company trappers. Although they may have recognized that a trading post at the Marias mouth was not in their best interest, their main consideration was loot, not stopping progress.

On 31 May 1823, perhaps as many as three or four hundred Bloods overtook the trappers near Pryor's Fork. After friendly encounters with the Piikani and Crows, the Americans were not expecting an attack. When Immell rode forward to greet the Bloods, he was killed. Jones and five of the trappers were also slaughtered, and five more were wounded as the terrified party scattered into the brush. The Bloods rounded up fifty horses and twenty-eight mules, which were loaded with packs of beaver possibly worth up to $16,000 in St. Louis.[174] Two months later, the suddenly wealthy Kainaa arrived at Edmonton House to cash in the booty.

The Siksika who had missed finding the Americans at the abandoned Yellowstone post now mistakenly trailed those who had gone up the Missouri River. This party belonged to another trading venture, the Ashley-Henry partnership. That old hand in the western hunt, Andrew Henry, hoped to approach the Three Forks by way of the Great Falls. The Siksika caught up with four men who were ascending the river in two wooden canoes. Killings a few miles above Smith's River blasted Henry's plan of slipping in unnoticed. Caching their traps, the shaken survivors fled downstream.[175]

The Gens du Large had now discouraged three attempts to penetrate the upper Missouri. Between them, the Kainaa and the Siksika had again foiled the Piikani opportunity to have a convenient trading house. Those Piikani who tried to salvage the situation by traveling down the Yellowstone River found that the Missouri Fur Company had abandoned the Bighorn post.

Toward the end of summer, some Piikani intercepted Andrew Henry's party, who were now trying to get into the Crow country by way of the Yellowstone. From the hard lessons of the summer, those trappers were not about to risk accepting the renewed invitation to come to the Marias. The disappointed Piikani were told that they were welcome and would be well rewarded for bringing beaver to the winter base set up in the old Missouri Fur Company house at the mouth of the Bighorn. As that meant a risky trip through Crow country, the option was no more attractive to the Piikani than the long trip to the Saskatchewan.

Finan McDonald and Mich Bourdon led the Snake brigade from the Flathead post in spring 1823. The twenty-four British trappers going back to the Snake country were now augmented by eleven men who had come over from the Saskatchewan the previous fall and who knew a bit about the Gens du Large. By the end of summer they had trapped as far south as the Bear River country and "had Saviral Battils with the nasion (Blackfoot?) on the other side of the Mountains." McDonald surely recalled the longstanding differences between his assistant and the Piikani when he wrote that "Poore Meshel Bordoe was kild with 5 more of the band." Those killings took place along Henry's Fork of the Snake as McDonald led the party toward the headwaters of the Lemhi River.

Later, McDonald and his abused men trapped a Piikani party in a defile leading to the pass into the Big Hole. In the open country of the eastern Snake Valley, beleaguered bands had a habit of going to ground in islands of trees. The revenge-seeking trappers set the brush on fire. Ten Indians were burned to death before the others broke cover and were mowed down by the guns of the unrelenting Snake brigade. McDonald later claimed that sixty-eight of a party of seventy-five were slaughtered "and those fue that askape our Shotes they had not Britch Clout to Cover them selves."[176]

Finan McDonald was no admirer of freemen hunters who "will not Lasin to that is told them, they never think of their own Profit nor the Company as long as they gate Bullaloe Meat." Nevertheless, he was sure that within four years, forty-five good trappers "wood rouin the Snake Cuntre." But a brigade of fifty men with six traps each required a large area to make sets. A large force might be desirable for self-defense, but "such a number of free Men will not agrey together and Playing dirty trick to each other setting off the traps of one another." The failed Bow

River expedition had been twice that size when it was turned back by Gens du Large hostility.

The Snake brigade lost another trapper, named Anderson, as it crossed into the Big Hole. That wide valley on the top of the continent was a favorite place of the Inuk'sik Piikani to hunt beaver. Perhaps the Small Robes met the trappers and promised McDonald that they would not return again to make war. McDonald was so encouraged that he led the brigade in an uncontested sweep down the Missouri as far as the Great Falls.

McDonald knew that the upper part of the Jefferson Fork had been trapped by Bourdon during the winter hunt and soon found evidence that the Jones and Immell party had been around the Three Forks in the spring. Still, the adventure was profitable—McDonald traded one thousand beaver pelts from Piikani who were unwilling to make the long trip to the Saskatchewan. Those were pelts that had been expected to turn up at Edmonton House, and McDonald's achievement gave him an early taste of intercorporate rivalry.

The Piikani who traded with McDonald near the Great Falls obligingly took a letter from him to deliver to fellow Baymen in the north. It was carried to Edmonton by the man with the Gens du Large, Hugh Munroe. The news held that "the Piegans have made a peace with the Flatheads although part have not sanctioned it." In November, Iron Shield made the chilly twenty-day ride from the Piikani winter camps to the British houses with his firsthand report of American activities. By then he could add that other Piikani had connected with and been clothed by the Ashley-Henry men on the Yellowstone.[177]

Because nearly three-fourths of the Indians had gone off to trade at the South Branch, Acton House and Mountain House were closed. In his definition of the market, Edmonton factor Colin Robertson estimated the present Gens du Large population. There were 500 tents of Siksika, 300 tents of Kainaa, 550 tents of Piikani, 450 tents of Atsiina, and 90 tents of Sarcee. That made over seven thousand potential hunters ranging in the south. It was crucial that they continue to bring their trade to Edmonton House.[178]

The party of thirty-two Piikani that accompanied Munroe on 25 November took fifteen sleeps to come from their winter camp. Nine of those days were over burned ground that afforded neither grazing for their weakening horses nor game to feed the travelers. Well might they complain that the Cree, Stoney, Blackfeet, Bloods, Sarcee, and even the Falls Indians had trading houses but they themselves had none.

The Hudson's Bay Company's answer to the American expansion was to send freemen to live with the Piikani. Those trappers were "to Hunt Beaver towards the Rocky Mountains on or above some of the waters that Fall into the Missouri, which is still represented by the plains tribes as abounding in Beaver." Having failed to impose direct trapping at once, the monopoly intended to insinuate it by degrees. When Iron Shield's followers departed on 1 December 1823, they took along Louis Brunnais, the half-Indian Primeau, the Iroquois mixed-blood Maurice Picard, language student Hugh Munroe, and Blackfoot interpreter Charles McKay. McKay was to ensure that the spring trade came to Edmonton. But by the time the traders got to the three winter camps on the Marias River, the greater part of the pelt harvest had already been traded to Finan McDonald.[179]

As the fur hunt intruded on the ranges of the Piikani, information about Piikani activities could be gleaned from the reports and gossip of the new breed of corporate fur traders. The British were straining to keep contact with customers who were drifting away beyond the international boundary. Though frustrated by their inconsistent production, the Saskatchewan traders had to admit that the Piegan were the best source of peltry from a region that seemed beyond reach by other means.

Contrary to the usual image of a grizzled trapper wading to set steel jaws beneath a fatally scented bent willow stick, Indians took beaver by whatever means was handy. Swimming beaver were shot and hopefully retrieved. A patient hunter might spear an animal emerging from the entrance to a bankside den. The Iroquois had taught western Indians the technique of walking out on a frozen pond to tear open houses, and traders even gave them ice chisels to help that hard work. The Siksika and Kainaa found a viable shortcut in taking packs from others. The looting of the Jones and Immell party, the biggest robbery to date, fixed a habit that would keep mountain men attentive for the next two decades.

The arena of these activities was the upper Missouri River and its three branches, particularly the Jefferson Fork and its near-mythic tributaries the Big Hole, the Ruby, the Beaverhead, the Blacktail, and the Red Rock. When an Edmonton House journalist wrote of Indians crossing the mountains to hunt, he meant they were going into those mountain-girted river valleys. Adventuring in that wonderland of snowy peaks and placid bottoms cut by willow-lined meanders made the Piikani into mountain men too.

John Rowand returned to Edmonton in fall 1824 to find the Siksika mourning severe losses. One hundred fifty men, women, and children had been massacred by the Beaver Hill Cree and Plain Stone Indians. A party of Kainaa and Atsiina, hoping to repeat last year's success against the Americans, bumped into a war party of Mountain Crows and lost 170 of their band. In addition, 120 Plains Indians were victims of upper Red River Assiniboine. After seeing a total of 440 go to the mythic Sand Hills, the Gens du Large were understandably depressed.

Meanwhile, the less aggressive Piikani were left unmolested on the upper branches of the Missouri, and they had successful hunts. But they continued to balk at carrying the pelts to distant Edmonton. By 16 December the three Piikani camps on the Bear River counted about twenty-four hundred men. Carrying fifteen hundred to two thousand beaver skins north in March 1825, they were "unquestionably the best beaver hunters" attached to Rowand's district. The peltry had been taken between their lands and those of the Snake and Flathead Indians, where beaver abounded. The Piikani planned to return there that summer.[180]

The bonanza beaver country lay within the United States, but Rowand got around the technicality by sending ten of his best beaver-hunting freemen with the Inuk'sik Piikani. The men he picked were the Canadians Jacques Berger, Pierre Berland, Louis Brunnais, Gardipee, and Hugh Munroe; the half-Indian James Bird, Musqua, Primeau, and George Ward; and the Iroquois Maurice Picard. Traveling with a party of 150 Piikani and Kainaa, Munroe, Bird, Picard, and two other Canadians were on the upper Beaverhead by 28 June 1825.

Instead of gainfully devoting themselves to the beaver hunt, aspiring young Indians persisted in riding south or west to seek rewards from a stealthy midnight creep into someone else's pony herd. The Crows were the most responsive defenders and would pursue the thieves for four days to recover their lost livestock. Horse-capturing parties avoided going against them during the blooming of the wild roses, when the Missouri River might become too high to recross. The Flatheads, Nez Perce, Pend d'Oreille, and other western tribes came to the semiannual buffalo hunts with herds for the taking. The broad grasslands along the Missouri below the Three Forks were coursed by floating communities of mobile horsemen and their travois families. There were no certified territories, but if those ochre plains belonged to anyone, they were Piikani and Inuk'sik domain as far south as the Big Hole.

The Piikani never managed to find a lasting answer to the question of intertribal and extratribal peace, nor an alternative to doing business with two-faced traders. Maintaining themselves in an increasingly dangerous world required a reliable source of ammunition. When Hugh Munroe accompanied the Inuk'sik during the winter of 1823/24, he watched his hosts run out of ammunition by spring and have to rely on their bows to kill buffalo.[181]

By 1824, the Hudson's Bay Company had learned a telling lesson in American intentions. That fall the determined Ashley-Henry trappers completed an end run around the screen of Crows and Shoshone and appeared in the Bear River valley. Seven unwelcome American guests followed the Snake brigade back to the Flathead post, where they observed the Salish trade. And at the end of the year, when Peter Skene Ogden took more freemen to the Snake country, the Americans trailed along.

As they passed the ominous Hellgate Canyon, Ogden's hunters were already shy of the Blackfeet. Two weeks into the new year they crossed into the Big Hole. At the end of January, an encounter with Atsiina returning from the Snake country cost the incautious freemen seventeen horses. The pass leading west out of the Big Hole was notorious as the defile that "war tribes" took in winter. The brigade was moving up the Lemhi River in mid-February when two men out tranching (trenching or digging out beaver) were fired on by seven men identified as Blackfeet. The attackers had only two guns and fled into the mountains when pursued.[182]

On April 1, the brigade was finally approaching the Snake River. Ogden allowed twelve men to go ahead to set traps. Most had already returned when two terrified trappers rode in shouting that ten or fifteen "Blackfeet" had rushed them. Antoine Benoit had been killed and scalped. Later, Indians were seen hiding in the brush, and the clerks William Kittson and Charles McKay risked going close enough to speak with them. The Bloods were probably responsible for killing Benoit; McKay, the interpreter, did not say that Piikani were involved.[183]

In spring 1825, the Inuk'sik Piikani and the Edmonton House "confidential servants" (corporate spies) were hunting in the Red Rock country. They met the Snake brigade returning from an unfortunate run-in with American trappers, in which the attractive prices offered by the Ashley-Henry men had seduced most of the freemen. McKay wrote a letter warning his friends on the Saskatchewan that two disloyal Iroquois had taken an outfit for trading with the Salish, and a former clerk, Nicholas Montour, had taken goods for the Slave Indians. The Edmonton House freemen convinced the discouraged Ogden that it was a bad idea to attempt to recover his losses by trapping toward the Three Forks.[184]

Sometime after that meeting, the Piikani found a way to reconcile with their Salish enemies. In the autumn of 1826, American entrepreneurs David E. Jackson and William L. Sublette made an uncontested trapping swing through the Three Forks. Although the initiate American clerk Robert Campbell had been understandably apprehensive, the trappers passed through that dangerous region with no serious incidents. Some of their men even took an outfit as far north as the Marias River and intercepted pelts that would have gone to Edmonton House.[185]

At the end of September 1825, the Hudson's Bay Company decided to briefly reopen Mountain House to receive the Piegan trade and to leave it as soon as the peltry was collected. Maurice Picard returned to Edmonton in mid-October to tell Rowand the news about meeting Ogden. Fourteen Piikani men and four women had made the long journey with him, but most of the Piikani traded at the Mountain House because they did not trust the Thickwood Stoney and Sarcee, whose territories lay on the route to Edmonton.

Picard reported that Gardipee, one of the trappers traveling with the Inuk'sik Piikani, had absconded with some of their horses and was now considered a bad man. Munroe, Bird, and Ward were still safe with them. Jacques Berger, who had gone to tent with the Piegan in spring 1826, reappeared in September with his wife, his Indian mother-in-law, and seventy-four beaver pelts, half of which belonged to his trapping partner, Louis Brunais. Berger said that the summer was half gone before the Piikani crossed the mountains, so it was unlikely that they would have many pelts to deliver.

The only Piegan to come in was Manecope (The Young Man), who delivered a letter from the former clerk Montour. Writing from the

Blackfoot River (a tributary of the Snake) on 18 April 1826, Montour boasted to his former associates that he was doing very well with the Americans. Hugh Munroe also came in with a few skins, but there was no news from young Bird or Ward, who were still traveling with the Inuk'sik.[186]

Three Blackfeet who had traveled near the mountains during the summer of 1827 delivered to Edmonton House the unpleasant news that Berger and Brunais had defected to the Americans. The Edmonton House journalist feared that they would use their influence to draw the Piegans to the competition. He took perverse satisfaction on 17 October in noting that Stoney had almost wiped out fourteen lodges of Blackfeet and Piegan. Later, this had to be corrected to just four tents of Bloods. But their fights with Salish buffalo hunters during the summer had cost the Piikani thirty-six dead.

After sending the clerk Henry Fisher to Mountain House with packs of trade goods, trader Rowand had to go there in November to deal with the defection of the freemen. Matters remained unresolved in March 1828, as "the Indians were making poor hunts and the Peigans were trafficking their furs with the Americans."[187]

The Plains tribes were in constant uproar, quarreling and stealing horses from each other. In the spring it was rumored that the Piikani had killed a Flathead chief and four hunters who were supposedly American.[188] Another, equally suspect report held that Berger and Brunais had been killed. In an unusual early August visit to Edmonton, Munroe and a Piikani known as Parfleche-pasant arrived as heralds for forty of their people. Munroe, who had given himself over to the Indian side of his new life, was a surly visitor who disparaged the Baymen to his Indian associates. Stommach-sopetah, head of the Buffalo Robes band of Bloods, was doing all in his power to excite hostility against the white men. Two months later, a Saulteur freeman arrived from the west side of the mountains with a story of a battle between the Piikani and the unlikely combination of Crows and Snakes.

The small band of Piegan headed by Tete qui Leve (Rising Head) who visited Mountain House in early February 1829 returned with the long-absent Jamey (Jemmy Jock) Bird. Because the plains were burned, the traders could not expect to get provisions from any of the Slave tribes and would probably have to abandon the place. Bird went back to the plains, promising to get his friends to cross the mountains early in the spring to work beaver.[189]

The potentially illuminating data in the house journals were often acrid tidbits written by sanctimonious bystanders. Traders responded to those comments without looking for deeper substance. Despite that narrowly focused record, it is important to remember that the Piikani world was not all beaver trading and horse stealing. The broad buffalo plains and pocket Edens on the upper Missouri were comfortable places for a wandering people who did not go out of their way to seek trouble. While the traders penned unintentional reflections of their own ambition and greed, the People were living complete, satisfying lives. Unfortunately, their travois were cutting trails that outsiders would follow into the heart of their homeland.

In October 1829, Henry Fisher was on his way to reopen Mountain House with twenty-two horseloads of goods. Four days after the outfit arrived on 18 October, the first eager customers appeared. By 24 October, there were forty Piegan, four freemen, and twelve suspect Stoneys around the house. Acting the unctuous maitre d', Jamey Bird made sure that his friends got rum, while Fisher was pleased to receive nine hundred beaver pelts. More Piikani pelts were delivered on 4 November. The bands must have wintered nearby, as Bird returned on 7 March 1830 with hunters who turned in fox, three beaver, and twelve dressed moose skins.

The outlook was darker when Bird returned in October 1830. The Piegan were now going to the Americans, who charged cheap prices for supplies and gave sixty balls and powder for a buffalo robe. Taking an outfit, Bird and Michel Patenaud hurried back to the Piikani camp, only to return on 19 December. They reported that the winter camp was on the Belly River, but the Piikani had been to the Kutenai and given them all their beaver skins for horses.

Fisher must have suspected that something was not right, because he sent the young Scot Donald McDonald to keep an eye on Bird. Bird had a way of evading supervision, however, and after a few days Big Donald returned, professing to be sick. But in fact, the real problem was with the dissident Jacques Berger. He had reappeared on Badger Creek with a sledload of goods from the American Fur Company post on the Missouri.

ELEVEN

"Teach Us to Love One Another"

Twenty-four years earlier, Meriwether Lewis had suggested that the advantages of commerce were a reason for Indian nations to seek peace among themselves. In 1808, former captain John McClallen, the freelance diplomat, died after trying to put that ideal into practice. About the same time, the British agent David Thompson was advising the Salish to reject patently unworkable Piikani peace overtures. When Piikani powder horns were full, a Flathead peace was unlikely.

Americans Bill Sublette and David Jackson were tough-minded pragmatists whose pricing policy for trapping outfits seduced the western freemen and won over Piikani. They traded beaver at the Marias River in fall 1826, but Sublette spoiled the relationship the next summer. At the 1827 Bear Lake rendezvous, he supported the Snakes in a fight with hovering Blackfeet. Piikani may have been involved, because John Rowand noted that "a small party of Peigans accompanied by a Blackfoot chief visited a place built by the Americans near a large lake . . . and saw the grand Camp of Snake Indians encampted about the house and Rum like so much water about them."[190]

Robert Campbell had gained enough field experience to conduct the Smith, Jackson & Sublette trapping brigade in the Beaverhead country. As they were returning to Cache Valley to winter, the trappers ran into trouble. In the Big Hole, Flatheads and Nez Perce were running buffalo along the Wisdom River, while Blackfeet kept to a fortified camp at the head of the Jefferson Fork. It looked like trouble, and the trappers tried to sidle past. The Blackfeet followed, and in a running fight a Flathead and the Iroquois Old Pierre were killed. Convinced that it was too dangerous to continue across the Snake plain, most of Campbell's party turned back to rejoin the Salish and winter with them.

In the spring of 1828, lurking Blackfeet attacked another party of Smith, Jackson & Sublette trappers, who had wintered close to Hudson's Bay Company's Snake brigade and near the Shoshone winter camps at the mouth of the Portneuf River. When Campbell brought his brigade back from the Salish country, there was another determined attack by the Blackfeet.[191]

American problems stemmed from their trade with enemies of the Gens du Large and from their association with the despised Iroquois free trappers. Smith, Jackson & Sublette continued to hunt and trade on the Blackfoot perimeter, but stiffening resistance was a factor in their decision to retire from the mountain business in 1830. Operations were turned over to a syndicate of desperately undercapitalized former trappers, who called themselves the Rocky Mountain Fur Company. To keep ahead of growing competition, the company had to risk penetrating the last reserves of bonanza beaver on the upper Missouri. From then on, the mountain men had a full dance card at the Blackfoot ball.[192]

It was sixteen years since James Hughes had drunkenly boasted about imposing a hard line to open the upper Missouri. Nine years later, the British traders were still stymied. After failing to penetrate the Gens du Large heartland with the Bow River expedition, the Hudson's Bay Company switched to the less costly alternative of infiltrating debt-obligated freemen trappers, or confidential servants, as Governor Simpson called them. But this was now proving to be a poor way of piggybacking the British empire on commerce.

Naturally, the loyalty of debt-obligated freemen was flexible. Although it is not clear what became of his trapping partner, Louis Brunnais, Jacques Berger joined the trappers who depended on Smith, Jackson & Sublette to resupply them in the mountains. When the outfitters were obliged to jack up prices, Berger readily transferred himself to the Upper Missouri Outfit of the American Fur Company. After the disputatious 1829 rendezvous, Berger appeared at Fort Union professing to enjoy an inroad with both the Bloods and Piegan.

The superintendent of the Upper Missouri Outfit, Kenneth McKenzie, recognized an opportunity. He advanced a trading outfit to Berger and gave him four engagees to help drag it upriver on the ice. The sublimely optimistic Berger and his apprehensive companions took forty days to get the sleds up the frozen Marias River as far as the head of Badger Creek. The seventeen Piikani they met were from the camp of Onestenatoue (He Who Eats Veal).[193] The old warrior Ach-sahp-akee (Pretty Woman)[194] recognized Berger and extended his protection.[195] On 6 March 1830, the party arrived at the Piikani winter camps on the Sun River, where Berger spent the next twenty-two days distributing gifts, dispensing liquor, and reciting the prices that McKenzie was willing to pay for beaver pelts.[196] In response to Berger's invitation, ninety-two men and thirty-two women escorted him back to Fort Union.[197]

The Piikani delegation arrived about mid-May. During their month-long visit, McKenzie was so generous with his hospitality that the (unidentified) Indian leaders invited him to come into their country with a trading establishment. The assignment was beyond Berger's abilities, so McKenzie called up his trusted Mandan trader, James Kipp. About the first of September, forty-four men set out to haul the supplies on a fifty-ton keelboat. The enterprise reached the Marias in a month and anchored where that stream opens into a small flat squeezed between hills. The keelboat was soon surrounded by five hundred lodges of Piikani clamoring to trade. Kipp wisely wanted to secure the post before he started the bung. He told them to come back when construction was completed and induced three principal Piikani men to remain and discourage annoying stragglers.

Seventy-five days later, Kipp was paying prices that were in some cases 300 or 400 percent above those usually given by the British. Those deals were oiled with a keg of pure alcohol that Kipp diluted into two hundred gallons of "Blackfoot whiskey." During a three-day carousal the reeling Piegans turned in 6,450 pounds of beaver, which would ultimately yield $46,000 for the American Fur Company.[198]

Back at Fort Union it was St. Andrew's Day, and as a true Scot, Kenneth McKenzie felt moved to make a memorable gesture. Apparently carried away with good intentions—and heady distillations—he drew up a grandiose treaty between the Assiniboine and the Blackfeet. Despite his high spirits, the king of the upper Missouri foresaw that the neighboring Assinboines might object. Drawing on a bottle of port from his private stock, McKenzie tossed this document:

> We send greetings to all mankind! Be it known unto all nations that the most ancient, most illustrious and most numerous tribes of the red skins, lords of the soil from the banks of the great waters unto the tops of the mountains, upon which the heavens rest, have entered into solemn league and covenant to make, preserve, and cherish a firm and lasting peace, that so long as the water runs, or grass grows, they may hail each other as brethren and smoke the calumet in friendship and security.
>
> On the vigil of the feast of St. Andrew in the year eighteen hundred and thirty-one, the powerful and distinguished nation of Blackfeet, Piegan and Blood Indians, by their ambassadors, appeared at Fort Union, near the spot where the Yellow Stone River unites its current with the Missouri, and in the council-chamber of the Governor Kenneth M'Kenzie met the principal chief of all the Assiniboin nation, the Man that holds the Knife, attended by his chiefs of council, le Brechu, le Borgne, the Sparrow, the Bear's Arm, la Terre que Tremble, l'Enfant de Medicine, when, conforming to all ancient customs and ceremonies, and observing the due mystical signs enjoined by the grand medicine lodges, a treaty of peace and friendship was entered into between the said high contracting parties and is testified by their hands and seals, hereunto annexed, hereafter and for ever to live as brethren of one large united happy family; and may the Great Spirit, who watcheth over us all, approve our conduct and teach us to love one another.
>
> Done, executed, ratified and confirmed at Fort Union on the day and year first within written, in the presence of Jas. Archdale Hamilton.

H. Chardon	Le Brechu, or Le Fils du Gros Francais
The Man That Holds the Knife	La Terre Que Tremble
Le Borgne	The Bear's Arm, or The Man
The Young Gaucher	L'Enfant de Medicine
The Sparrow	That Lives Alone
K. M'Kenzie, on Behalf of the Piegans and Blackfeet[199]	

There were no Piegan or Blackfeet present, but McKenzie readily appropriated their diplomatic prerogative. Actually, the document had very little to do with them, it was really meant to forestall Assinboine apprehension that the new upriver store was selling guns and ammunition to their enemies.

Meanwhile, James Kipp conducted a good trade in fatal hardware and munitions. He was not overly concerned when those customers hefted the weapons and vowed to use them on the Flatheads. After a quarter century of asking for it, the Piikani finally had a trading house that brought the riches of the *naapiikoaiksi* to the lodge door. But what did they need beyond a few bits of cloth, a new butcher knife, or a handful of blue beads? A way to deny those intrusive western hunters access to their buffalo and their beaver. And that was just fine with Kipp. Supplying expendables like munitions was the best way to stimulate the production of ever more pelts.

After the first of the year 1832, the Bloods showed up. Kipp spun a wide loop in his recollection, but he wrote that he had noticed some Piegan headed north after trading and concluded that they would carry the bad news of the new American post to the British traders. As Kipp told it, the Bloods were primed by British traders "to undertake the reduction of [his] fort."[200] In February, after a friendly Piegan had warned Kipp of the Blood intentions, the traders holed up in the fort with a good supply of wood and a stock of ice to melt for water. About five hundred Blood lodges settled in around the claustrophobic place, taking occasional shots from long range. Kipp refused to be drawn into an exchange but, after eleven days under siege, demonstrated the power of his four-pound cannon against a tree.

The Blood envoys who soon opened negotiations admitted that they had traded their peltry to the British, but they said they had a lot of buffalo robes, which the northern traders refused. Kipp took in three thousand buffalo robes, about three hundred packs, because he could profitably transport skins that were too heavy for the competition to handle. The Bloods must have been as concerned as the Assiniboine about the growing Piikani capacity for war, but their fear of falling behind in the arms race was eased when the robes insured parity at the gun store. Who could have realized that Kipp's concession was the beginning of the end?

At the same time, Kipp also debauched a key man in the Hudson's Bay Company's Piikani trade. Since 1825, the half-breed James Bird Jr.—also known as Jemmy Jock Bird—had been employed in a role that Governor George Simpson discreetly described as "confidential." Bird traveled with the beaver-hunting Small Robes band into United States territory, where British traders were prohibited, and tried to keep their catches flowing north to Edmonton. Employing Bird had seemed cheaper than building and maintaining a trading post near the border but it was a false economy. The confidential servant turned his influence against the company.

The spook that got into Bird on Halloween 1831 led him to write to his employers, kissing off that relationship and promising to take the Piegan trade to the Americans. The next spring Kipp put Bird and eight of his Piikani kinsmen aboard an express pirogue and hurried them down to Fort Union, where McKenzie bestowed a fabulous bribe on the mixed-blood. Bird had been traveling with the Piegan for over ten years, and at least one of his wives was the daughter of a chief. The influence he enjoyed among the beaver-hunting Inuk'sik seemed to justify his generous salary. Perhaps McKenzie saw an opportunity to expand on his deceitful November treaty. Bird and his companions were sent on to Fort Tecumseh (now Pierre, South Dakota).[201]

Bird was one of those men on the margin who never quite left the world of his trader father nor fully entered into the life of his Inuk'sik wife. His activities of the past few years had drifted from the dutiful into areas of self-interest. His native kinsmen understood this subtle metamorphosis better than did the transplanted Canadian traders. It implied something that the Piikani could grasp: a refusal to be used any longer.

Since 1780, the French term "Soulier Noir" (Black Shoe) had been applied to certain neighbors of the Hidatsa. Bird and the mock-diplomatic mission immediately went to the Black Shoe lodges. What took place behind the buffalo-hide curtain was not recorded, but it must have been a heady moment in Missouri River Indian politics.[202] Afterwards, Bird and his companions returned upstream on the first steamboat to make it all the way to Fort Union.

At the same time, other important events had taken place upriver. Unable to induce men to stay at this dangerous post among the Piegan, Kipp abandoned the place when he took down the returns. Alert Assiniboine quickly moved in and burned it in an emphatic demonstration of their mistrust of McKenzie's peace agreement. Meanwhile, a Blood delegation, which included the proven warrior Petohpekis, hurried to Fort Union to catch up with the new world order.

The American Fur Company's Piegan establishment intruded on ancient enmities. The trading upset the touchy relationship between the Gens du Large and their Crow and Assiniboine neighbors. But the immediate effect of Kipp's trade was felt west of the post. After procuring guns and ammunition, the young Piikani were a ticking time bomb.

Piikani had always raided for Salish horses and battled western buffalo hunters. At worst these were contests of attrition without lasting effect. But in spring 1832, the tide of malevolence that was sweeping westward took on a new dimension. Early in the year, "Blackfoot" raiders hovered around the Shoshone camps near the mouth of the Portneuf River, where American trappers liked to winter. Two trappers going to other American camps in Cache Valley walked into a Blackfoot ambush. The American Robert Montgomery was killed; his Iroquois companion John Gray escaped but suffered horribly from frostbite before reaching friends.[203]

By May the Bloods had also traded robes for munitions and hurried to get in on the fun. Leading elements of Piikani aggression were already materializing before the Bloods had finished trading with Kipp. Just beyond the Big and Little Lost Rivers on the north side of the Snake Valley, a Piikani band bumped into John Work's Snake brigade on 10 January 1832. In the exchange of shouted insults, the Piikani claimed to have an unlimited supply of weapons and ammunition as well as the insatiable desire for Flathead scalps. Work estimated that three hundred warriors attacked his camp twenty days later. After turning back three determined charges, the British had the good luck to bring down a war chief. However, the battle drained the Snake brigade of all enthusiasm for trapping in Piegan beaver preserves. They turned west and ceased to be a factor in the hunt.[204]

The battle between the so-called Blackfeet and the Flatheads began on 18 May 1832 with the usual preliminary shouted threats and heroic posturing. The invaders vowed to fight until "they should get their stomachs full."[205] The multiplication of terror may have led the Salish to believe that they faced over a thousand enemies. The initial Blackfoot charge broke among the barricaded Flathead lodges. After several attackers were killed inside the camp circle, the Blackfeet's expectation of overrunning the camp turned sour.

Two days of fighting cost the pugnacious Blackfeet sixteen warriors and convinced them to give it up. Defending their camp cost the Salish twelve warriors and a thousand horses. When an American trapper arrived a few days later to lead the Flatheads to the fur traders' rendezvous in Pierre's Hole, eight or ten wounded men were dragged along on travois. Three sufferers died during the hot crossing of the eastern Snake plain.

That summer the Flatheads found no love in their hearts for Plains Indians.[206] As the rendezvous was breaking up, one of their leading men and an Iroquois killed the chief of a relatively innocent band of Atsiina who were returning from the Arapaho country. The Atsiina were cornered in trees growing around an old beaver dam and nearly exterminated. That episode went into the mythology as the infamous battle of Pierre's Hole.

Meanwhile, that spring Jemmy Jock Bird's defection had struck a sensitive spot at Edmonton House. Damning Bird for disloyalty, chief trader John Rowand had to do something. On 26 May 1832, the clerk at Fort Sanspariel on the upper Saskatchewan began preparing for a trip to the Piegan "who have lately gone to the American's Fort established about the mouth of Medicine River before the Great Falls of the Missouri."[207] Ten days later, Rowand took with him two dependable clerks, George McDougal and Henry Fisher, and fifteen other men. They rode south as far as the "Mississouri" River and located the Piikani near the Sweetgrass Hills. The dissident Bird came right over to the British camp, armed and accompanied by singing Indians. Ignoring what he knew was a typical entry display, Rowand stormed out of his tent snarling "traitor" and threatening to shoot the defector. After years as an Indian trader, Rowand was conditioned to hold his temper in the face of any provocation; this was a calculated confrontation staged to discredit Bird.

As nearby Indians stepped in "endeavoring to appease his anger & stop him from shooting," Rowand had a bit of luck. Bird spun his horse so violently that it crashed into a tree, throwing him to the ground. Quickly remounting, the mixed-blood trader "rode off at full speed."[208] To the watching warriors, it was a significant embarrassment to see their champion driven from the field.

His commitment to raw power demonstrated that Rowand was the harder man, but the encounter did not display the decorum that most

Indians expected of a chief. They were shocked, and embarrassed, to see two former friends fighting like children over a few lousy beaver skins. There was no doubt that the Hudson's Bay Company was not in favor of the peace agreement of the American Fur Company.

Riding homeward in mid-August, Rowand stopped to trade in his worn-out horses for fresh ones from the Kutenai. Those westerners were still bringing stock to the head of the Oldman River, where Fidler had seen them in 1792. No doubt they also hoped to visit the new American trading post. The leader of the party of thirty-three received Rowand with good will. He was repaid with tobacco, and ammunition to boot.[209] Within a few days the Kutenai would be attacked by a thousand(?) Bloods and Blackfeet. Seven Kutenai were wounded defending themselves, but they managed to kill seven attackers and wound twenty others.

Rowand left Fisher and nine men at the head of the south branch of the Bow River to build a more convenient store for the Piegan Indians. By the first of September, fifteen horses were on the way there with thirty pieces of goods for the Piegan trade.[210] But it would require a considerable readjustment of prices to entice them.

The eventful year 1832 ended with a new British post planted in the Piikani heartland and a lot of Piikani neighbors upset. The disparity between Piikani and Kainaa martial accomplishments became a simmering source of jealousy around the new establishment. Too bad that one of the bravest of the Bloods was down at Fort Union having his portrait painted.

TWELVE

Petohpekis and the Blood Barrier

When Ol' Joe Meek said, "Keep a bright eye fer the Blackfeet," Ol' Cotton and Ol' Gabe nodded sagely. They had their own thrilling yarns about Bug's Boys, as the old trappers called them.[211] Incautious mountain men often met with iron arrowheads that other whites had traded to their nemesis. Ignoring "sign" could result in a terminal haircut. As far as most trappers were concerned, Blackfeet were ornery varmints with a wide streak of mean.[212]

Although the hair of his enemies that decorated the seams of his painted war shirt included the scalps of eight white men, Petohpekis (Piitaa-mohpikis, or Eagle Ribs) was not considered a chief. He was so impressive, however, that the artist who was visiting Fort Union in late June 1832 felt compelled to paint a standing portrait. George Catlin's painting captured the image of a self-assured warrior standing with one arm crooked belligerently on his hip. The other arm was extended to display his decorated lance and two medicine bundles. The curved horns on his white fur cap created a silhouette that enemies could readily recognize in battle.[213]

George Catlin's portrait of Eagle Ribs in war attire
—Courtesy National Museum of American Art

Catlin called his subject a Blackfoot, but Petohpekis was actually a Blood warrior, the son of Menestokos (Father of All Children).[214] Given the conflicts at that time between the Piikani and Kainaa, it seems unlikely that a Blood would have accompanied the eight Small Robe Piikani who went to Fort Tecumseh with Bird in May. That delegation returned to Fort Union on the same steamboat that carried Catlin, and by June those men were back in the Sweetgrass Hills. Catlin recalled that some Blackfeet had come to Fort Union shortly before the steamboat arrived, so Petohpekis must have come then.[215]

In the citadel of fur trade diplomacy, Petohpekis was the latest target of hospitality. So he was probably hung over when he came to Catlin's studio in the north bastion. The small, dark place was crowded with unreconciled warriors from several tribes who took turns boasting of the atrocities they had inflicted on each other.[216] While posing for his portrait, Eagle Ribs recited his accomplishments, enough to chill the hearts of most men.

The prestigious Kainaa chief Stomick-sosack (Bull's Back Fat) had been ridiculing the Piikani for a lack of martial enthusiasm.[217] But it was well-armed Piegan who had seized the initiative and driven off the Snake brigade that year. Later, a combined force of at least three hundred Kainaa, Piikani, and Siksika attacked the Flatheads at the Salmon River on 19 and 20 May 1832 and created a military embarrassment in which sixteen Bloods were killed. Petohpekis escaped responsibility for that fiasco because he had been on the way to Fort Union at the time.

While waiting for the boat at Fort Tecumseh, the Piikani had seen a supply brigade being organized to reoutfit the mountain trappers.[218] Later, at Fort Union, the experienced trapping brigade leader Etienne Provost was also preparing to pack supplies to the American Fur Company brigade operating in the mountains. Another old enemy, the former Smith, Jackson & Sublette brigade leader Samuel Tullock, was taking an outfit to the mouth of the Bighorn for a Crow post.

Fort Union had also been the staging point for three previous invasions of the Three Forks. Blackfeet remembered the American Fur Company trapper William Henry Vanderburg as the leader of fifty hunters they had intercepted at Bozeman Pass in October 1830. When one trapper was killed, two wounded, and many horses destroyed, Vanderburg's party was forced to fall back and winter on the Powder River.[219] That brigade was the same one now being resupplied at Fort Tecumseh and supported from Fort Union. Wiser from experience, Vanderburg and his associate Andrew Drips intended to make a long detour through the Crow country that would avoid the ever-vigilant Blackfeet.

Kenneth McKenzie, the mastermind of the American Fur Company's Upper Missouri Outfit, had used the Inuk'sik-friendly Jemmy Jock Bird to advantage with the Piikani. Seeing McKenzie pampering Bird and his Piikani companions at Fort Union did nothing to endear them to a proud Kainaa like Petohpekis. Nor was McKenzie's expansion to the Marias as harmonious as he had hoped. That great step trod on the moccasins of the Crow and Assiniboine, who quickly moved in to burn Kipp's post after his boat left. Perhaps Eagle Ribs had come to Fort Union to report that outrage to McKenzie, because the Scotsman began outfitting another boat. Eagle Ribs may have had his own reservations about the management of the Upper Missouri Outfit. McKenzie was duplicitous and became ridiculous when drinking. His presumptuous St. Andrew's Day treaty ignored the basic requirement of Indian diplomacy, full participation by all parties.

Tension increased at the fort when a loitering Cree took the opportunity to shoot a Blackfoot chief as he stood in the compound talking with McKenzie, and Catlin was delighted to record the futile ministrations of a real Indian medicine man. Now a shadow fell across trade diplomacy.

After the Assiniboine destroyed his post, the liquor-trading James Kipp pusillanimously refused to go back to the mouth of the Marias, leaving McKenzie high and dry. So at about the same time that Petohpekis was posing for his picture, McKenzie threw a gentlemanly but relatively inexperienced Virginian named David D. Mitchell into the simmering cauldron.

Another boat was sent upstream. In addition to rebuilding materials and the new outfit, Mitchell's keelboat carried McKenzie's gifts to the Blackfeet. When the boat swamped and sank in a violent wind, the expectant Indians were understandably upset by the loss of their presents. Matters almost came to blows when Mitchell equivocated about replacing them. But after getting a new outfit from the bottomless well of American Fur Company capital, Mitchell returned upriver in late July and began rebuilding six miles above the ashes of Kipp's post. The Indians observed that Mitchell seemed afraid to live ashore while the new place was being built. Meanwhile, the Gens du Large were in the Sweetgrass Hills waiting impatiently for trading to begin.[220]

The Upper Missouri Outfit was unaware of what had developed at the latest trappers' rendezvous. Back in the mountains, the American Fur Company pack trains had arrived too late to claim the trade of the thirsty trappers, so the field men Drips and Vanderburg stood by while the Rocky Mountain Fur Company sucked in beaver pelts. They then decided to trail the mountain-wise Rocky Mountain Fur Company hunters to the best trapping. But treading on the heels of expert competitors like Tom Fitzpatrick and Jim Bridger was more risky than Drips and Vanderburg realized.[221]

In later years Warren A. Ferris, formerly a mountaineer working for the American Fur Company, published his memoir, *Life in the Rocky Mountains*. Ferris recalled an episode in which ignoring a warning almost cost him his life. After the rendezvous and the later battle at Pierre's Hole,

Ferris moved north with the American Fur Company brigade of trappers. They were crossing the Deer Lodge plain when they found a map drawn in the dirt at a conspicuous open place near the trail. It apparently depicted the Three Forks and surroundings. Within the drawing was a square enclosure of little sticks—a model fort—surrounded by several conical heaps of dirt. A stick with a bit of rag fluttering at the top obviously represented a flagpole. One of the two stick figures planted before the gate wore a hat, smoked a pipe, and had a little wad of horsehair and tobacco at its feet. The other figure had a little piece of dressed skin containing a few grains of gunpowder. Near the many smaller figures surrounding the stick fort was a bundle of thirty red-painted sticks. There were other sticks planted at angles, scattered pieces of cloth, and seven representations of horsemen.

The mountaineers were stumped until their Flathead companions interpreted the message:

> Flatheads, take notice, that peace, amity and commerce have at length been established in good faith, between the whites and our tribe; that for our benefit they have erected a fort at the three forks of the Missouri, supplied with every thing necessary for trade that our comfort and safety require; that we have assembled in great numbers at the fort, where a brisk trade has been opened, and that we shall hence-forth remain on the head waters of the Missouri. You will please observe that we scalped thirty of you last spring, and that we intend to serve the rest of you in the same manner. If, therefore, you consult your own interests and safety, you will not venture on our hunting grounds, but keep out of our vicinity. You may depend on the truth of what we now tell you. Done by a party of seven Blood horsemen, now on our way home to the Forks.[222]

Meanwhile, the lack of communication between the central mountains and Fort Union meant that Kenneth McKenzie had no way of announcing to the Blackfeet that American Fur Company trappers were coming into their country. The best he could do was give Eagle Ribs a letter to deliver to Vanderburg recommending that he approach wary Blackfeet displaying a truce flag.[223] McKenzie may have encouraged the Indians to be less receptive, however, of the Rocky Mountain Fur Company. Returning upriver, Petohpekis stopped to attend the sun dance, which kept him north of the Missouri until fall.

In September, Drips's and Vanderburg's groups trailed the Rocky Mountain Fur Company trappers across the Deer Lodge Valley to the divide, where they found the warning from the Bloods. Vanderburg surely realized that his party was under surveillance, but he ignored the warning and kept on the trail of the competition. In early October the trapping parties finally separated. Drips broke off to work the Jefferson Fork, Vanderburg stopped on the Madison River, and Fitzpatrick and Bridger pushed on to the Gallatin River. When beaver proved scarce and Indian signs grew ominous around the Gallatin, the Rocky Mountain Fur Company trappers switched over to the Madison, where Vanderburg's party could be a handy cushion against surprise. Feeling outmaneuvered, Vanderburg decided to rejoin Drips.

As they crossed toward the Jefferson, Vanderburg's party saw so many signs of Indians that the trappers refused to continue until the situation was clarified. Taking six men, Vanderburg rode ahead to check things out. His little party had just crossed a dry gully when they approached one of those little islands of trees where war parties liked to hide. Suddenly, what seemed like a hundred warriors tripped the ambush. The startled Frenchman Pillou lost his seat, his horse, and his life. Vanderburg's horse was shot, but he pulled himself free and called to his companions to stand fast. Instead, they stampeded. Standing up to deliver his last shot, Vanderburg was so scared that he forgot to cock the pistol. One of the attackers was known as Akitsikan (Woman Moccasin) because he had once been caught wearing his wife's shoes. He claimed to have killed Vanderburg, and in later years he would be known as Ninastako (Mountain Chief).[224]

Later, sympathetic Flatheads helped the other trappers locate the bodies. Vanderburg's corpse was horribly mutilated and the bones had been thrown in the creek. Taking this emphatic gesture to heart, the survivors decided to look for beaver in other places. The Bloods, however, trailed the Rocky Mountain Fur Company brigade toward the head of the Madison.

While trading ammunition to sixty or seventy friendly Piikani, the Americans were warned to beware of the large party of Kainaa in the vicinity.[225] When the trappers discovered some Indians bathing in a mountain lake, they could not resist taking potshots. The bathers turned out to be stragglers from the main Blood party, who then rushed the trappers. Joe Meek and those reckless comedians had to race for their lives. Soon the parties were at a standoff.

It was a bad beginning, but Petohpekis rode forward displaying his white flag and signaled for a council. Taking the Piegan wife of one of the trappers as an interpreter, Jim Bridger rode forward to confer.[226] Depending on who tells the yarn, Bridger carried his rifle either in plain sight or concealed beneath his leg. When Bridger cocked the gun, the alarmed Eagle Ribs made a grab that forced the trapper to fire into the ground. The warrior was trying to tap a little sense into Bridger's skull when the American wheeled and raced for safety. Ol' Gabe Bridger took two arrows in his back, and in the ensuing melee the Americans lost three men and the Bloods nine.[227]

Back at Mitchell's outfit, thousands of Indians hovered impatiently while the crew built the new post, which would be called Fort McKenzie.[228] The trader had just recovered his confidence when Petohpekis and the Bloods arrived. Eagle Ribs presented Mitchell with the trophies of his latest martial accomplishment. The horrified trader recognized the brace of pistols as Vanderburg's.

Portrait of Petohpekis (Eagle Ribs) by George Catlin
—*Courtesy National Museum of American Art*

Eagle Ribs ingenuously explained that he and his warriors had only wanted to deliver McKenzie's letter. They had been as surprised by the trappers as the trappers were by them, and they were only trying to restrain the startled horses when Vanderburg panicked. The trapper had tried to cock his pistol and the Blood finished him.[229] As far as the Bloods were concerned, it was a clear case of mistaken identity and self-defense.

Mitchell was in no position to judge the murder. He immediately started an express to Fort Union. The bad news reached Fort Pierre (the renamed Fort Tecumseh) on 9 January 1833, and the St. Louis proprietor, Pierre Chouteau Jr., knew by 26 March. The incident confirmed what Chouteau had already concluded about direct trapping after speaking to Bird and the visiting Piikani at Fort Tecumseh a year before. From his grasp of how the Piikani felt about those intrusions, Chouteau added, "I am convinced that these [trapping] expeditions have been an annual loss . . . If [they] had confined themselves entirely to the trade [at regular posts] returns would have been greater and expenses much less."[230]

The Indian elders who conferred during the summer sun dance surely favored a more conciliatory attitude toward American traders. The energies of their young warriors were better focused on traditional Snake and Flathead enemies. It also seems unlikely that a well-known warrior like Petohpekis could have raised a hundred-man war party without being noticed. Perhaps the Vanderburg incident really was an unexpected situation that got out of hand, and the later encounter with Bridger a frustrated attempt at placation. But would Petohpekis have acted differently in different circumstances? The killings could have been another expression of the old Kainaa role of spoiler. Bloods liked to act as arbitrators of policy. As the son of the leader of a rising Blood faction, Petohpekis may have made a play for power on his people's behalf.[231]

Mountaineers maintained that during 1832 as many as fifty-eight trappers were killed by hostile Blackfoot bands. But the Americans were the interlopers after all, and the Gens du Large were defending their own determined perimeter of valuable beaver preserves. In his trade at Fort McKenzie, Mitchell collected 6,450 pounds of beaver from the Piikani. That was more than half of the 11,000 pounds of beaver shipped from the upper Missouri that year. Indian hunters were very much part of the production of the great cash commodity.

The adventures of Petohpekis were many, and this is not a full account of his coups. Instead, these episodes are meant to show how vulnerable the Gens du Large world was to accident, false interpretation, and preconception. In this volatile world, the choice between tranquillity and destruction seemed to hang from a single horsehair, twisting vexingly in the winds of change. But whether Eagle Ribs's motives derived from political necessity or selfish ambition, his audacity failed to upset the new trading relationship. And just in case the Americans could not find it in their hearts to forgive, many Kainaa traveled north that winter to mend fences with the Hudson's Bay Company.[232]

By the beginning of September, seventy tents of Siksika were camped about the Nose on a tributary of the Battle River with the Bloods nearby. Piegan were still hanging around the Sweetgrass Hills and beginning the winter buffalo hunt. Assiniboine and a few Cree lived near the Bears Paw woods, with Crows not far removed. A month later, a sickness among the plainsmen's herds began killing Indian horses and mules.

Mid-month, a few Blackfeet arrived at Edmonton House with a convoluted account of the deaths of two Americans, presumably Vanderburg and Pillou. That led Edmonton's journalist to speculate that the Indians "are not so satisfied with the Americans this season as they were last." But his was a false hope, as the total Hudson's Bay returns from the Piegan, Bloods, and Cree from Bear River amounted to only 108 beaver.[233]

In the continuing wars on the northwest plains, Bloods and Blackfeet were rumored to have killed eighteen Stoneys, including the notable war leader The Chief That Holds the Knife. That casualty count was later amended to ten slain Assiniboine and four Blackfeet. Hudson's Bay Company trader James Edward Harriot, who was well acquainted with the Gens du Large, thought that "the Indians are in a most dreadful state of malice amongst themselves and that war will soon break out throughout the plains tribes, owing to the envious mind of their chiefs." When hovering Assiniboine threatened Fort McKenzie, the American trader rolled out eight kegs of rum and bought them off.[234]

Places as far away as Fort Carlton and Fort Pelly also reported conflicts. Combined bands of Cree and Assinboine went south to attack thirty tents of Slaves, killing a great many and taking ninety-six horses and six women. In May 1835, the Fort Pelly journalist documented a

visit by the renowned Assiniboine leader he recorded as The Man Who
Holds the Knife. The reports of his death had been premature. With
other Stoneys, he now planned to join the Cree going to war on the
Blackfeet. It took an outbreak of smallpox at the forks of the Qu'Appelle
River in December 1837 to slow down those depredations.[235]

THIRTEEN

Skin Games

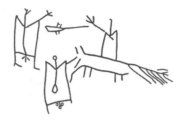

As John Jacob Astor ate oysters, he congratulated himself on his rise from petty pedlar among the Seneca to the lordly state of *the* pioneer American capitalist. Pulling himself up by the bootstraps, he had founded a great fortune. Nothing suggests that he was much concerned about the impact his personal achievement had on Indians. If questioned, the New York mogul would have said that he did not invent the system. He himself left the beaver business on 1 June 1834. Henceforth, the operations of the western department were the concern of Pratte, Chouteau & Company of St. Louis.

Before Astor went among the Iroquois of northern New York as a young pedlar, a visionary known as the Seneca Prophet had recognized the addictive threat of metal tools, woolen cloth, and liquor on his people and preached a return to the old ways. Over the sad course of eastern American Indian dispossession, that litany was repeated many times. Now, as the people of the northwestern plains heard it moaning relentlessly on the winds, it was already too late. They had become addicted to steel arrowheads, guns, powder, woolens, and alcohol.

The focus of the Indian trade to this point had been on what was then the most lucrative peltry—beaver—but these rodents were not otherwise essential to tribal life. As the European markets for beaver fur began to dry up, however, traders had to come up with another commodity that would allow them to continue their business. In the shift to the buffalo-robe trade, commerce began to impinge on the very basis of Plains Indian life.

In his instructions to the American Fur Company's upriver traders, James Archdale Hamilton, the earlier witness to McKenzie's treaty, let slip a clue to the changing Upper Missouri Outfit strategy. Hamilton told the upriver traders to "sell traps cheap to Indians, say two Robes each rather than loan them . . . and articles in great demand by Indians should not be sold to the men. . . . As the beaver trade for the last three years has been regularly declining, not withstanding every facility & encouragement we have given the Piegans, it appears to me that our sheet anchor will be the Robe trade and by encouraging the Blood, Blackfeet & others to make Robes, articles which they now obtain as luxuries will become necessaries and they will be compelled to remain on the Missouri in order to procure them."[236]

By now the Gens du Large understood that the American "medicine line" locked the British to fixed forts north of the border. To get beaver, the British were dependent on their confidential servants who traveled with the bands.[237] The establishment of the American Fur Company had intruded on the old beaver trade, but the new business in buffalo robes—which seemed to have developed overnight—put their buffalo-running plainsmen back in the market.[238]

Hides were a by-product of Gens du Large subsistence hunting. Women worked them into soft robes, which made excellent carriage or cariole wraps for a waiting market that rode behind horses instead of astride. Saskatchewan traders had accepted a few robes in the past and drew a modest profit from them, but hauling those bulky packs down the Saskatchewan in York boats and wrestling them across the many difficult portages to the bay was a labor-intensive chore. Because shipments from Hudson's Bay had to go to London, the robes were carried across the Atlantic and then back again to the shivering Canadian buyers.

The American Fur Company's keelboats, on the other hand, took tons of robes on board and simply floated down the Missouri River on the spring freshet. From Fort Union the robes could be shipped farther east in newfangled steamboats. An eager market awaited the first three thousand robes, which weighed about fifteen tons.[239] Three years later, the Upper Missouri Outfit shipped nine thousand robes, weighing forty-five tons. Fort Union was deep into the buffalo trade with the Assiniboine and Crow. From now on, that commodity would dominate business on the upper Missouri.[240]

Although a robe was worth only $1.35, James Kipp's first trade pumped as much as $20,000 into the northwest plains economy. There were no banks in Indian country, no investment system, and nomadic life precluded burying cash in a tin can in the backyard. Believing that credits were meant to be spent, Blackfoot customers paid $18.00 for a common trade gun that cost $9.35 in St. Louis, and they loaded up on expendables like powder and balls. From the beginning, the robe trade was interconnected with the profitable arms trade. Coupled with the sale of alcohol, the new business would prove to be deadly for the Blackfeet.[241]

After years in the chancy role of extorting beaver from other Indians or unwary trappers, the Kainaa were suddenly catapulted into a new legitimacy. Four years earlier, their pugnacious war leader Stommach-sopetah had advocated robbing the Flatheads as a means of obtaining tradable beaver. That strategy not only failed miserably in 1832 but started a series of events that severely punished the unlucky Atsiina. The next blow was about to fall on the relatively innocuous Inuk'sik Piikani.

The upper river was the epicenter of trade-war tremors felt as far away as Fort Union. The Assiniboine who traded there went forth to compete with the Gens du Large for buffalo. The plainsmen were understandably upset to see the Upper Missouri Outfit pumping arms and munitions into the enemy war machine.

The Stoneys had wasted no time moving to burn Kipp's abandoned house in 1832. Kenneth McKenzie had foreseen the developing problem and tried to head it off with his peace treaty. But it did not help the tense situation to send the placative David D. Mitchell to rebuild the American Fur Company's upriver emporium. Posted among a people who expected strong leaders, Mitchell was a bit too willing to endure the Atsiina and Kainaa, who appropriated a dominant role around Fort McKenzie.

In August 1833, upper-river affairs came under the scrutiny of a visiting German scientist. Alexander Phillip Maximilian, prince of Wied-Neuwied, was so determined to accurately record what he saw that he brought along the artist Karl Bodmer. Bodmer's astonishingly accurate drawings and watercolor paintings captured images of the

Great Camp of the Piekanns near Fort McKenzie
by Karl Bodmer —Courtesy Arthur H. Clark

Gens du Large at the peak of their glory. Those portraits and landscapes fixed forever the world of the Piikani boy who was standing on the shore when the visitors arrived.

If the pictographs on the Piikani's painted elk skin speak truly, this boy, Ninokskatosi (Three Suns), was the son of a distinguished warrior. His father, Ketsepenn-nuka (Spotted Elk), was so successful in attacks on the Flatheads that he felt justified in changing his name to Ninoch-kiau (Bear Chief). Three Suns's great-uncle Natoie-poochsen (Holy Word) was another respected Piikani elder.

The family was tenting near Fort McKenzie when the stocky little Prince Maximilian and Bodmer came ashore. Eight hundred Piegan turned out to greet the supply boat and gawk at the passengers. All the Piikani greats were there, including Iron Shield, who wore a red and blue uniform as he sat on his bay charger. The present bearer of the famous name Kutonapi (Kootenae-appe) came later with his people. The boy was thrilled to see his father among these heroes.

Maximilian and Bodmer were impressed by Ninoch-kiau's recital of his coups. The body count from his adventure wars of spring 1833 was forty-five slain Salish warriors and two unlucky French Canadians who got in the way.[242] Bear Chief's campaign was considered a success because his band had suffered only six dead and some wounded.[243]

David Mitchell had favored Bear Chief with a special outfit of clothes. But the trader failed to realize that awarding him the handsome uniform, red felt hat, and double-barrel percussion gun insulted other considerable men such as Blood leader The Sun. Their resulting alienation probably contributed to the subsequent shooting of an American Fur Company engagee. No one was taken in when drunken Bloods killed the engagee, named Martin, and tried to pass it off as an accident. The enraged Bear Chief drove the killer out of the fort, beating him with his pistol while publicly damning the Bloods for jeopardizing the harmony of the trading house. The murder was an insult that could not be overlooked.

On 16 August, Ninoch-kiau's quiet, well-disposed nephew went out looking for horses and was killed by Bloods. The boy was an innocent

Karl Bodmer portraits of (left to right) Stomick-sosack (Bull's Back Fat); Ninoch-kiaiu (Bear Chief); and Homach-ksachkum (Kutenai Man) —Courtesy Arthur H. Clark

sacrifice to the differences between the Kainaa and Piikani, which had been exacerbated the previous year when the Piikani seized the initiative in trade, diplomacy, and war. Bear Chief's Salish war trophies and new name were a direct repudiation of the insults Stommach-sopetah, head of the Blood's Buffalo Robes band, had made around the trading post.

Ten-year-old Three Suns could sense the tension. The funeral of his slain cousin was a double grief because a brother of the murdered youth was also put into the same grave. A keening old woman cut off a joint of her finger. David Mitchell was also burying his little son, whose mother was an Indian woman, and the trader received the honor of giving drinks all around to clear their hearts. Although Bear Chief put on old clothes, he stopped short of cutting his hair and covering himself with ashes, as did his uncle The Word of Life. Instead he loaded his new double-barrel gun with ball and waited through the speeches, vows, and lamentations for the Bloods to reappear. The boy could not understand why the artist Bodmer would want to paint a portrait of his father in his mourning clothes.[244]

Three Suns was happy to see his sister return with her husband, Jemmy Jock Bird. After inducing the Piikani to bring their beaver to Fort McKenzie last spring, Bird had been insulted and threatened by Rowand. The indignant Jemmy Jock took his family to the Red River settlement (present-day Winnipeg, Manitoba) and had it out with the governor of the great Hudson's Bay Company. Now Three Suns's sister hinted that they returned with a secret.

Bear Chief's band of eighteen or twenty lodges was settled in a grove of poplars near Fort McKenzie. Suddenly one morning, fusee balls cracked through the lodge covers. Hundreds of painted Cree and Assiniboine were attacking. The howling killers rushed through the community, slashing the hide covers with knives and blindly firing their guns inside. Thirty Piikani warriors tumbled out to return the fire while herding their terrified families to the fort. Women and children scattered like rabbits, seeking safety inside the palisades or fleeing into the bushes. In a few moments, four women and several children were killed.

The compound became a bedlam of shouting men, wailing women, and stampeding horses. While warriors climbed on the roofs of the houses to fire over the palisades, a woman was cutting a ball out of the knee of old Otsequa-stomik. Wounded in the back of the head, The White

*Bodmer's portrayal of the fight at Fort McKenzie on
28 August 1833* —Courtesy Arthur H. Clark

Buffalo howled and cried as they rattled his death medicine. Three Suns's
father raged at Mitchell's reluctance to assist them, but not until Indian
reinforcements came galloping from nearby camps did the traders venture
outside the fort.[245]

Bodmer's depiction of the 28 August 1833 attack may have con-
densed the action, but it is a vivid snapshot of the grim reality of Indian
warfare. The attacking Assiniboine and Cree may have lost six dead and
twenty wounded, but they admitted to only half that number when they
returned to Fort Union. Fort McKenzie's Alexander Culbertson misdated
the event 28 August 1834 in his journal, which he later allowed artist
John James Audubon to copy. The attack was seen in a different light
by that young trader. He felt that the fort people did all the fighting
and that it was the Piikani and Kainaa who hung back.[246]

The cooperation displayed between the Piegans and Bloods during the emergency was short-lived. As the tribes moved to their winter camps, Piegan killed two Blood chiefs. One of the Piegan camps was destroyed in retaliation, and the survivors fled to Hudson's Bay Company's new Piegan Post for sanctuary. The returns for the Piegan Post Outfit in 1833 were only 543 large and small beaver. In recognition of the new competitive situation, the trader also accepted 377 buffalo robes.[247]

Neighboring tribes feared that the Upper Missouri Outfit was creating a dangerous war machine. If the message of the August attack wasn't clear enough, the Crows came again in the summer of 1834.[248] On 13 June, the Bloods started to war against the Crows. Two of old Bull's Back Fat's sons and a daughter and her husband decided to return to Fort McKenzie, but they were intercepted by lurking enemies and killed.

On 25 June, four hundred Crows arrived, intent on taking Fort McKenzie by stratagem. Culbertson resisted their overtures of smoking and offers of their best horses, refusing to let them inside the fort. The next day, after taking sore-headed shots at the fort, they went off. In the meantime, the Bloods had captured fifteen Crow horses and returned on 30 June with meat for the hungry traders. Then twenty "Blackfeet" who could not resist another adventure this time stumbled into the enemy. Unwilling to settle for only two scalps, the Crow war leader led a charge against the entrenched eighteen. The Crow leader was killed, but the raiders were overrun.[249]

Trying to prevent further disturbances, the Upper Missouri Outfit resorted to the same dispersal of posts that the British traders had tried years before on the Saskatchewan. After 1834, the American Fur Company built a post for the Crow well down the Yellowstone at the mouth of the Rosebud River. This convenient store, as well as the attractive Fort Union, was meant to inhibit those roamers. The Crows camped near the posts during the fall and winter, killing buffalo and dressing hides, but in the spring and summer they continued going to war and trading with the transmontane tribes.[250]

Maximilian's observations of the savage warfare missed the politics behind the incidents. He caught the Gens du Large when their culture was changing to fit the new robe trade. The Piikani were losing the advantage they had previously enjoyed in beaver hunting. Ironically, the commercial conquest of the Missouri River was finally completed just when the two-hundred-year-old beaver market finally softened. Hot competitors would continue to pay high prices for a few more years, but during the third decade of the nineteenth century, the North American skin game finally found the bottom of the well. The robe trade that replaced it would carry still deeper implications for the Gens du Large world.

FOURTEEN

Small Robes, Big Hearts

*n the often violent world of the Gens du Large, one band of
Piikani consistently displayed a placative streak bordering on
pacifism. The Inuk'sik were known to the traders and the priests
as the Small (or Little) Robes.[251] Frontier folk are likely to become
hybrids, and the Inuk'sik may have been Piikani blended with the Cree
who had traveled with them for almost a century. They also mixed with
the western people they encountered in the high beaver marches.[252]

James Kipp, recently returned to Fort Union from the mouth of the
Marias in 1832, described the Inuk'sik to the visiting painter George
Catlin. According to Kipp, they were a distinct body of 250 lodges to
be distinguished from the 500 lodges of the Piikani proper.[253] British
agents had known and traveled with them for many years.

When the Muddy River Indians came to trade at Edmonton House
in spring 1823, they were asked to take along and look after the promising
young apprentice Hugh Munroe. Enlisted in Montreal, Munroe began
his service at Edmonton House during the outfit of 1815. Eight years
later he was no stranger to Indians and was sent to learn the Piikani

language and keep an eye on the American traders. Munroe's guardian was the Small Robe leader known as Tete qui Leve, or Rising Head.[254]

Although Edmonton House records show that he returned in November 1823, Munroe (or his uncritical biographers, George Bird Grinnell and James Willard Schultz) later backdated that first trip with the Indians by seven years. Although the old man's memory may have failed in specifics, his report of his first impression of the Small Robes Piikani remained generally correct.

Munroe described a three-mile-long column of families, horses, and camp gear that left Edmonton and traveled south along the mountains to Cut Bank Creek. Although his adopted father was Rising Head, later stories emphasized another colorful character called Lone Walker (Nitai-wa'wuhk).[255] That familiarity became intimate, because Munroe later took Lone Walker's daughter (Suyikaiyiahki or Mink Woman) as his wife. Since the chief accepted the responsibility of five lodges and sixteen wives, the young Bayman was connected to a significant family. As a son-in-law, he was also expected to help during their hunt.

Munroe's introduction to the war games was not long in coming. Before going to Badger Creek to participate in the summer sun dance, Tete qui Leve's band intercepted and killed seven Crow Indians. At the annual gathering, they heard reports of meetings between the Piikani and Americans who promised to open a trading house at Bear River. Two parties of American trappers had been attacked and defeated by Bloods and Blackfeet. Returning to Edmonton House in November, Munroe reported that Finan McDonald of the Snake brigade had visited the Piikani and carried a thousand beaver pelts to the rival Spokane District.[256]

Munroe's story of travels with Lone Walker's family may have dated from December 1823, when he rejoined them for the winter. Tete qui Leve's band traveled down the Sun River and to the Great Falls of the Missouri. Crossing the river, they went on to Arrow Creek, a stream that rises in the Belt Mountains about sixty miles below the falls. Unfortunately, the Crows were waiting to take revenge for their seven slain warriors and claimed the lives of forty-eight Piikani men, thirty-two women and nine children. Sixty-one Crows also fell, including a chief slain by the illustrious Lone Walker.

Undaunted by their losses, the Small Robes pressed east to the Judith River and camped on a creek in the Bears Paw Mountains. When reinforcements arrived, the Small Robes trailed the Crows as far as the Musselshell but found only a deserted camp. After that, they went into winter camp along Warm Spring Creek, near present-day Lewistown, Montana, and spent the rest of the winter hunting beaver. After convincing his hosts to make peace with the Crow, Munroe accompanied them across the Missouri at Cow Island and on to the Marias River.[257]

The Edmonton House journal for this period is missing, but interesting data are found in John Rowand's 1824/25 Saskatchewan report. His version of the Plains Indians' fighting with the Crows set Blood and Gros Ventre losses at 170 dead. Another 150 "Blackfeet" were also killed by the Beaver Hill Cree and Plain Stone (Assiniboine) Indians. Red River Stone Indians accounted for twenty scalps. Rowand thought that the gory total of 440 "has given [the Plains Indians] a blow of which they are not likely to recover for some time to come." The Blackfeet were understandably despondent.[258]

The conflict Rowand recorded, which Munroe may have later appropriated, seems to describe a combined Atsiina, Kainaa, and Siksika war experience rather than one of the Piikani. Because the Piikani operated toward the south or west, most of their problems should have involved Shoshone, Salish, or Sahaptan buffalo hunters. Records show that they were producing valuable beaver pelts and balked at carrying those packs to distant Edmonton. In mid-December 1824, for example, Rowand had to send his mixed-blood clerk, Henry Fisher, to the Marias River camps, where he induced the Piikani to bring in fifteen hundred to two thousand pelts at the end of the following March.

Rowand estimated that the twenty-four hundred Piegan beaver hunters were an industrious people working "a tract of land between their lands and the Snake and Flat Head Indians, which abounds in beaver." He prevailed on them to return there, accompanied by ten of his best freeman trappers. The combined parties left in the spring and were expected to be gone for a year.[259] It was Munroe's duty as a Hudson's Bay Company agent to ensure that the beaver hunters delivered their packs to the English posts. That those debt-obligated freeman trappers would be taking furs in American territory did not inhibit Rowand's plan.

In addition to Munroe, the Small Robes hosted James Bird Jr.— Jemmy Jock Bird—the Metis son of the former Edmonton chief factor, and another young mixed-blood named George Ward. The Iroquois freeman Maurice Picard, who was somehow related to Peter Skene Ogden, may have gone along in hope of connecting with the Snake brigade.

Munroe was an old man when he shared his reminiscence with George Bird Grinnell and the yarn-spinning James Willard Schultz. Regarding the events of the summer of 1825, three other descriptions confirm Munroe's account of a meeting on 28 June. The meeting place was in the drainage divide between the upper Missouri and Snake Rivers. Ogden's Snake brigade had recently taken a severe blow when about two-thirds of the trapping force went over to the better-paying Americans. Ogden had come north hoping to make up Hudson's Bay losses by trapping on the Missouri headwaters. His Piikani fellow travelers told him that the large numbers of Indians working those streams were unlikely to respond positively to rival trappers. Munroe and Bird succeeded in turning the remaining freemen west.[260]

The impact of the generous American prices that had seduced Ogden's trappers were felt as far north as Edmonton House when the Inuk'sik came to trade that fall. Munroe left soon after a falling out with his mentor Tete qui Leve over Hudson's Bay Company prices, but Jemmy Jock Bird and Ward continued to travel with the Small Robes.[261] The Americans' liberal pricing continued to undermine the loyalties of the Hudson's Bay Company freeman, and in 1827 Jacques Berger and Louis Brunnais went over to the opposition. Only Jemmy Jock Bird continued the role of confidential servant to the English company.

Those were exciting times in the mountains. The Piikani, Inuk'sik, and Salish were struggling to reconcile the attractive prices that the Americans offered with the serious disadvantage of tolerating competitive trapping. The Salish received goods through several Iroquois trappers bringing outfits from the American rendezvous. It is possible that the Piikani also received American goods from Bird's uncle, the former Nor'wester Nicholas Montour. Hoping to offset the advantage their neighbors were gaining, the Muddy River Indians concluded a peace with the Flatheads. In the fall of 1826, they even received some American traders at the Marias River.[262]

In addition to both exploiting and defending the upper Missouri beaver preserves, the Piikani had to contend with western buffalo hunters. Those contests must have been a consequence of their own drift southward. But there are also hints of earlier, amiable exchanges with the

Les pieds noirs et les bêtes plates font amicalement des échanges mutuels

Friendly trade between Blackfeet and Flatheads;
drawing by Father Nicolas Point, circa 1846
—Courtesy Jesuit Missouri Province Archives

Kutenai and Salish. One marriage between a Kutenai man and a Piikani woman produced the internationalist later known as Makuie-poka (Wolf's Son). In about 1820, he formed a union with a Salish woman that had a lasting effect on intertribal exchanges. Nez Perce captured in fights were also integrated into the band.[263] Couples visiting their relatives became links to more understanding relations.[264]

The brief peace between the Salish and Piikani lasted just long enough for a Smith, Jackson & Sublette sweep through the Three Forks. The next summer in 1826, at the Bear Lake rendezvous, Sublette offended Blackfoot raiders by taking the part of the Snakes. By late fall the Smith, Jackson & Sublette clerk Robert Campbell began to have trouble. Jackson added to the distrust by wintering with the Flatheads in 1828/29. But that did not prevent Piikani from trading with Americans the following spring.[265] The truth was that the beaver-productive Big Hole was a better place for compromise than for conflict. For twenty years, the Piikani had made gestures toward an amiable relationship with their Salish neighbors.

But they could never accomplish anything lasting because there was no way of guaranteeing the good behavior of the other Gens du Large.

In the winter of 1830/31, a former traveler with the Bloods came to the Piikani winter camps on the Sun River. Jacques Berger carried an introductory offer from the Upper Missouri Outfit of the American Fur Company to open a trading store at the mouth of the Marias River. Of course this was favorably received, and the next summer James Kipp came with a full outfit. With his role as a British agent moot, Jemmy Jock Bird pragmatically sold his influence among the Small Robes to the company for a considerable bonus. By the time the chagrined British got around to rehiring him two years later, the Americans had consolidated their foothold.

Bird's primary loyalty seems to have been to his Inuk'sik relatives by marriage. Glimpses of the Small Robes from Hudson's Bay journals over the next years are discolored by the Saskatchewan management's disenchantment with Bird. The mixed-blood returned to the British in 1833 as something of an agent provocateur, with a healthy dose of self-interest. Perhaps his standing among the Inuk'sik obliged Bird to accompany several warriors to Fort Hall, a trading post on the Snake River in the summer of 1836.

Fort Hall represented the failing interests of an independent Yankee trader named Nathaniel Wyeth. The place didn't have much to do with the Inuk'sik, the Piikani, or even distant Baymen. The post interpreter was an Iroquois named Antoine Godin. Godin and a Salish warrior had been responsible for instigating the battle of Pierre's Hole. Atsiina were the sufferers in that attack, so it is difficult to see what reason Bird had for confronting Godin. Bird's party induced the interpreter to cross the Portneuf River to confer with them. An Indian shot him, but Bird was said to have carved Wyeth's initials in the scalped man's forehead.

Early the next spring, fifteen Piikani prowling on the west side of the Big Hole killed a Salish beaver trapper and wounded another. But that was not enough to deter the Salish and Nez Perce summer buffalo hunt. In 1837, the hunters were accompanied by the Hudson's Bay Company trader Francis Ermatinger and an unusual traveling store. Their tactic was to obtain peltry from the Salish before they could take it to the American trappers' rendezvous at Green River. After the significant threats encountered in 1832, the Hudson's Bay Company had abandoned the risky direct-hunting brigades. The Columbia Department was resigned to sending mobile trading outfits with the Indian hunters to claim pelts as soon as the Indian trappers took them. The twelve lodges of Nez Perce that joined the Flathead buffalo hunters came by way of Fort Hall. Ermatinger was also escorting the American missionary William Henry Gray, who had illusions of starting a Protestant effort among the Salish. Gray meant to go on to the Green River rendezvous.[266]

After crossing into the Big Hole, the conglomerate party became more interested in keeping tight security. Rumors told of roving Blackfeet exchanging long-distance fire with the westerners. Then the group discovered five Small Robe horse thieves, whom they overtook and killed, capturing the woman traveling with them. Gray described her as fair with round full features and a masculine frame, but not at all of a vicious countenance. She bore up under the horror of having her husband's and brother's bloody scalps flaunted in her face by the exhalting Salish women. Gray was appalled by her treatment.

Although the buffalo hunters believed that they were surrounded by three camps of Piikani Blackfeet, they held nightly scalp dances as rites of passage to the hunt and moved past the hot springs in the middle of the valley. Nearing the plains on the southwest side, the Piikani Wolf's Son, who was married to a Salish woman, tried to guarantee a safe conduct. At night Wolf's Son called into the darkness for his tribesmen to come and reconcile differences.[267]

Wolf's Son (Makuie-poka) was a second-generation internationalist and broker between the tribes. The artist Karl Bodmer had painted his portrait and that of his father Homach-ksachkum (Kutenai Man) at Fort McKenzie four years earlier. Kutenai Man had married a Piikani woman and had lived for so long among her people that he had considerable standing. In 1833 he had asked Mitchell to arrange for him and Jacques Berger to carry an American Fur Company outfit to the Kutenai. The Bloods effectively stifled that enterprise, killing a company employee for emphasis.[268]

When Bodmer painted Wolf's Son's portrait, he captured the image of a young man elaborately decorated with beadwork, bear claws, and imported dentalium shells that showed how widely Indian trade networks extended at that time. Wolf's Son wore a striped southwestern trade blanket instead of the buffalo robes favored by other subjects. His marriage to a Salish woman may have produced a son who later Jesuit missionaries would know as Sata and think of as Satan.[269] Bodmer may have painted this boy, too, under the name Packkaab-sachkomoa-poh. The French translation approximates as "Wicked Boy."

Late in the afternoon of 20 June, two rightfully apprehensive Piikani and a middle-aged Kutenai woman approached the British party's camp. Two hundred Piikani lodges intended to stop near the Beaverhead Rock, and these three had risked coming as heralds. They handed over a note from their Small Robe fellow traveler Jemmy Jock Bird. Bird, who was also trying to arrange a meeting, warned that his tribesmen were mainly interested in horses and the Salish had best guard their herds.

Turning west, the Salish hunters and the Hudson's Bay Company traveling store crossed the other horse plain toward a well-known Blackfoot war camp where the pines began. They intended to follow the dangerous defile across the mountains to the Lemhi River. Rumors held that several parties of Blackfeet planned to unite and exact revenge for the killing of the five raiding warriors, but the hunters threaded the pass safely. They were camped on the Lemhi River when Bird and three companions caught up and reassured them that the Little Robes were determined to keep the arrangement they had concluded with the Salish the previous year. It was war parties from other bands who were causing trouble.

In addition to his Inuk'sik friends, Bird mentioned "Pagans," Bloods, Falls Indians, Sarcee, and "Squashins" (Gray's apparent misunderstanding of Siksika). The Small Robes were willing to forgive the killing of their five young men because those fools refused to listen to their elders and deserved what they got. But their tribal leadership was disappointing. Salish and Inuk'sik leaders and elders were frantically trying to deal with crises generated by thoughtless rustlers and murderous opportunists. They hoped to avoid some ill-considered act by other Gens du Large or westerners that could blow up a fragile understanding. Inuk'sik leaders made conspicuous demonstrations of solidarity by sitting down on robes and blankets and ceremoniously passing the pipe. The camp chief strode among the lodges in the evening haranguing his followers, but there was no guarantee that his words would be heeded by those reluctant to give up old habits.

The Kutenai woman who had brought Bird's message returned with Bird to the British camp. Her name, at least at one time, was Qanqon-kamek-klaula (Sitting in the Water Grizzly).[270] For a brief time she had been the wife of one of David Thompson's engagees at Kootenae House. That arrangement was over by 1811, when she presented herself as a man, with a wife of her own. That odd couple had preceded Thompson down the Columbia and later wandered widely, with Qanqon posing as a mystic or sometimes as an Amazon warrior. In a culture of narrow, specific roles Qanqon had lasted for almost a quarter of a century, but now her spirit power was running down. A few days after the parties parted, Gray heard that the Blackfeet she was with had killed her, but he could not state the reason.[271]

During the three days that the two bands camped together, Jemmy Jock Bird spoke with Gray and gave the Protestant missionary some interesting insights into the Blackfoot world. Raised as a nominal Anglican, Jemmy Jock seemed to encourage the missionary expansion that Gray was proposing. Bird suggested that the best way to penetrate into the Gens du Large world was from either the upper Missouri or the distant Saskatchewan. Bird thought that there should be two missionaries each for the bands of the "Squashin, Bloods and Pagans," as well as for the Falls Indians who traveled with them for a portion of the season. He also included the "Cercees," who spoke a different tongue but were peaceful like the Flatheads and generally well disposed.[272]

Only a year after his atrocious act at Fort Hall, was Bird trying to dilute the savage reputation of his friends? Or did he hope that their conversion to Christianity might stifle the negative impact of other Gens du Large? Gray's associates, Marcus Whitman and Henry Spaulding, seemed to be bringing the Cayuse and Nez Perce to heel. Or was Bird concerned that Iroquois freeman had induced the Salish and Nez Perce to send another delegation to St. Louis in search of Catholic teachers?

Leaving the Hudson's Bay party traveling to Green River, Gray fell in with the latest Salish delegation to St. Louis. But when that party was surrounded by hostile Sioux at Ash Hollow, Gray withdrew, leaving four beleaguered Iroquois to their fate. That cowardly act ruined the hope of Protestant inroads among the Salish and left them open to the Catholic effort from St. Louis.[273] Still, Gray had taken his conversations with Bird about the Protestant missions seriously enough to bring them up to former Fort McKenzie trader David D. Mitchell at Council Bluffs. Mitchell "seemed to favor the proposition, and said he would forward a letter, giving a bill of prices for supplies to the care of the Company at St. Louis."[274] But the mission was not to be.

Meanwhile, another deadly warrior was on its way to the mountain Indians. It chuffed up the Missouri River on the American Fur Company steamer *St. Peters*. On 14 July 1837, the American Fur Company trader at Fort Clark noted that a Mandan died of what appeared to be smallpox. A month and a half later, eight hundred Mandan, Hidatsa, and Arikara were dead. At Fort Union, E. T. Denig desperately resorted to the direct introduction of live smallpox matter as an inoculant, but the effort failed to prevent the reduction of one thousand Assiniboine lodges to four hundred.[275]

From Fort Union, Alexander Harvey proceeded upriver with the keelboat. When one of his boatmen, a Blackfoot passenger, and a Metis fell ill, Harvey halted at the mouth of the Judith River and forwarded a message to Alex Culbertson at Fort McKenzie that he did not think it wise to continue. Culbertson thought likewise, but the assembled Blackfeet were vibrating in anticipation of the fall trade and threatened to bring the keelboat on by force. Against his better judgment, Culbertson ordered Harvey to continue. After the boat arrived, the Blackfeet took five leisurely days to complete their trading, then they departed. The disease soon spread among the fort personnel. Even Culbertson was infected, but of the twenty-seven who died, twenty-six were the Indian or Metis wives of the traders.

As the summer waned, the traders thought it was odd that no Indians returned. Culbertson finally went up toward the Three Forks to see what had become of his customers. The stench from a grove of cottonwoods led him to a silent camp. Hundreds of rotting bodies were scattered among flapping lodges and abandoned gear. Only two old women, who had probably acquired immunity in the 1781/82 epidemic, survived among their fallen families and friends.[276]

During the epidemic, the Indians broke up into small bands and fled to the mountains and the insulating prairies, never comprehending that the deadly conqueror rode with them. As they moved into the mountains, the infected Indians left the bodies of their dead along the trail. The Small Robes were not spared. One abandoned lodge contained nine hideously swollen corpses. On 5 June 1838, an American Fur Company trapping brigade followed a grim trail to an infected Small Robe camp on the Madison River. The leader of those fifteen lodges admitted that his people were perishing from the smallpox. After trading a few horses,

Portrait of Nen–na–i–poh–sy (Chief Talker), chief of the Little Robes, by Gustav Sohon[4]
—Courtesy Washington State Historical Society

the trappers left the skeletal survivors to their fate.[277] Ultimately, the Small Robes were reduced to about eighty lodges.[278]

An admirer of Jemmy Jock Bird later promoted a story that Bird brought Indians in to be inoculated. But Bird did not reappear at Rocky Mountain House until 31 December 1838. During the traditional holiday festivities, John Rowand took time to write to a York Factory correspondent that "Master Bird has at last made his appearance at R Mountain House after an absence of nearly two years, he arrived with nothing, he got about 60 Beaver, of that number he gave forty, to our people across the Mountains and twenty to his old friends the Americans for supplies for himself which he told Mr. Harriot he could not do without. In his abscence he got the small pox who has marked his face well, he also had the misfortune of loosing one of his Piegan wives by that same disease however it is nothing for him as he got another for a horse which cost him but a small trifle, besides this he has a tent full of them for sale."[279] John Rowand was not a forgiving man.

The Inuk'sik were positioned in a conciliatory role from early on. This was probably attributable to geography. Their territory made them both intermediaries when it was advantageous for other Blackfeet to seek accommodation and a cushion against retaliation for those raiding into neighboring lands. During the time of the intensified beaver hunt, these pacific attitudes were undoubtedly encouraged by British agents traveling with the Inuk'sik. However, the pattern persisted after the decline of the beaver hunt and was a significant factor in the brief inroads made by the Jesuits among the Inuk'sik and Piikani. Certainly the once-large Small Robes band did not deserve the designation applied broadly to the Piikani, "raiders of the northern plains."

FIFTEEN

A Black Robe Decade

*I*n 1840, Jesuit Father Pierre-Jean De Smet attended the annual rendezvous of American trappers. He was scouting the possibility of establishing a mission in Salish country, and he met with a Salish delegation there. But he also began to hear of the Piikani.

By now the beaver hunt was in decline. As one of the last hunting brigades was organizing for a quest toward the southwest, the Shoshone made conspicuous threats against their old nemesis, the Blackfeet. The women threatened, "Oh Blackfoot bitches . . . if we could only eat the hearts of all your young ones and bathe in the blood of your cursed nation."[280] Hearing this combined with the gory yarns the mountaineers spun about "Bug's Boys," De Smet did not get a flattering introduction to the Gens du Large.

De Smet heard reports of a five-day fight that had taken place sometime during 1839. The Salish and Pend d'Oreilles whom the priest met in Pierre's Hole boasted that seventy of their warriors had repulsed two hundred Blackfeet from four assembled camps, killing fifty of them.[281] The only western casualty had been a man who took an arrow in his head. The barb could not be removed and he lingered four months before expiring. What made this conflict significant to the missionary was that the Salish were said to have knelt and prayed before the battle.[282] Assured that enemies of the Salish would not trouble him when he came into their country, De Smet nevertheless prayed for divine protection as he accompanied the Salish through the Red Rock country toward the Three Forks.

But the Blackfeet he met along the way weren't as bloodthirsty as expected. De Smet believed that they recognized him as an interpreter of the great spirit, and they carried him into their camp on a buffalo robe. As they sat in council, the leading men struck the earth with one hand while raising the other toward heaven, "to signify the earth produces nothing but evil, while all that is good comes from above."[283]

Taking no chances, sixteen Flatheads escorted the Black Robe from the Three Forks to the Yellowstone River on 27 August 1840. That was risky for them because the Blackfeet "give them no quarter when they meet them, but massacre them in the cruelest manner," while the Crows were merely robbers.[284]

In the race for benighted souls, the Protestants had an edge. The Reverend Robert Rundle, chaplain to the Hudson's Bay Company, piety personified, was already in contact. He traveled to Rocky Mountain House on 22 February 1841 and met his first Bloods and Blackfeet. The Bloods soon made themselves scarce out of fear of hostility from their confederates. Two days later, a party of Piegans arrived, camping a bit apart in order to make an impressive procession. They presented a fine white horse striped with red ochre to trader Edward Harriott.

Rundle thought the dresses of the chiefs were quite handsome and that the needlework was creditable "to civilized communicants." Describing the dress of one of the Blackfoot Indians to his sister, Rundle wrote, "His coat was profusely adorned with porcupine quills and beads and his leggings were also adorned with beads. Nothing on his head, and a Buffalo robe which serves for an outer article of clothing, just like a greatcoat for an Englishman." The prospects for sowing the seed of Eternal Life among the Indians of the plains were so exciting that the learned innocent missed their pointed queries about "double barrel guns."[285]

The second Jesuit mission party was still muddling about on the coast of the Missouri when Rundle left on April Fool's Day 1841 to visit the Cree and Slave Indian camps on the Bow River. It took seventeen days to reach the first camp, where Rundle was treated to successive feasts of berry pemmican, buffalo tongues, dried berries, buffalo marrow fat, berry soup, and prairie turnips. The chaplain was somewhat disconcerted to learn that his host kept seven wives, who lived in a twenty-six-skin lodge large enough to hold a hundred people. That pavilion was crowded when Rundle began preaching, but his interpreter, the ubiquitous Jemmy Jock Bird, showed a sulkiness that developed into a full balk. Unable to communicate, the mystified Rundle had to give up and go back to Edmonton.

An overland party of Catholic missionaries arrived at the northern end of the Bitterroot Valley on 18 October of that year. Seeing a new spirit power, the Salish there pitched in to help build St. Mary's Mission. Father De Smet was optimistic about saving the souls of the western bands but feared that "the Blackfeet are the only Indians of whose salvation we would have reason to despair, if the ways of God were the same as those of men, for they are murderers, thieves, traitors and all that is wicked."[286] That harsh judgment was due to the twenty horse raids made by Piikani during the year, which ran off about a hundred animals.

Within two months, a promising connection was forged. On Christmas Day 1841, Wolf's Son, the Inuk'sik intermediary, allowed himself to be baptized with the Christian name Nicolas. His son Sata, by his Salish wife, became Gervais. They were the first Piikani to receive that grace at St. Mary's Mission.

Father Gregory Mengarini described Piikani visitors to the mission with charming innocence. In attempting to differentiate between the Short Robed and Long Robed, he found the latter were dedicated "to kill men, and steal horses" but the small-statured, wiry Short Robed were inclined to peace. That theory was later questioned when the priests apprehended and thrashed a Short Robe horse thief and told him to get out of town. Returning with the explanation that he could never reach his people on foot, the unrepentant sinner made himself at home until the missionaries gave him an animal and sent him off with some buffalo hunters. Another time, Father Mengarini welcomed a visiting Piikani chief and his twenty followers with a loaded banquet table. In his desire to make a good impression, the priest had failed to grasp that Indian manners required guests to eat everything set before them.[287]

To the attentive neophytes, the Catholic chronology used to instruct them in the history of the church must have seemed like an astonishingly complex winter count. It reached back beyond anything ever depicted on an animal skin, but it overlooked important events drawn on their own winter counts. That past did not seem to matter.

Father De Smet hoped to ensure progress with the Salish by sending Father Nicolas Point on their winter buffalo hunt. While acting as a traveling chaplain, he could also test the possibilities for reaching out to the Piikani. The priest spent eight days in retreat and prayer before undertaking that challenge. Passing the Hellgate on 4 January 1842, the hunters had their first hint of lurking Blackfeet within two weeks.

Sometime between 1842 and 1844 Point made a portrait of Wolf's Son. He was depicted as a pipe-carrying chief of the Little Lodge who was missing his left eye.[288] That small man was still trying to bridge the great gap between the two sides of his family background. One time, the newly baptized Nicolas rode off on a seventeen-day search for the Small Robes. That quest was unsuccessful, but when he returned home he posted himself away from the camp, calling into the darkness for his people to come.[289]

In early February 1842, the Salish made a buffalo run that killed 153 animals in one afternoon.[290] The next day, Piikani who'd been watching came in to smoke and spend the night. When a horse thief was killed that night trying to get away with four Salish horses, the visitors were coolly indifferent because he was not of their people. The body was left to the wolves.

Pend d'Oreille riding ahead of the Salish hunters met some Blackfeet. The Blackfoot chief's son tried to appropriate two Pend d'Oreille horses, and in the resulting scuffle the father was killed. His demoralized followers were trapped in a box canyon and massacred to a man. Of the twenty-six corpses left strewn on the field, Point noted that only six heads were still attached to the bodies.[291]

Fearing the consequences of their rash behavior, the Pend d'Oreille kept closer to the Salish, and the rest of the hunt was conducted without further incident. After three months in the dangerous buffalo country, the westerners repassed the Hellgate in April 1842. They harbored no hard feelings toward the Blackfeet, and in mid-July twelve Small Robes came to St. Mary's. Ostensibly the visit was made to arrange the return of a horse that Point had abandoned in the mountains, but they really wanted to check out the place. Because the Salish summer buffalo hunters were leaving the next day, the priest had an excuse to refuse the Small Robes' invitation to return east of the mountains with them.[292]

Father Point kept a document curiously labeled "Lettre indienne ecrite en 1842." It is unlikely that it was a Salish production because it depicts Fort McKenzie, with the keelboat riding at anchor. Across the river, on the north side presumably, are the lodges and standing poles of twenty-two tents. An Indian appears to be delivering a message to the trader who came to meet him outside the palisades. The hoof prints leading up to the gate suggest a trail. Surrounding the post are bird-tracklike symbols that could represent the hostile Crows.[293]

By midsummer the provisions made during the winter hunt were used up. The summer hunt was on the Tobacco Fork of the Yellowstone in the beginning of August, so that the Salish could enjoy a friendly smoke of buffalo dung with the Crows. During the hunt, two young Small Robes who had fallen in with the Salish had an exciting encounter with bears. There was only one minor incident, a horse theft, until a Salish woman wandered away from camp and was cruelly murdered by a lurking Blackfoot. Even the killer's people repudiated that cowardly crime. By 26 September, when the first snow started the westerners for home, Father Point had experienced one complete cycle of the Salish hunting rounds.

Point's observations suggest that the Salish and associated western tribes were spending at least half of the year hunting east of the mountains. That competition for protein must have tried the patience of the Gens du Large, who were sensitive to the disturbance of the herds. The market for buffalo robes was growing, but Point does not indicate how or whether the Salish got in on it at Fort McKenzie, the only place to trade. Beyond the perpetual problem of the horse games, the Small Robes seemed to be staying their hand. They were not living up to the negative reputation that Father De Smet had prematurely fixed upon them.

Leaving on 9 January, the 1844 winter hunters took twenty hungry days to cross the mountains. Starving Salish dogs ate their pack straps— and the priest's pants—before they reached buffalo. Hungry Pend d'Oreille riding ahead even dragged drowned cows out of the river. When thin ice discouraged the hunters from crossing the Missouri, they turned north toward the Blackfoot winter camps. Within a week they were feasting on fresh meat that Father Point claimed was due to God's grace.

The hunt was declared over on 3 March 1844. A week later, the devout Salish convert Ambrose convinced a Blackfoot friend to accept baptism. It was unfortunate that the candidate was also made an offer by a Salish widow who promised more earthly rewards, creating something of a scandal in the camp. Father Point saw that the couple was properly legitimized "before the altar of the sacrament of matrimony."[294] Peter, as the Blackfoot was renamed, became the first Blackfoot to be baptized in his own land.

Traveling through the snowy Piikani territory, the Salish hunting chief Victor and a small point guard bumped into thirty-seven Piikani. The Piikani were on foot, which suggested a horse-capture expedition. When Victor and four mounted men rode boldly forward, the disadvantaged pedestrians threw down their arms and broke out their pipes. After smoking on a buffalo robe, the Salish took their new friends up behind them and rode double back to the main body.

Victor meant to ingratiate his guests, but the other Flatheads found no enthusiasm for turning the other cheek. With four belligerent Flatheads and Blackfeet seeking an excuse to quarrel, Ambrose strained to placate the parties. After the guests departed, promising to bring their people to confirm the new understanding, Victor tried to put as much distance between them as possible.

An unnamed white trader traveling with the Salish insisted that those Blackfoot devils were not to be trusted. "If others steal from us," he said, "we are at liberty to steal from them." He was passing out ammunition for an attack on the first Blackfoot camp they encountered. Point concluded that "He loved war more than peace, for the simple reason that during times of peace he sold less gunpowder than during war."

On 19 March, Cheslesmalakax, the grand chief of the Small Robes, appeared at the Salish camp to smoke and improve on the good beginning.[295] The Inuk'sik Three Crows, who was related to Victor by marriage, was so impressed with the work of the priest that he promised to bring his twenty-eight lodges to St. Mary's within a month to be baptized. But that night a Blackfoot was killed trying to raid the horses. The incident discouraged Three Crows, and he never came to St. Mary's.

The Salish and Piikani were unaware of an atrocity that had been inflicted at Fort McKenzie a short time before. The previous year, a Blackfoot party led by Big Snake on its way to raid the Crows had taken cattle from the fort and then compounded the insult by killing an engagee sent to recover them. In February 1844, a band of Piikani unconnected with the troublemakers brought five hundred robes to trade. Determined to have revenge, the traders Francois Chardon and Alexander Harvey loaded the post cannon with shrapnel, and when the Indians were grouped before the gate, Harvey fired. Four were killed and seventeen wounded. Fearing retaliation, the traders burned the old place and floated the goods down to the mouth of the Judith. Ironically named Fort Chardon in honor of the murderer, the new post they established there was damned from the beginning.[296]

On the last Sunday of the Salish winter hunt, 24 March 1844, Father Point was pleased to receive 103 Salish at the communion rail and to leave a cross overlooking the pagan lands.[297] The summer hunt took place without unpleasantness, and the one-eyed Wolf's Son apparently stayed around St. Mary's to make sure that the place was secure.

On the Saskatchewan, most of the Methodist Chaplain Robert Rundle's success was with the Cree and Assiniboine who dominated the region as far south as the Red Deer River. Those Indians liked to call the trail to the Bow River the Slave Indian Road. What it held for intruders was posted in a tree just north of the Red Deer. The skull of a Slave who ventured there in summer 1844 was prominently displayed for the edification of others.[298] But with the buffalo-robe market booming on the Missouri, why would Gens du Large even risk going so far north?

After several trips with the Salish, Father Point was shuffled off to the Coeur d'Alene mission. In January and February 1845, he hunted deer with the Coeur d'Alene in the vicinity of Lake Pend d'Oreille. Point had courage and a dreamy innocence together with an artist's close observation, but he lacked the organizational intensity of De Smet. Still, both men were soldiers in Ignatius's army of light, trained for battle against the forces of darkness. Where better to find that than in the Blackfoot country?

De Smet had a focused man's vision of what was good for Indians, and he resolved to attempt a flank attack. In late 1845, the priest traveled north and crossed the mountains to the upper Bow River. The Thickwood, or Mountain, Stoney (Assiniboine) who hunted in those woods were still using dog travois. The twenty Cree camped at Rocky Mountain House on 4 October wore crosses given to them by Father J. B. Thibault and had ignored the preaching of the Reverend Mr. Rundle. Although De Smet and the chaplain had some challenging conversations there, the Jesuit neglected to mention Rundle in his letters to headquarters.

The Cree bragged that they had taken six hundred Blackfoot horses in raids between the two branches of the Saskatchewan the previous year. But most of them were careful to be gone when some Piikani arrived on 28 October. Later, thirteen more Muddy River Indians came with a leader who wore an elaborate outfit decorated with eagle feathers and a blue-figured breast plate.

De Smet was gratified to be invited to visit the Piikani camps. Unable to obtain the dedicated Catholic Hugh Munroe as a guide and interpreter, he had to settle for the Inuk'sik fellow traveler, Jemmy Jock Bird. De Smet's past experience with Bird had been disappointing. Bird had shown a Protestant inclination in his earlier meeting with William H. Gray, and he was becoming more supportive of the Hudson's Bay Company chaplain. Before Rundle's departure on 29 October, he outfitted Bird with a hymn book, the Apostles' Creed, the Lord's Prayer, and an evening hymn, all in Cree. Rundle left lamenting, "Popery! Popery! Alas that the pure light of Protestant Xty should be hid from them."[299]

Jemmy Jock Bird had fallen into the role of broker between intrusive religions. He soon revealed a bias against the visiting Jesuit, perhaps because De Smet might have shown an unfeeling reaction to terrible news about his Small Robe friends. From the report that the Piikani brought to Rocky Mountain House, De Smet concluded, "The year 1845 will be a memorable epoch in the sad annal of the Blackfoot nation. . . . The Crows have struck them a mortal blow—fifty families, the entire band of the Little Robe, were lately massacred, and 160 women and children have been led into captivity."

That report was confirmed by the Fort Union trader Edwin Denig after he heard a firsthand account from one of his traders, who had been with the Crows. Denig believed that all the men of forty-five lodges had been destroyed while the women were taken as wives and the children adopted.

Only twelve families remained after the attack. Three Crows, the grand chief of the Small Robes, apparently perished with his people. De Smet, always looking for an illustrative example, heard that the captive women got revenge when the Crow became infected with smallpox. The canny women advised the affected Crow to use the sweat lodge, followed by a cold dip, as the best treatment for the disease.

Two or three months after the attack, an intercessor had managed to obtain the release of fifty women, who were sent back to their people.[300] But when Denig wrote about the incident twelve years later, the captured children had grown to manhood and now "carry the tomahawk and scalping knife against their relations."[301]

In spring 1846, the Salish and Pend d'Oreille were in Blackfoot country again. They had been joined by about four times their own number of Blackfeet to make a cooperative buffalo hunt. But tension was heavy, and both sides took the precaution of barricading their camps. Armed warriors lounged in the open space between the two camps pretending to be at ease. Unable to bear the growing tension, a Flathead aimed and fired, killing a leading Blackfoot. With a whoop the Blackfeet charged and had the Salish on the run. Realizing that their fate was in the balance, the westerners rallied and drove the Blackfeet from the field. For all the heroic posturing on both sides, the westerners lost only four while the Gens du Large would mourn twenty-one warriors left on the field. Significantly, the surviving Small Robes among the Blackfeet refused to be drawn into the fight.[302]

After his guide Jemmy Jock Bird became surly and abandoned him in the wilderness in fall 1845, Father De Smet returned to winter at Edmonton and travel down the Columbia River in the spring. Packing supplies for the inland missions, he picked up Father Point, who was unhappy with his associates and was rusting in disuse at the Coeur d'Alene mission. The two left St. Mary's in mid-July 1846 accompanied by two young Small Robes. Near the Three Forks they recognized the travois trail of the surviving Inuk'sik as well as evidence that Nez Perce were also in the country. Matters began to look darker when they caught up with the hunt on the Yellowstone River on 6 September.[303]

The camp included Flathead hunters, thirty Nez Perce lodges, and the twelve remaining Small Robe families hunting with the Flathead. The day before, they had withstood an attack by a Crow force believed to be five times their number. The priests described a face-off between bands who set up fortified camps before coming out to engage.

During the nine-hour fight, the surviving Small Robes helped kill ten Crows and wound fourteen. They claimed the privilege of leading the victory dances and taking part in the pipe ceremony, which was conducted by a red-garbed chief and three women. Because the participants carried green branches in procession, Point concluded that crowns of greenery had replaced bloody scalps.

Belligerent posturing by the Crow had deflected the hunters north toward the Musselshell River. The Nez Perce and Pend d'Oreille could not conceal their antipathy toward the Small Robes, and to escape an increasingly uncomfortable situation, the Inuk'sik decided to separate from their Salish friends. The priests rode away with them, hoping to connect with the main body of Piikani. Not far along that trail, the old peacemaker Wolf's Son slipped from his saddle. Under his Christian name Nicolas, the first convert died along the trail. The role of the priest's intermediary now fell on Nicolas's son Sata, or Gervais.

Soon the Small Robes were killing buffalo on the upper Judith River just east of the Little Belt Mountains. A Piikani pipe-stem bearer came to greet the newcomers while his leader modestly stayed in the rear. When the formalities were concluded, Omahksikimi (Amakzikinne, as Father Point spelled it, or Great Lake) came forward. When the trailing Salish and Nez Perce caught up with them on 15 September 1846, there were about two thousand Indians feasting together. With grease dripping down his chin, one Small Robe ridiculed the gluttonous Nez Perce who gobbled their meat like dogs and spent whole days painting and adorning themselves.

Great Lake welcomed the Salish chief Victor's friendly attitude. To prevent the Nez Perce from creating a situation, the Salish leader Ambrose and his young men patrolled the camp, moving potential troublemakers on, even beating an uncooperative Nez Perce and then giving his outraged chief a taste of the same. When the parties separated the next day, these Flatheads hung back to ensure that the Nez Perce did not try something that might spoil the peace.

The Piikani had been to the Cypress Hills collecting buffalo tongues for the sun dance, but it is unlikely that the Black Robes saw that important rite. In his journal, Father Point named Lone Wolf as a Small Robes leader and Masopeta as a chief who had received the mystery of the Yellow Buffalo Lodge. Sata and his children still traveled with the twelve surviving families of the Small Robes. Great Lake claimed the leadership of the Piikani, with Little Plume as the chief of the Worm clan. Citing old age, a Piikani chief resigned his role in favor of his brother and accepted baptism under the name Ignatius Xavier. He was notable for having always lived with one wife.

Father De Smet estimated that there were fourteen thousand souls in the six tribes of "Peagans, Surcees, Bloods, Gros-Ventres, Black-Foot proper and Little Robes."[304] The Blood war party that rode in on 17 September 1846 had known other Black Robes on the Saskatchewan who had baptized sixty of their children. A gathering of that size ensured disruptive incidents: troublemaking Nez Perce were run out of camp; two Atsiina pursued and killed two Crows; Cree hotly pursued five Piikani lodges. On 21 September Bloods returned with twenty-seven Crow horses. Meanwhile the priests baptized ninety-six children and two aged people.[305] Dancing occupied the entire camp the next day while the Indians waited for the arrival of the supply boat at nearby Fort Lewis.

The removal of the trade to Fort Chardon at the mouth of the Judith was unproductive and showed the Upper Missouri Outfit that it needed to have a post closer to the Blackfoot heartland. Competitors had made earlier attempts before Alexander Culbertson successfully planted a new place on the south side of the Missouri River above the abandoned Fort McKenzie. The new post was christened Fort Honore Picote, but it was known during its short life as Fort Lewis, in honor of the explorer Meriwether Lewis. But low water during the autumn made the place difficult to reach, expensive to staff, and on the wrong side of the river to please the Blackfeet.[306]

The missionaries went to Fort Lewis on 24 September, hoping to clear up a quarrel among the Gens du Large. The much-feared Blood warrior Aponista had killed a Nez Perce who was under Piikani protection. The man's humiliated host shot the offender but failed to kill him. Now Aponista had planted his lodge on an island near Fort Lewis, waiting like a gunfighter on Main Street and vowing, "I must kill a Peagan. If it is not a chief, it will be another."

De Smet and Point rode with the apprehensive Piikani host to see if it was possible to arrange a reconciliation. According to inventive spelling, the leaders sitting in on these risky negotiations included Amakzikinne (Great Lake), Onistaistamik (White Bull), Masleistamik (Bull Crow), Aiketzo (Grand Roulette), Sata (The Wicked), and Akaniaki (The Man Who Was Beaten). Faced by an eminent gathering and placated with a suitable gift from his enemy, the Blood softened and magnanimously let the incident pass.

The touchy situations convinced De Smet that there was room for social improvement:

> Assuredly it is a work well worthy of the zeal of an apostle: to reclaim these savages from the soul-destroying idolatry in which they are plunged, for they are worshippers of the sun and moon: and to teach them the consolatory truths of the Divine Redeemer of mankind, to which they seemed to listen with utmost attention, and heartfelt satisfaction. Allow me the reflection, the ultimate fate of these fierce and lonely tribes is fixed at no distant date, unless looked to in time. What will become of them? The buffalo-field is becoming narrower from year to year, and each succeeding hunt finds the Indians in closer contact. It is highly probable that the Black-Feet plains, from the Sascatshawin to the Yellow-Stone, will be the last resort of the wild animals twelve years hence. Will these be sufficient to feed and clothe the hundred thousand inhabitants of these western wilds? The Crees, Black-Feet, Assiniboins, Crows, Snakes, Rickaries, and Sioux, will then come together and fight their bloody battles on these plains and become themselves extinct over the last buffalo-steak.[307]

The Jesuits came to the buffalo country as soldiers of God in the old war for souls. Fathers De Smet and Point had been preceded by a handful of converted Iroquois who introduced Christian concepts to the Salish. Now the Salish and Inuk'sik brought them to the Piikani. On 4 October 1846, ten days after the traveling bands of Indians had assembled within trading distance of Fort Lewis, the supply boat set off to return downstream. De Smet was aboard, but Point, who did not work well with other missionaries, was left to stay during the winter and try to improve on the Small Robe connection.

It was almost a month before Great Lake condescended to enter Fort Lewis. The next day, Father Point returned to his camp with him. On 28 October, they heard that there were only ten survivors of ten Piikani lodges that had been destroyed by the Assiniboine.

The fifty families Point accompanied still used the buffalo drive and pisskan method for the winter hunt. The slaughter was indiscriminate, but it allowed the harvesting of the most preferred hides, which were taken from heifers in winter. When the hunt ended on 23 November, a thousand animals had been killed "for commercial purposes."[308]

Winter gave Point an opportunity to visit other Gens du Large camps. He met the Fish Eater band of Bloods who enjoyed a connection at Fort Lewis because the daughter of their chief was married to the post master Alexander Culbertson. Accompanied by the uneasy Sata and the post interpreter Augustin Hamel, the priest went to their lodges. The host, Panarkuinimaki, was an abrupt, boastful man who wore a little black-and-yellow stuffed bird on his headdress. Laying back on his willow-stick backrest, bracketed by a dog on one side and a caged rooster on the other, he bragged that he had killed about forty Crows with gun and bow. White men, he thought, were hopeless liars. Point came away feeling that the trip had been worthwhile because Panarkuinimaki allowed that he would be friends with the Flatheads, and that he would confine his aggression to the deserving Assiniboine. Later, he opened the way for Point to conduct over a hundred baptisms. And, finally, a near-fatal encounter with lurking Assiniboine led Panarkuinimaki to accept baptism. As a demonstration of his commitment to Christianity, he handed over the exotic headdress of bird feathers that once signified his spirit power.[309]

Point put aside his prejudice against the licentious and plundering Siksika to visit their camp. After several visits and smoking with their elders, his view changed. Many adult Blackfeet allowed themselves to be baptized.

Two hundred lodges of Atsiina found a lukewarm reception at Fort Lewis on 9 October 1846. The newly enforced prohibition against giving liquor to Indians led to them being served water flavored with molasses. Even the understanding Father Point thought the change was unfortunate because the Gros Ventre mellowed and became affectionate when they drank—it was when they were sober that they were dangerous. Their fifty-year-old chief Eagle went into battle draped in an American flag.

On 15 October, Eagle's son left to raid the Crows. Point risked meddling by giving these warriors a letter to deliver to the Crow trader. The priest pretended that it was an introduction, but he actually asked the trader to refuse the Atsiina ammunition and to promote peace.[310]

In December, Father Point and the interpreter Hamel rode ten hours through the snow to the Gros Ventre camp, tucked away in the bottoms of a small river. The leaders of the band were gathered around a boiling kettle over a very welcome blazing fire. Conspicuous was The Bearded One, La Barbu, who wore a cowl and may have been a mixed-blood.

He had helped facilitate a reconciliation in what turned out to be a double case of mistaken identity. The Atsiina had been insulted by Pend d'Oreille during a friendly visit to the Flatheads. The confusion pointed out the problem that the Gros Ventre found it difficult to distinguish, even face-to-face, between friends and foes. The westerners mistook Atsiina for culpable Piikani horse thieves. As always, irresponsible young men caused the dispute.

Among the Gros Ventre, it was the coifed pipe bearers, men associated with grave spirit powers, who were willing to have their children baptized. The drawings and watercolors Father Point made are wonderful illustrations of the native men, women, and children he knew. These are supplemented by a series of drawings probably made by one of the converts. This naturally talented artist had the eye and perception to put down a series of visions of the whites as seen by an Indian. Over a drawing of a trader regarding an elaborately decorated shield bearing the pictograph of a black buffalo on a red ground, Point lettered the name

This drawing by Ksistekomina (Eagle Chief) records his impression of Fort Lewis. Note the attention paid to the costumes of the traders and their Indian wives, who are obviously sharing in the chores.
—Courtesy Archives de la Compagnie de Jesus

Ksistekomina. That may have been the name of the Siksika who shared his palette and brushes, Kiskkihkini, or Bald Eagle. This native artist was clearly familiar with drawing tools. Perhaps he was a painter of the elaborately decorated lodges.

On ten expressive pages, the artist drew his impressions of the trader's world.[311] His drawings reveal how the Gens du Large perceived the other half of the robe-trading symbiosis. The artist accurately represented the animals he knew, including a moose, and made telling depictions of the strangers' cattle and hogs. In one drawing, a keelboat with an elk-skull figurehead is being pulled with a cordelle. The cargo includes a domestic milk cow being brought into a world teeming with buffalo. Other sketches show voyageurs rowing or poling and their dogs harnessed to a toboggan.

The artist painted the traders wearing long and short coats, striped shirts and pants, and a wide variety of hats and caps. A clay pipe was always clamped between their teeth. Those standing with axes on their shoulders performed women's chores. Engagees drove the wagons that circulated between camps collecting loads of robes. One leans casually on a cutlass. Another group surrounds a visiting chief who has been outfitted in white men's clothing and is smoking a ceremonial pipe with his new friends. In the complete depiction of Fort Lewis, a white man stood in every opening.

Two drawings slyly pick up on the hypocrisy of the traders. Since the priests were around, the traders were circumspect about their liquor trade. But the Blackfoot artist knew the practice all too well and drew an engagee in a striped shirt dispensing the stuff to a customer who had taken care to bring buckets to carry it off. In another drawing, a chief in an elaborate old skin costume seems to be shaking hands or exchanging something with a seated trader, while holding a jug in his other hand.

Nothing abstract seems intended in these drawings, but the traders always stand in the tight little doorways looking out. The vertical lines that represent the palings of the walled fort look not unlike bars on a jail cell. Was this resemblance an unconscious recognition of the claustrophobic nature of those places, where the traders were penned inside some crude retreat while their savage customers roamed at will?

In spring 1847, the circuit-riding Reverend Mr. Rundle traveled south across the Bow, Steep Rock, and Highwood Rivers to a camp on the Bull Pound River not far from where Peter Fidler had wintered fifty years before. Now the twenty-four Piegan families who followed The Bull's Head were balanced against twenty-five lodges of Cree and Assiniboine. Rundle's prayers were delivered in the Cree tongue, but Jemmy Jock Bird, who was again acting as interpreter, brought in a Piikani chief who displayed several emblems of Catholicism.

After leaving the Bull Pound camps, the missionary party passed Pheasant Pond River on the way to Hugh Munroe's tent on the Sly Shooting River. As they rode past, Bird and The Bull's Head pointed out the place where there had been a great battle fifty or sixty years before. About five hundred Piegans, Bloods, Blackfeet, Cree, Sarcee, and even a few Strongwood Assiniboine met a like number of Kutenai, Flatheads, Snakes, and Crows. The retreating Kutenai were pursued for forty or fifty miles.

Malevolence was the one constant of Piikani life. A year earlier, on 16 June 1846, twenty-eight young Piikani fought with the Pend d'Oreille and Kutenai. They gained the field without loss, and the next day twenty of them returned to the field singing. They walked into a Flathead ambush, and in the six-hour fight that followed, the Piikani chief Mikistuki, a warrior named Sak-pu (Sinew Piece), and two others were killed.[312]

After six years, Rundle still considered the Slave Indians "gross idolators," who went to the mountains and hilltops to remain for days without food "praying and crying to their familiars." Back at Edmonton by 21 July, he heard that Slave Indians had avenged a horse stolen from them on the Bow River. About eleven northern Indians had been killed, including a little Catholic convert girl who was scalped but was still praying when they finished her off.[313]

When the boat left Fort Lewis on 19 May 1847, Father Point was aboard. The whole fort was being dismantled and floated three miles downstream to a more favorable location on the north side of the river, which in time would be known as Fort Benton. When, in later years, Point wrote about those eight months with the Gens du Large, the old man still felt a sentimental attachment. But there was no place for idiosyncratic individualists like Point in the rigid disciplines of the Jesuit order, and he was due to be shuffled off to Sandwich, Ontario, to serve the surviving Hurons. The 651 souls he had saved for heaven were mostly children; only twenty-six were adults, and many of those were baptized *in articulo mortis.* Missionaries would not come to the Piikani again for several years, and then they were driven away in the hysterical furor of the Sun River war.

The legacy of Father Point's tenure is the understanding of the Salish and Blackfeet caught in the almost comic-strip sequence of his innocent drawings. As an artist, Point was no Bodmer or Catlin, but he was more intimate with the Gens du Large and more understanding. The Jesuit also made a remarkable contribution to Indian history by encouraging the Blackfoot artist to record the Indian view of the trader's world.

Point had recognized the one-eyed Wolf's Son as an influential Small Robe elder. After Wolf's Son's death, Kinuks-inah (Little Chief) led those twelve families. By summer 1848, their leader had been disparaged by the trader Charles Larpenteur with the name Little Rogue. He continued to lead the band until his death in 1865.

Horses caused a quarrel that broke up the peace between the Piikani and Salish in the summer of 1848. One man from each party was killed. That fall, a party of fifteen Piegan was returning from a hostile adventure in the west when they ran into Charles Larpenteur and his partner James Bruguiere. With the Piikani Sata as a guide, the traders were trying to locate a wagon road along the old Road to the Buffalo. On Father De Smet's suggestion, they meant to open a trade from Fort Benton to the Flatheads. However, the returning Piegan warriors said it was impossible to cross so late in October. They also warned the traders that they would kill any beaver trappers they found in the mountains.[314] It was no surprise, then, that Sata failed to find a way.[315]

During the winter, the whole Blackfoot tribe remonstrated against the proposed wagon trade with the Flatheads. They vowed to stay south of the Missouri the next summer to seek war with the Flathead buffalo hunters.[316] In addition, the recent rising of the western plateau tribes against the Whitman mission in the Walla Walla Valley, and the white settlers' strong response, had many native people upset. By 1850, the Salish were disillusioned and the bright promise of St. Mary's was guttering out. On 7 September of that year, fifty Blackfeet attacked the St. Mary's mission compound, killing some of the retainers and running off horses. Fathers Ravalli and Mengarini were terrified. On 5 November, Father Joset gave them permission to abandon the place and retrench in a tighter perimeter.

Sata's mixed heritage and confused Christianity did not prevent him from leading a raid into the Flathead country. Near present-day Evaro, Montana, the Small Robes ambushed the Hudson's Bay Company outfit that Angus McDonald was sending to the Flatheads in the lower Bitterroot Valley. In the attack, two Kanaka servants were killed. The incensed McDonald put out a $200 contract on Sata's head.[317]

The Small Robes were now considered just another Piegan band. Three years later, when the artist John Mix Stanley went to the Cypress Hills, he put their number at thirty lodges. By 1855, the Small Robes were deprecated as unwelcome loafers hanging around Fort Benton. Their great sin seemed to be failing to dress enough buffalo robes to please the traders.[318] As dedicated beaver hunters, they may have found it difficult to adapt to the new emphasis on the robe trade. Slipping down the economic ladder and diminished in many small ways, they seemed to be drifting into oblivion.

The Piikani were late in feeling the impact of missionary Christianity, but when it came, the intrusion was from two fronts. The remaining Inuk'sik should have been easy converts, but the initial Catholic inroads did not last very long, and Protestant efforts were largely north of the line. And as long as the tribes remained mobile, it was unlikely that outside religion would replace their perfectly workable belief system.

SIXTEEN

"Our Women Flattered Us to War" [319]

omplex human forces enveloped the Piikani. The continental drift of native peoples created collisions among the Gens du Large long before contact with Europeans started the great earthquake.[320] Sometimes those old war cries still echo in the winds, an intense and distant vibration in a magnificent vastness. But these endless spaces had room enough for all, and the herds that grazed were meat enough for all. What was the need for violence?

The term "warrior" does not appear in the traders' early vocabularies because they weren't concerned with Indian infrastructure. They recognized the prominent men by clothing them in red captain's uniform coats. The Blackfoot term *ninaa* means someone who is foremost, but not necessarily privileged. *Ohkinniinaa* is literally the necklace leader, or head chief, and *ninaipokaa* could be his offspring with a favored status, a chief child. Several terms dealt with war: preparing to go to war was *saihpiyi;* war itself, *awahkaootsiiyssin;* war against each other, *waawahkaotsiiyi;* and returning from war, *o'tamiaatayayi.* But there was no word for those who went.[321]

In such a self-reliant society, people were pretty much who they were, but they were always guided by the learned sense of what was right. One's independence and freedom were accompanied by a leveling sense of responsibility. Although these tribesmen were not ones to brood over the gravity of taking a life, even when big egos came into conflict they felt that it was better to settle differences by stepping aside. If a confrontation came to the knife, the killer risked being despised, and knew it.

Still, lacking judges, juries, or public executioners, the Piikani too often relied on personal revenge to settle real and imagined offenses. Egoists stalked among the lodges as threateningly as gunfighters in a frontier town. Father Point recounted how the fearsome Aponista killed a man who was under the protection of a Piikani lodge, then threatened to kill the offended host or one of his tribesmen. And Big Snake's rash actions at Fort McKenzie in fall 1843 had led to the slaughter of innocent Piikani.

Men's societies enforced camp order, sometimes giving license to the enthusiasm of bullies. In an unconstituted community, social disapproval as a way of governing behavior could also result in families simply clearing out when the system failed. This social churning led to new coalitions and new bands, but distance usually kept such divisions from getting too political. The big power moves grew from individual ambition rather than from factions.

Counting martial accomplishments as a means of selecting leaders carried some large social disadvantages, so close attention to public responsibility confirmed tribal leadership.[322] Standing tall, speaking straight, exuding dignity and unshakable self-confidence were the attributes that won respect. Notoriety came to those who had killed, even if for the public good.

While the Piikani recognized the limitations of the military mind, they allowed that skillful leadership in civil matters was valuable. Just as the words of an English country squire carried more weight than those of an unlanded farmhand, so the words of a respected chief were heard with consideration. Perhaps that role might be passed to his son, but inheritance was no guarantee. Both foolish old men and reckless youths were seen for what they were. According to the admiring David Thompson, the proven Piikani strategist Kootenae-appe was more levelheaded than the hereditary civil leader Sakimo. Historian Ted Binnema has unraveled the polarity of two Siksika band leaders: Big Man, who exuded xenophobic resistance, and Old Swan, who was learning the art of compromise.[323] This shows that leadership roles were as much an expression of personality as they were of social structure.

At the turn of the nineteenth century, Piikani boys coming of age fixed their aspirations on obtaining horses to use as bridal gifts by making frequent raids on their neighbors. The Piikani elders, who tried to find peace with the Salish, fought against the tide of impetuousness. Legitimate objectives of band defense and community security became perverted into endless cycles of raiding and revenge. The preemptive blow meant to ensure security really kept families in perpetual apprehension of its inevitable return.

Driving the Gens du Large war machine was competition among bands for status and control of reliable food supplies and horses, and for trading advantage. Adding to the group rivalries were various personal vendettas and the individual desire for expression and recognition, creating a growing atmosphere of violence.

Mere statistics of the bloody encounters do not give a full impression of the grotesquely painted raiders coming out of the dawn to ruthlessly slaughter surprised men, women, and children. There are so many casual descriptions of those attacks, even by eyewitnesses, that they seem like ordinary expressions of a violent culture. Portrayals of the stoic acceptance of the victims is misleading. In those murderous exchanges, loved ones were lost for no good reason and lives were scarred forever. Perhaps it was a deadly habit that had gotten out of hand, or the layering of revenge upon revenge beyond recall, but there is no denying the tragedy and no way to respect its history.

After carving a martial reputation out of Snake hides, the Muddy River Indians drifted into the role of march lords, facing two fronts. They had to contend with westerners hungry for buffalo and with easterners lusting for beaver. Drawing arms and munitions from the traders to keep up a balance of terror meant an inescapable dependence on these trading houses. But going to the store meant leaving families exposed to attack. Karl Bodmer caught the horror and confusion of one attack. In a blinding moment of pure terror, attackers slashed lodge covers and fired guns at those cowering inside. The slaughter was indiscriminate and, so to speak, unchivalrous.

This Karl Bodmer work depicts a Piegan man wearing a painted robe.
—Courtesy Joslyn Art Museum

But women, who did not expect to be spared, were themselves unsparing. Recall Gray's account of a captured woman abused for three days by Flathead sisters who danced with her slaughtered husband's scalp. And when De Smet came three years later, he reported Snake harpies dancing and damning Blackfoot bitches.

A few militant Piikani women were always willing to go beyond the desperate defense of the camp. A Piegan woman named Running Eagle earned fame and death as an amazon. And during the August 1846 fight with the Crows, mothers were seen imposing themselves between their sons and the enemies, young girls scrambled to retrieve arrows for empty quivers, and a celebrated woman warrior chased the Crows from the field with an ax.

Pandering to the folklore of women warriors, Father Point took unchristian pride in describing the female fighter Kuilix leading a charge on twenty-eight cornered Blackfeet and then helping to slaughter and mutilate them. According to Charles Revais, an eighteen-year-old Piikani girl named Lance Woman accompanied her brother and a war party that traveled as far south as Taos. In a similar tale, James Willard Schultz related the story of Otter Woman, whose sweetheart was killed by the Crows in 1879. After years of going to battle, her personal vendetta was finally diverted into raising warrior sons.[324]

The militancy of Indian women is exaggerated, however. Looking to exploit the popular market, journalists sensationalized such events. But women's real role in the war games did help perpetuate the myth.

Many early white observers, bred to Old World illusions of chivalry and honorable murder, had found the conduct of Indian battles wanting in murderous commitment. Even Father Point, when he had the leisure to compose his *Souveniers des Montagnes Rocheuses,* wrote that "Indian fights are very similar to a *jeu de barres,* and for this reason last a long time without spilling much blood. Thus, instead of saying, 'We shall fight,' they say, 'We shall have sport.'"[325] True, the manly contests between mounted warriors were often a lot of show. Any understanding of that bravado, however, needs to be balanced by remembering such acts as the cowardly murder of a woman who had gone out to gather firewood.

In later years, the romantic impressions of outsiders changed. During the Pacific Northwest plateau wars, the brash shavetail Lieutenant Philip Sheridan described his first impression of Indian warfare as "picturesque barbarianism, fascinating but repulsive." Behind the sensational gore was something unlikely to command the attention of itinerant observers. The same camps that launched marauders also yearned for peace and some measure of security. A wife or a husband, attentive children, and wise elders were more important than feather heroes. The romantic label "raiders on the northwestern plains" overlooks that for the last forty years, the Piikani had been seeking peace with their neighbors. But accommodations with the Salish were often sabotaged by other Gens du Large, whose hunger for western horses left the Salish with little interest in making life easier for the Piikani. The apparently inescapable habit of horse stealing left too much room for violence.

During the Gens du Large buffalo wars with the western Indians, or with the Crows who jealously guarded the Yellowstone herds, warring bands stopped and erected barricaded camps before engaging. Both sides then came forward for as many as nine hours of heroic posturing, riding demonstrations, and occasional unlucky casualties. The big victories were the result of ambush or surprise attacks.

After combined Salish, Nez Perce, and Inuk'sik forces routed the Crows on the Yellowstone River in 1846, the twelve surviving Small Robe families celebrated their revenge for the destruction of most of their kinsmen. They led the procession to the dance, which Father Point described:

> The more bizarre the costume, the more admiration it attracted. One man was wearing strings of small bells all of different tones; another had put over his ordinary clothes a raiment fit for a military parade. So as not to be outdone by the men, the women attached to their clothes some of the items that had contributed to the victory—here, an ornate bag carrying the shot or the powder; there a medicine pouch. But the most striking was a headdress of eagle and other feathers wreathed with blue, red or green ribbon, according to the artist's taste. All of this regalia was put over the leather tunic that, designed to insure female modesty, the women always wore. There was something magical about the towering headdress as its undulating movement harmonized with the dance, which consisted of a little hop, more or less lively, depending on the beat of the drum. This instrument was played only by the men, but the singing, the very soul of the performance, was for everyone. From time to time to break the monotony of the chant, the sharper sounds of the whistle could be heard. If, in spite of this encouragement, the action appeared to be slowing down, there were broken cries produced by striking the mouth with the hand, lively harangues accompanied by pantomime, grotesque faces made by an old coryphaeus—all of which livened up festivities. There were two old women with black smeared all over their faces who attempted to achieve this same effect. They threw aside the staves with which they were supporting their trembling hops, swung their arms about with all the force they could muster, and jumped up and down until they could no longer move.[326]

The Flathead women, who once danced with Blackfoot scalps, were also invited to take part. After the dance, there was the procession of the calumet by the four most distinguished members of their tribe, one man and three women. Point obviously enjoyed the spectacle but feared that others might condemn a man of God for those feelings. He rationalized, "with the Indians particularly, it is better to graft than to fell."

Symbols were important. The Indians wore parts of creatures that were laden with special significance. Eagle feathers, for example, were not easy to acquire. Eagle catchers lay in camouflaged pits baited to attract the soaring scavengers. When one of the great birds descended, the warrior would draw it down upon his chest, ignoring the raking talons, and wring its neck. Proud veterans liked to wear the tall feathers in their hair to telegraph to intimidated enemies what they had done. Each feather marked a heroic deed, and the greatest warriors among them collected enough feathers to make a tall, upstanding bonnet. No self-respecting warrior dared lie about these accomplishments.

Young men kept the world of the Gens du Large in uproar. They rode afar on deadly excursions that were as exciting and as pointless as a present-day drive-by shooting. Old men, who should have known better from bitter experience, incited them by reciting the adventures that marked their own ascent to manhood. Years later, they were still repeating those gory details to goggling anthropologists, pretending that they had somehow made themselves the mystic warriors of the plains without becoming vicious.

The extreme extent of the ferocity during skirmishes was recorded by a Canadian who visited the upper Saskatchewan in 1848. When artist Paul Kane was at Rocky Mountain House in April, gossip confirmed the heartless murder of a girl, the same incident that appalled the Reverend Rundle. Retaliating against a Cree pipe-stem carrier, the Blackfeet skinned his body and left his outsides stuffed with grass along the trail.

Descending the Saskatchewan in June, Kane met a large war party of Blackfeet, Bloods, Sarcee, Gros Ventre, and "Pay-gans" who were making a circuitous cruise for Cree scalps as they moved toward Edmonton. One of the leaders was the notorious Piikani Omoxesisixany (Big Snake), whose brother confirmed that he had been behind the cattle-stealing incident at Fort McKenzie in fall 1843. This war party became the subject of a Kane painting, which in addition to Big Snake included the Bloods Mis-ke-me-kin (Iron Collar) and Little Horn, and the principal Sarcee chief Wah-nis-stow (White Buffalo). In a later fight with Cree, those same cruising marauders killed nineteen and wounded forty.[327] Kane had glimpsed the dark cloud of hostile activity that now shadowed the plains from the North Branch of the Saskatchewan to beyond the Yellowstone. Malevolence kept the ranges of the Gens du Large free of intruders, but at a terrible cost.

Just before mid-century, what had been known as "the Blackfoot barrier to the fur trade" played out. It had been specific: confiscate pelts, enforce prerogatives, claim revenge, and enhance a dangerous prestige. But the fur trade evaporated and the trappers left. In the contest for buffalo, the Gens du Large were set against one another. As Father De Smet foresaw, the buffalo wars were expressions of a movable territorial prerogative that was likely to get even more intense as pressure on the great herds focused on an ever narrower range.

Intrusive mercantilism also helped drive the war games. The trade was pragmatically profane, and its best-selling expendables were liquor and munitions. The natives used both in ways destructive to their own tribal world.

Nowadays some complain about the lack of war memorials to Plains warriors. Modern apologists, Indian and white, conveniently overlook the self-destructive flaws of that "sacred" tradition. But the bands participated in their own destruction, and that culture needs to be called to account. Those war games laid a dark shadow over the brilliance of the northern plainsmen.

Given the numerous incidents of violence, not all of which can be attributed to the social forces of the horse-capture game, it seems impossible to completely justify Blackfoot brutality. The cult of Blackfoot aggression became a truism of the mountain hunt, a lingering apprehension during the pioneer period, and an excuse for far more fictionalized retellings than the actual record justifies. In order to judge it fairly, it is necessary to divide the violence into that with inward manifestations and that with outward—to reassess what was simply a grotesque perpetuation of outmoded cultural patterns and what was natural resistance to increasingly deadly intrusions from outside the native community.

It was other plains tribes that harried the pioneer roads to Oregon and California and attempted to exploit the distraction of the Civil War. Their excesses reflected on the northwestern plainsmen, who were mostly removed from the pressures of an expanding frontier. Primed by the myth of the Blackfoot barrier, overland pilgrims couldn't differentiate between opportunistic Bannocks and curious bystanders from the north.

Soon a new breed of trailside entrepreneurs began intruding into the Big Hole. Obtaining worn-out cattle from the overland wagon trains, they drove them north to recover on the grasses where buffalo once roamed and then resold them to the next year's batch of pioneers. Such was the beginning of the cattle frontier; gold miners soon followed, and a concerned federal government began to think that it was time to bring the free-ranging Gens du Large to heel.

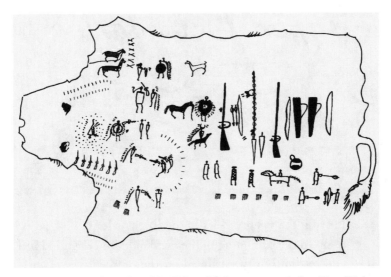

This sketch of a painted buffalo robe that was traded at Fort Union in 1832 was redrawn from an original in the 1833 field journal of Prince Maximilian of Wied-Neuwied.[5]

SEVENTEEN

Paper Boundaries

During the twenty years of the Rocky Mountain beaver hunt up to the beginning of the overland pioneer period in 1841, no real authority infringed on the prerogatives of the Gens du Large. The white man's differences, individual and corporate, with the native peoples were either negotiated, swallowed, or settled by direct action. The upper Missouri had always been the most distant part of Louisiana Territory and, for almost half a century, the concept of American sovereignty rested lightly there. When the grip of the United States finally tightened, it still seemed reluctant to take a firm grasp.

Alexander Culbertson's younger half-brother Thaddeus described his expedition to the "Mauvais Terres" (Bad Lands) and upper Missouri in 1850. Young Culbertson didn't get as far as Fort Benton, but he did get reliable information from the trader Malcolm Clark. Clark had come down to Fort Union to receive the new outfit, but when the steamer was stalled by low water he had to land his goods eight miles above the mouth of the Musselshell. He would have to build boats or barges to carry the outfit the rest of the way.

Clark described to Culbertson, with some disdain, the Blackfoot custom of leaving the dead and their possessions in lodges. Wolves invariably got to the bodies. He also took a dim view of the treatment errant wives received from husbands, or from their own brothers if the husband failed to revenge an indiscretion. Adultery could be punished by cutting a woman's nose. On the other hand, the adopted relationships between young men were remarkable for their closeness. Any warrior who lost his friend for want of bravery or skill in battle was disgraced.

Based on the information from Clark, young Culbertson tabulated the several Indian nations of the upper Missouri. It was still difficult to distinguish among the Gens du Large. He believed that the Blackfeet were broken down into the north Blackfeet, who traded with the Hudson's Bay Company, and the south Blackfeet, whose business was with the American Fur Company. The Bloods were divided into the Fish Eaters, Depuvis, and Robes with Hair on the Outside bands. The "Piedgans" broke down into the North Piedgans, the Little Robes, the People Who Don't Laugh, the Bloody Piedgans, and the Cow Dung band. Culbertson had not ascertained the divisions of the Gros Ventre du Prairie, but all together the Gens du Large numbered ninety-six hundred.[328]

Culbertson's work was partially sponsored by the Smithsonian Institution, and part of his journal was published in March 1851. His comments on the Blackfoot helped formulate opinions in the states about that "large and warlike nation." By summer 1851, as many as ten thousand central-plains tribesmen had congregated at Fort Laramie. They rode in to hear the words of the American government, which meant to secure the vulnerable Oregon Trail by inhibiting the roaming tribes. One step would be to delineate territorial divisions between rival tribes and mitigate their hostility toward each other. Once that was accomplished, later negotiations would begin restricting them to definite areas.

Several men closely associated with the Piikani figured in that preliminary step. The St. Louis Indian superintendency was administrated by former Indian traders. Ten years earlier, the failed Rocky Mountain entrepreneur Joshua Pilcher had yielded the office to the man who built Fort McKenzie. Now superintendent David D. Mitchell would gerrymander the Piikani ranges from Fort Laramie.

Father De Smet, whose missionary work in the mountains had ended in 1848, came to Fort Laramie at the invitation of Superintendent Mitchell. He brought his "sketches and the outline of maps of the Prairie & Mountain country . . . and information on the habits, history and other interesting matters appertaining to the Upper Indians." When the agreements were concluded, De Smet returned to St. Louis and drew the great map that delineated the new territory. Interestingly, the southern bounds of the Blackfoot country were set about where the buffalo hunters had battled the Crows five years earlier.

Alexander Culbertson, the upper-Missouri River trader, was charged with bringing Piikani representatives to the great council. He was unable to locate them in time, so there were no Blackfeet present when the bounds of the Crow country along the Musselshell that limited their eastern ranges were established.

"Commencing at the mouth of the Muscle-shell river, thence up the Missouri river to its source, —thence along the main range of the Rocky Mountains, in a Southern direction to the head waters of the northern source of the Yellow Stone river, —thence down the Yellow Stone to the mouth of Twenty five Yard Creek, —thence across to the head waters of the Muscle-shell river, —and thence down the Muscle-shell to the place of beginning."

That description, written on meaningless paper, meant nothing to the horsemen, who always rode where they chose. But in 1853, a party came up the Missouri River to examine a northern route for a railway to the Pacific. The young military engineer in charge was Isaac Ingles Stevens. He met thirty chiefs at Fort Benton on 21 September and let it be known that the United States wanted the horse raiding to stop. It was time to give up hostile exchanges with the Crows, Assiniboine, Cree, and Snakes, and to stop troubling Blackfoot, Sans Arc, and Auncepapas bands of Sioux.

Stevens hurried on to assume the government of the newly created Washington Territory and the superintendency of the western Indians. He left his young assistant, James Doty, to winter at Fort Benton, to make weather observations and do a bit of exploring. Doty made a trip to the Marias River and realized how the People divided themselves. Two hundred lodges of Piegans, 600 men or 1800 persons, were the inheritance of the United States. Another ninety Piegan lodges, 270 men or 500 hundred souls, living north of the line, had no authority other than the Hudson's Bay Company.

Because Stevens's proposals threatened peace, the winter of 1853/54 became a time of increased activity. Doty guessed that more than five hundred warriors went out against the Flatheads, Shoshone, and Crows.

The Fort Benton journalist recorded the passage of forty-eight outward bound and returning war parties.[329] Presumably, their main interest was capturing horses before the opportunity was lost.

During his seven years as an upper river trader, David D. Mitchell had amused himself by collecting the yarns of "the old savans of the tribe." Those sly old guys fed suckers some astonishing versions of their origin, naming, and history, which suggests that outside influences were already infecting tribal mythology. But Mitchell was generous when he wrote in early 1854,

> The Blackfoot has always been regarded as a treacherous, bloodthirsty savage; this is a mistake, growing out of our ignorance of his true character. It is true, they killed and scalped a great many of the mountain trappers; but it must be considered, that they were under no treaty obligations, so far as the United States were concerned. They found strangers trespassing on their hunting grounds, and killing off the game upon which they relied for subsistence; any other tribe, or even civilized nation, would have done the same with less provocation.[330]

In May 1855, commissioner of Indian affairs George W. Manypenny instructed three commissioners on how to proceed in corralling the Blackfeet:

> The principal objects to be attained by the proposed negotiations are, the establishment of well defined and permanent relations of amity with all the most numerous and warlike tribes in that remote region of the country, both between the Indians and the United States, and between the tribes as among themselves. . . . A cordial, firm, and perpetual peace should be established; a well understood recognition by the Indians of their allegiance to the United States, and their obligation to obey its laws, should be obtained, and a high regard on their part for its justice, magnanimity and power, should be fostered or inculcated.

Manypenny optimistically continued,

> The Indians should assent to remain in the regions of country respectively occupied by each tribe, and not to commit depredations or make hostile excursions against other tribes. . . . The Indians should be induced, if it is practicable, to assent to remain within the United States, and not to pass into the British possessions, either to hunt, trade or fish; and their communication with agents of the British government should be terminated.[331]

That agenda pretty well repudiated a hundred years of Gens du Large experience and placed a good deal of confidence in the abstraction of the boundary line. After concluding a similar treaty with the Salish, Kutenai, and upper Pend d'Oreille in the Bitterroot Valley, Commissioner Stevens returned to Fort Benton on 26 July 1855. But it took until 17 October to assemble the scattered bands of Piegan, Bloods, and Blackfeet at the mouth of the Judith River. Nez Perce and Flathead observers came to see if the Americans could deliver peace with their old enemies. The resources of the nation were finally being concentrated on the ideal that Captain John McClallen had first unsuccessfully attempted forty-eight years earlier.[332]

What had the international boundary that had been agreed on in 1818 and completed in 1846 meant to the plainsmen? The Indians ignored the medicine line until the government men, unfamiliar with the true way of things, came with their unintelligible gibberish and curious papers. The formal construction of this new treaty did not survive the interpretation of traders like Alexander Culbertson and Benjamin Durocher (De Roche). Given his past performance with missionaries, who can say what information the unpredictable Jemmy Jock Bird passed on to his old friends?

A basic terminology for the Gens du Large was finally written into United States law, which proclaimed that the Piikani, Kainaa, Siksika, and Atsiina constituted the "Blackfoot Nation." The treaty that Congress ratified on 15 April 1856 defined two degrees of territorial restriction. The first described the extent of the Blackfoot hunting range as a large area following the main divide of the Rocky Mountains from the forty-ninth parallel south and east to the sources of the Yellowstone, and down as far as Twenty-five Yard Creek where it struck north to the Musselshell. Reflecting the Crow treaty of 1851, that boundary followed the Musselshell to its mouth and north to the British line. Addressing the troublesome problem of the western tribes' access to buffalo, the treaty provided that for the next ninety-nine years, parties traveling there to hunt were not supposed to infringe on the exclusive Blackfoot reserve.

The commissioners designated that the reservation would comprise the country north from a line running from the head of the old Salish Road to the Buffalo (Stevens's Hellgate, or Medicine Rock Pass) across to the headwaters of the Musselshell. To avoid trouble, hunting nations

Portrait of Mek-yapy (Red Dye), a Piegan warrior, by Gustav Sohon, dated 9 October 1855, about a week before the conclusion of the Judith treaty. Mek-yapy did not sign the treaty, but his portrait shows the elaborate dress of a young Piegan man of that period.[6] —Courtesy Washington State Historical Society

and the resident Blackfeet would refrain from camping within ten miles of the line. The commissioners expected that the plainsmen would forgo hostilities except in self-defense and redirect their energies into agricultural and mechanical pursuits.

On 17 October 1855 Lame Bull, the "only chief," led the acceptance of the treaty paper. His mark was followed by those of Mountain Chief, Low Horn, Little Gray Head, Little Dog, Big Snake, The Skunk, Bad Head, Middle Sitter, and Kitch-eepone-istah. Another band of Piikani that signed included Running Rabbit, Bear Chief, Little White Buffalo, and Big Straw.

Ever the Blood, the chief Seen from Afar questioned if it was really possible to keep the young men at home.[333] As he foresaw, peace between old enemies was a delusion. According to the first report of the new Blackfoot Indian agent, Major Edwin A. C. Hatch, ten days after the treaty was signed a Blood party left to attack Crow camps. At least the Piikani and Atsiina refused to join them.

In 1857, Blackfoot raiders were still going as far as the Platte River to harry the Sioux, Arapaho, and Cheyenne.[334] The next year they also fought the Kutenai. Those hostile adventures were munitioned through the Fort Benton robe trade.

Major Hatch's successor as Blackfoot agent was Major Alfred J. Vaughan, who had a young Indian wife and spent a lot of time among the Piikani. Although he was suspected of being in the pocket of the American Fur Company, Vaughan made a startling recommendation in his 1858 report: the trade in buffalo robes should be prohibited. Vaughan foresaw that the ruthless slaughter of animals for their hides jeopardized the Blackfoot food supply. But the prohibition would mean breaking the American Fur Company's lock on the lucrative upper Missouri robe trade, and the trust had too many influential friends in Washington for it to go through.

A Pend d'Oreille raiding party bypassed the Piikani in 1861 and took Atsiina horses on the Milk River. As they fled west, the rustlers dropped a few animals near a Piikani camp on the Marias River. Without asking questions, the pursuing Gros Ventre attacked the Piikani, their former friends. To guard against retaliation the Atsiina formed a new alliance with the River Crows.

While the Blackfoot Treaty was being negotiated, a war between the whites and Indians had broken out in the western plateau country. Within three years, however, the hostile Yakima, Walla Walla, Spokane, and Coeur d'Alene had been defeated by the government. Still, the unrest continued elsewhere. In September 1858, two soldiers of fortune were outfitted at Fort Walla Walla to cross the mountains to the east and test the Blackfoot attitude. They reached the Piikani camp of Little Dog on the Marias River in October and were treated kindly. But, returning home in company with some Kutenai, they were attacked by Bloods in the vicinity of St. Mary's Lake.

Father Joseph Menetrey made the 294-mile trip from St. Ignatius mission to Fort Benton in September 1855, but it was not until autumn 1859 that the Jesuits tried to return to the Blackfoot reservation. Father Adrian Hoecken and Brother Vincent Magri built three squat log cabins near the present-day Choteau, Montana. But the place was too removed from the usual haunts of the Indians and they soon moved to the Sun River. Because the Blackfeet remained standoffish, the place was abandoned in August 1860. Four Jesuits led by Father Giorda wintered at Fort Benton in 1861/62 and were joined by the peripatetic Father Menetrey. In February they relocated not far from the famous pisskan near present-day Ulm.[335] Surely the wandering bands would come there.

The 1855 treaty had been written with a potential railway route in mind. Ensuring the free passage of U.S. citizens was a reasonable requirement, but it was bad luck for the Blackfeet that in 1863 gold was discovered east of the Rocky Mountains. The disreputable prospectors who flooded into the country were sure to cause trouble and the government was distracted at the time by the Civil War.

Ten years after the treaty, Bloods were still keeping the country in an uproar. In spring 1865, they took forty horses from the Fort Benton herds. It was no surprise that a month later three visiting Kainaa were gunned down in the street. Two days later, Calf Shirt and his followers killed ten wood cutters twelve miles from town and fled across the Canadian border.

The tensions of the "Blackfoot War" may be attributable in part to the Indians' new understanding of the border. That abstract line had the spirit power to keep bluecoats from pursuing across it. For those who could not give up the rustler's road, the medicine line was a magic sanctuary.

It seemed an inappropriate time to negotiate a land cession, but deputy agent Hiram D. Upham had instructions from the commissioner of Indian affairs to pull the southern boundary of the Blackfoot reservation back to the line of the Teton River. For promised annuities of $50,000 spread over the next twenty years, Little Dog and the other chiefs were pleased to sell between 200,000 and 300,000 acres in 1865. But roving Piikani and Kainaa war parties reacted by killing several miners, and that was enough to convince the commissioner to recommend against ratification of the land cession.

There was no holding back the tide of five hundred miners that stampeded to the reputed gold discovery on the Sun River. Frustrated, most soon went home, and those who tried to stay through the winter were forced to rely on the antelope hunting of Little Dog to sustain them. The kindness was repaid with violence when a dedicated Indian hater conspired with other miners to shoot a passing Piikani and hang his three companions. The following April, an old friend of the Blackfeet was visiting Fort Benton, Father De Smet, who declared that "a fresh and furious war has broken out between the whites and the Blackfeet, in which the whites have given the first provocation."

Little Dog, Lame Bull's successor, had earned the respect of his people in adventures as far south as the waters of the Colorado River. At the treaty council, Little Dog had advocated peace and held to that view by refusing to retaliate when Cree and Assiniboine attacked his camp shortly afterward. In May, Little Dog rode to Fort Benton to return twelve stolen horses to Agent Upham. Believing that the chief was too friendly with the whites, some of his own tribesmen intercepted and killed him and his son four miles from the agency.[336] The murders expressed once again the major flaw of Indian leadership. Its internal rivalry has been likened to a basket of crabs: when one climbed too high the others pulled him down again. Such conditions did not encourage the emergence of strong leaders.

The Blackfoot War dragged on from 1865 to 1870. But the Civil War was now over, and the U.S. Army could draw upon experienced officers and available troops. Soldiers moved into garrisons on the Judith River and at Fort Shaw, which was planted in the middle of the Sun River country to protect the east end of the Mullen Road, a newly constructed military route across the Bitterroot mountains. Most disturbances during this period of unrest took the familiar forms of horse raiding and acts of revenge. But incidents that started as just police problems too often escalated into tragedy.

Another commissioner came to Fort Benton in September 1868, to renegotiate the failed 1865 agreement. Mountain Chief signed on behalf of the Piikani, Calf Shirt for the Bloods, and Three Bulls for the northern tribes. Although there were no special payments to the chiefs this time, the second agreement also failed ratification due to the continuing violence.

Malcolm Clark was a former trader who had started ranching not far from Helena, Montana. He had married a Piikani woman whose cousin was Owl Child, Mountain Chief's son. When Owl Child visited the ranch in spring 1867, Clark managed to insult him. The young warrior nursed that grudge for two years and, on 18 August 1869, returned to the ranch to kill Clark and wound his son. Outraged citizens of Helena promptly impaneled a grand jury and swore warrants for the arrest of the Indian murderers, who were thought to be hiding with Mountain Chief's people. Not so foolhardy as to attempt serving the process himself, the United States Marshal turned the paper over to the Montana superintendent of Indians, General Alfred Sully. When Sully's meeting with four concerned chiefs at the new Teton River Agency produced no action, the matter was turned over to the army at Fort Shaw.

During the Civil War, the Colorado militia had set a tragic precedent by attacking Cheyenne winter camps at Sand Creek. In 1868, federal troops had done much the same on the Washita River. Now, two years later, their most effective strategy was to attack the uncooperative Piikani while they were fixed in their winter camps. Colonel E. M. Baker was ordered to move from Fort Shaw and apprehend the fugitives that were being harbored in the camp of Mountain Chief. After marching through punishing weather, on 23 January 1870 Baker's column attacked a sleeping camp. But Mountain Chief had moved to another location, and it was the smallpox-ridden camp of Heavy Runner that came under fire. Running out to stop the terrible mistake, the chief was cut down. The soldiers continued to fire blindly into the lodges. There wasn't much return fire and only one soldier was hit.

It was two months before the embarrassing official report revealed that 173 Indians had been killed; it said that all were able-bodied men except for fifty-three women and children who were shot accidentally. This outraged the Indian agent, Lieutenant W. A. Pease, who reported that in fact most of the camp's men had been away hunting, and only fifteen of the dead could have been considered fighting men in even the broadest definition. Ninety of the bodies were women and fifty were children under twelve years of age, most suffering from smallpox. There was no way to explain why the soldiers had turned 140 surviving women and children loose into the winter after burning their lodges and driving their horses away.[337]

The casualties inflicted on Heavy Runner's innocent camp were not unlike the countless atrocities that the Gens du Large had visited on each other since time beyond recall. Mountain Chief realized that the innocents had died for the misdeeds of his relative, and other bands seemed to accept yet another tragic blow. Many of the Piikani who moved north carried with them the most recent bout of the dreaded smallpox.[338] Loss of leaders, loss of lands, and the indignities they suffered from the robe trade had dispirited the Piikani.

In July 1870, an old friend set out to locate the Piikani. Although Alexander Culbertson's marital affiliation was with the Bloods, he went looking for the Piegan in the vicinity of the Cypress Hills. Passing between the Three Buttes (Sweetgrass Hills), Culbertson saw immense herds of buffalo—cows and bulls together at that time of year. Two hundred lodges, about two thousand people, were what remained after last winter's epidemic had reduced the rising generation by about a third. The old trader feared that the disease, coupled with the recent army attack, was hastening "their inevitable extinction from the face of the earth." That grim forecast overlaid his observation that the Piikani showed no hostile or unfriendly feeling toward the whites "whom they know are the whole cause of their misfortune."[339]

Cree had moved into the Cypress Hills region by 1865. Within four years there were 350 lodges of twenty-five hundred people, including five hundred warriors, competing with the Piikani for the buffalo. In spring 1869, the well-known Cree Maskepetoon went to negotiate differences between his people and the Blackfeet, and he was murdered while smoking in council. In the fall of the following year, encouraged by the Blackfoot losses to smallpox, soldiers, and whiskey, revenge-hungry Cree chiefs led a combined army of six to eight hundred of their own warriors and their Assiniboine allies against Kainaa and Piikani camps near the junction of the Oldman and St. Mary Rivers. Ignoring nearby Piikani, the invaders struck a small camp of Bloods. The victims were armed with repeating rifles, needle guns, and revolvers, and they repelled the assault. The attackers were driven across the Oldman River onto a tree-covered bluff. The Blackfeet later claimed they killed as many as two or three hundred enemies, but the actual Cree casualties were probably closer to seventy-five, at the cost of forty defenders. According to Culbertson,

> The battle of Oldman River ended the last plains war. The Crees sent tobacco to the Blackfoot in the spring 1871, and a formal peace was concluded at the meeting of chiefs at the Red Deer River in the autumn. Both sides had been exhausted by the conflicts, the epidemics, and the whiskey trade. They now hunted across the plains without regard for territorial limits, pursuing the remnants of the buffalo herds, while the spectre of a white Canadian invasion was slowly translated into reality.[340]

The notorious liquor trade flourished north of the U.S. border until the Canadians turned off the spigot in 1874. Plans to send in the North West Mounted Police had already been under way when in May 1873 wolf hunters (whiskey pedlars) attacked a bothersome Assiniboine camp in the Cypress Hills. The Mounties appeared that autumn and soon formed a buffer against white invasions, but the extension of Canadian authority over the northwestern plains tribes was a bit tardy. It was now twenty-two years since the United States began the difficult process of bringing the northern Gens du Large to reservations.

The British Empire had always been parsimonious in its North American Indian affairs. For two hundred years the British allowed the Hudson's Bay Company, a mercantile corporation, to control the northwest. After the company sold Rupert's Land to the Canadians, a long-retarded expansion of pent-up northern pioneers burst upon the Metis and Indian world almost overnight. The mixed-bloods—who were the first and the last to react—never managed to drag more than a few Cree into their resistance. The Gens du Large stood apart, historic warriors refusing the final battle.

Isaac Stevens's treaty of 1855 had been an initial gesture toward establishing a legal relationship between the United States and the assembled tribesmen. It used the term "Blackfoot Nation" to imply a unified tribal identity, and over the next decades that phrasing became set in the minds of not only a distant government, but of the people themselves. Individuals had been compressed into a workable abstraction.

The treaty process began in earnest in 1869, when Civil War general U. S. Grant became president. Upon his inauguration, Grant set up a commission to address "the Indian problem" in a humanitarian way. He confirmed that intention by appointing the Seneca Indian, Civil War veteran General Ely S. Parker to head the commission. But that administration was corrupted by opportunists sprouting like weeds from the razed fields of the national ordeal. Parker was falsely accused of corruption, while scandals about the diversion of Indian Bureau funds rocked the administration. When the Plains tribes refused to be herded onto reservations, Grant sent in the army.

After the Battle of the Little Bighorn in June 1876, five thousand refugee Sioux fled over the border and relocated in Canada's Wood Mountain area. That made them unwelcome competitors with the Blackfeet for the dwindling buffalo herds. In summer 1877, nonreservation Nez Perce were also being pursued by the army. They tried to retreat to familiar buffalo ranges using the same trails their predecessors had followed for generations. Most of Chief Joseph's followers were finally run down in the Bears Paw Mountains, but a few of White Bird's people made it across the medicine line into Canada. Those dramatic events further underscored a process that had been going on in the area since 1871.

In September 1877, before the winter hunt, representatives of the Siksika, Kainaa, Aapathosipikani (North Piegan), and Sarcee came to the Blackfoot Crossing of the Bow River. A few Assiniboine also joined them. Tribal leaders and their followers were gathering to hear a proposal from the Canadian government. The camp eventually grew to hundreds of leather lodges and a herd of ten thousand horses. Feathered headdresses and scarlet tunics contributed to the pageantry that both the Queen's men and Naapi's people loved.

The Canadian treaty ingloriously named Treaty Number Seven intended to resolve the problem of aboriginal possession so that those lands could legally be passed into private ownership. The tribes were being asked to give up title to the land in order to gain attention to their needs and protection from the onrushing world. The leaders would trade the sovereignty of their societies for "a direct relationship with the Crown."[341]

Many of the People feared that change. Some historians still argue that those being asked to agree were incapable of understanding the implications of the treaty. In a sense that was true, because those plainsmen were part of a world that seemed indivisible. What they took from it was sustenance; their territorial disputes had to do with important things like access to the buffalo herds. Their tipi rings and travois tracks rested lightly on the expanses that unrolled beneath the hooves of their ponies. But in 1877, there were few innocents. The Indians had learned the concept of property and its transfer through trading. Now, in the face of starvation, they were pragmatically willing to sell an abstraction for immediate needs. Tomorrow couldn't be that much different from today.

Fifty thousand square miles were at stake, but Queen Victoria would be generous with her wards. She would reserve one square mile for each five persons and give them an allowance of twelve dollars each the first year and five dollars each thereafter. She would provide ammunition to hunt on government land, and cattle, seed potatoes, and plows to produce food after the buffalo were gone. When the interpreter, Jerry Potts, was incapable of translating the complexities of the elaborate treaty language, a blind old man was called out of his tattered lodge. Out of the darkness of his vision—and the midnight of his soul—Jemmy Jock Bird relayed the terms that would end the world the People had always known.

The Kainaa elder Red Crow resented the attention paid to the Siksika leader Crowfoot. But Crowfoot withheld his opinion until Red Crow spoke against the treaty and then he tipped the balance. On 21 September 1877, the tribal leaders came to the treaty pavilion. They touched or pointed to a pen and the recorder made a mark for them. The band played "God Save the Queen," and the leading delegates received red coats, flags, and medals to commemorate the occasion.

The Siksika were installed close to the Blackfoot Crossing. The Kainaa eventually ended up with the largest reservation, 541 square miles of rolling grassland between the Belly and St. Mary Rivers. The North Piegan were strung along the barren uplands of the Oldman River.

The mild winter of 1877/78 failed to move the buffalo into the foothills where the winter camps could reach them. Those starving Blackfoot communities had to move to the west edge of the Sand Hills and compete with other Blackfeet, Bloods, Cree, Assiniboine, and refugee Sioux. That summer the grasslands were parched and the herds drifted south. The Siksika returned to the Blackfoot Crossing to hold the annual sun dance and receive their treaty payments: five dollars to individuals, fifteen dollars to minor chiefs, and twenty-five dollars to chiefs. The enterprising I. G. Baker Company from the Missouri River was on hand; it was said the company took in $3,500 in three hours after the first disbursement.

Two years after the treaty was signed, the Ottawa government appointed a respected civil engineer from British Columbia as Indian Commissioner of the North-West Territory. Edgar Dewdney traveled west to Fort Benton and up the former Whoop-up Trail, now a major freighting road to Fort Walsh. He soon began meeting hungry Indians. At Fort Macleod, Dewdney heard that starving Siksika at the Blackfoot Crossing were eating gophers, mice, and badgers. By mid-July the chief, Crowfoot, had his hands full keeping his young men from killing cattle around Fort Macleod. Some of those who followed the North Piegan chief Eagle Trail and the minor chief Running Wolf were even ready to try farming.[342] Dewdney asked the Queen's men to drive away the Sioux, whose hunting seemed to prevent the buffalo from coming north. If anyone crossed the border it would cause trouble with the Americans.

By then many Canadian Blackfeet had already moved south of the line, hoping to find buffalo in United States territory. Only about eight hundred Bloods lived on their Belly River reserve.[343] On the south side of the medicine line, Piikani were camping on the Badger Creek branch of the Marias River, the Kainaa on the Belly River, and the Siksika on the Bow.

To those who live within walls and never tasted real meat, those rolling grasslands would look inhospitable, dry, and dusty. Spring, of course, brings a wonderful greening and leafing. But the northern plains are relentlessly combed by the wind, and even snow needs a foothold among the bowing grass or stubble in order to stick. The warm Chinook wind is famous, but cold winds from the glacial mountains can still lash out in early July.

The People had always known these places as buffalo country, and their ideas about where to locate reservations reflected their conditioning as hunters. The Queen's treaty drawers were more than willing to go along with the Indians' requests for these near wastelands. They simply wanted to corral those wandering wild folk, and were glad to leave the better real estate for the settlers coming in on the railroads. But the American treaty with the Blackfeet failed to consider fully the approaching fate of the herds. Though the agreement outlined a huge territory for them, the Blackfeet would have to share it with their western competitors. Still, who could have foreseen that the intensified sustenance hunting, combined with the insatiable appetite for robes and hides, could ever use up that endless multitude of animals? Eventually, the American Blackfeet would face reservation readjustments and shrinking territory. And, finally, the reality that the buffalo were going, going—gone.

By the time the Canadian treaty was made, two decades after the American treaty, that grim fact could no longer be denied. The Queen's men needed to concentrate the tribes where they could be administered— and fed, when it came to that. Although southern Alberta is a marginal place for grain farming, it is a wonderful place for ranching. For the tribesmen, ranching might have been the first step away from the hunt. Unfortunately, the same idea occurred to white settlers, and lands the Indians might have used were often leased to outsiders.

Even today, from a hilltop in that country it is difficult to understand the necessity of dividing those great spaces. That was the last and perhaps most telling of the European impositions on the Gens du Large. Maybe the treaty boundaries were ghosts of ancient clashes over water holes, of the lingering Anglo-Saxon resentment of the conquering Normans, of all the mean and grabby traditions that Western civilization could not leave behind. The People had lived from time beyond recall in those vast ranges, but now lines drawn on a paper cost more than anyone, even the intruders, could have imagined.

Times change, the earth gets taken up, the vast gets smaller. Laid against the wall of the great mountains with its pleasant piedmont fringe of forests, the Blackfoot country is a scenic place to pass through. But most tourists often do not see the underlying poverty and the dependence. It takes a prairie people to fully appreciate these places, where more is concentrated than the modern world will ever know.

EIGHTEEN
Jackals and Hides

The Fort McKenzie robe trade put the Bloods in a more competitive position. When Mitchell accepted fifteen hundred pounds of beaver for $4,500 but then took nine thousand buffalo robes worth about $12,150, the Piikani suddenly lost the advantage they had enjoyed. The quarrels between leading Indians that Maximilian noticed in 1833 reflected some of those readjustments, and that was only the beginning.

The robe trade converted the foundation of tribal life into an obscene commodity. Those who participated in the coming slaughter were damned (if a Biblical concept is appropriate) because they violated the ancient hunting symbiosis. They traded their connection to Naapi's world for a self-destructive relationship with the traders. How did that greedy killing seem to the Sun, to Old Man who made them out of mud, to the spirits of the *iinii* wandering in the Sand Hills?

Taking provisions to the post-bound traders had seemed like a mere extension of their normal lives, a step beyond their own subsistence hunting, but still food for men. In the north, Blackfeet learned to manipulate that business by deliberately burning the grasslands, preventing the traders from subsisting themselves. Trading dried tongues was like collecting them for the sun dances. If no other meat was taken it was wasteful, but there were so many animals that it did not seem to matter.

The buffalo herds were never a continuous mass of animals stretching from horizon to horizon, as folklore would have us believe. Herds were scattered in the valleys and over the sloping plains, and hunting required locating them. There were solitary bulls almost everywhere, owing their survival to their tough undesirability. It was easy to miss the disaster taking shape. It was an interlocking system of traders, hide hunters, and tribal robe makers that was eroding the herds.

After fifty years or more, "naive" no longer described Indian relationships with the northern merchants. It had never applied at Kipp's first post, nor at the succeeding posts, Fort McKenzie, Fort Chardon, Fort Lewis, and Fort Benton. Surely the upper river traders displayed the full spectrum of human depravity. Many were types unwelcome in any other society. Whetting the skinning-knife edge of that business, most intended to get theirs and get out. Those who stayed on were not going to contribute very much to the Indian world.

Traders were frustrated because Indians were conservative consumers and produced only enough robes to satisfy their modest requirements. Hunting buffalo demanded mobility, so even rich families found it inconvenient to pack too many material possessions. The market for arms and expendable ammunition was limited to actual need. While the easy availability of trade beads and cloth created changes in the decorative arts, ornaments were not a major economic factor.

How could traders stimulate production of robes, and what could they entice the Indians to buy with the excess capital it generated? Liquor was a marvelous expendable. A good part of the infusion of capital flowed through the Indian gut.[344] That kind of economics made the robe trade deadly. New weaponry sealed the bargain.

From 1833 until 1859, the American Fur Company standard of trade was based on the buffalo robe. A prime robe was taken from a cow or heifer during the winter when the fleece was fullest. The dressing, done by women, usually took two or three days of hard labor, first chipping off flesh and then softening the hide. A complete head and tail robe was worth $12 in St. Louis. For convenience in butchering or working robes, the women sometimes split a hide and sewed it back together after it was properly treated. Split robes brought $5 downstream. But at the trading post, one robe bought a cup of sugar, a pound of tobacco, or a cup of coffee beans. It took ten robes for a gun and one to get twenty-five loads of powder and ball. After 1859 the payment for robes rose, so the traders were giving three cups of sugar and one of coffee for a dressed robe that had the nominal value of $4 in St. Louis.

There are no reliable figures on the growth of the upper-river robe trade. The Upper Missouri Outfit of the American Fur Company traded three thousand robes from the Bloods in 1831. During the outfit of 1834/35 they took in nine thousand. Ten thousand robes were received in 1838, and that doubled three years later. After the American Fur Company. suspended operations in 1842, the firm of Pierre Chouteau Jr. & Company inherited the Upper Missouri Outfit. Ten years later, their main competition, Harvey, Primeau & Company, shipped 16,409 cow and calf robes. After the Blackfoot Treaty, the Upper Missouri Outfit sent down 34,789 cow and calf robes. In 1857 they shipped 36,000.

In the north, the British were unable to share in that business because they lacked the means of easy downstream transport. In 1857/58, the Canadian surveyor Captain Palliser saw the Rocky Mountain House trader turn away bands of eighty or a hundred Blackfeet bringing bear skins, wolf pelts, and buffalo robes. Each refusal cost traders the confidence of their customers.

Beaver trapping had been less environmentally damaging because apparently cleaned-out colonies usually recovered after a few years. But the buffalo-robe trade produced a devastating effect. The preference for cow or heifer hides, taken in winter when the animals were carrying next year's calves, had double the impact. Left with a range sprinkled with grazing bulls, the herds were already doomed.

By participating in the robe trade, the tribes were cooperating in the destruction of their way of life. Failing to foresee the consequences might be excused because the herds were so immense. Perhaps the hunters lacked the perspective, or pessimism, to recognize what was happening. Perhaps they blocked it from their minds, just as we blind ourselves today to the environmental inevitabilities of acid rain and the vanishing ozone layer. A perfectly adapted animal population was being cleared from its natural ranges.[345] What use would there be for horses if there were no herds to run? There is a burial myth worth considering. To scare children, or one another, some have told stories of the Sand Hills where there are only fleshless bones—skeleton hunters on skeleton ponies pursue skeleton buffalo.

Coyote, that Loki of the western prairies, was back to his old tricks, drawing the guileless, the gullible, and the greedy into a cultural disaster.

NINETEEN

White Man's Water

ompared to the ethical pretenses of the English and the boisterous enthusiasm of the Canadians, most of the American Fur Company factors seemed aloof and single-minded, brought in as middle managers but determined to get theirs and get out. Was it their fault the Indians clamored for *naapiaohkii* (white man's water)?

Alcohol was nothing new to the Indian trade. When the Upper Missouri Outfit started the bung at James Kipp's post and floated Fort McKenzie on a sea of liquor, the Gens du Large eagerly bellied up to the bar. The West Indian rum and Monongahela rye they served were just as individually and socially corrosive as the later-day Colombian import. The consequences of drinking for native communities included chemical addiction, family disruption, erosion of authority, and death. Hunters reeling away from the store sometimes died in snowdrifts along the trail or killed each other in camp. Little tragedies like those didn't make the papers or get into the memoirs.

About the same time that Kipp converted thirty-two gallons of almost pure alcohol into two hundred gallons of "Blackfoot Whiskey" in 1830, the federal government in distant Washington was drafting new, stricter regulations on the liquor trade. Already there had been a confiscation of illicit American Fur Company cargo. In 1834, liquor trading in the

United States was prohibited. But who was actually going to enforce that? Upper Missouri traders justified their breaking the law by arguing that they needed to compete with their well-oiled British rivals on equal terms.

Recognizing that a gallon of this concoction of water, ginger, red pepper, and black molasses equaled between twenty and thirty-two beaver skins in value, Kenneth McKenzie imported a still to Fort Union and began converting Indian corn into naapiaokii.[346] But there were too many frustrated competitors floating down the Yellowstone for McKenzie's still to remain a secret. Although the rival operation, Sublette & Campbell, was said to have carried a hundred kegs into the Indian country in 1833, they took perverse delight in confirming reports of McKenzie's still to the Fort Leavenworth authorities.[347] Exposed, the trust bought its way out of a charge that might have cost it its trading license.

In 1844, the disgruntled American Fur Company bully Alexander Harvey informed the new commissioner of Indian Affairs in St. Louis of the continuing violation of government regulations among the traders. Charges were brought against Francois Chardon, his fellow culprit in the Fort McKenzie Piikani killings, as well as such old hands as Jacques

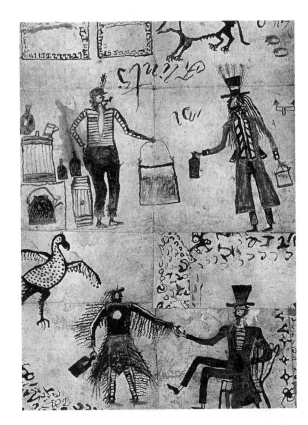

This is Ksistekomina's depiction of liquor trading at Fort Lewis. Note the details in the artist's rendering of liquor-store activities, such as the containers the customers bring to carry away their purchases.
—Courtesy Archives de la Compagnie de Jesus.

Berger, James Lee, and Malcolm Clark. A fine of $12,000 should have inhibited the American Fur Company business, but apparently it didn't, judging from the records. Father Point's Blackfoot artist was remarkably familiar with the "*traite et distribution de liqueur,*" and during the winter of 1846/47, the missionary did not report any outcry over the lack of hospitality at Fort Lewis.[348]

The inventory of stock and goods at Fort Benton in 1850 and 1851 neglects to note the presence of alcohol, even for medicinal purposes. The only barleycorn mentioned refers to a size of bead. But during the visit of the Northern Railway exploring expedition, and the later treaty party, liquid refreshment was enjoyed by the white men and presumably by the Indians as well. Anyone who has ever put in many miles on a horse understands the value of being anesthetized.

The elimination of competition for the northern Indian trade allowed the Hudson's Bay traders to reduce their liquor trade to something commensurate with the dignity of a British corporation. That their motivation was humanitarian is open to question.[349] The plains-rambling Earl of Southesk glossed over the practices of his Saskatchewan hosts in 1859, but a former Hudson's Bay Company employee, W. S. Gladestone, confirmed that liquor was traded at Edmonton House and Rocky Mountain House in 1860.[350] South of the Red Deer, however, Hudson's Bay trade was weakening because of its reluctance to accept bulky buffalo robes.

When Indian agent Gad E. Upson arrived at Fort Benton in late December 1863, he found agency affairs deplorable and whiskey being traded to the Indians.[351] In that era, gentlemen capitalists overindulged, the masses swilled on payday, and dust-dry frontiersmen slaked their thirsts at the bar. Who could refuse an Indian a bucket of bust-head to carry home to the tipi? Inebriated warriors did not take to the war trail, although excesses in town often turned into saloon quarrels. Irresponsible whites sometimes just shot drunken Indians. The upper Missouri drinking culture was like a tightening noose squeezing out the breath of human decency.

Ritual, taboo, habit, family, and community all contributed to band unity. Drinking destroyed that unity as it brutalized the lodge and family and put fellow tribesmen in jeopardy. The physiological effect of alcohol on Native Americans has become a popular area for scientific speculation. In truth, the disastrous results of Indian drinking reported by the fur traders were not much different from what they might have seen among the dispirited working class of the industrial revolution. As these proud men realized that their world was slipping away, liquor accelerated its disintegration.

Until 1868, there was little effort to enforce prohibition on the reservation. In that year, however, the Blackfoot agent George Wright had some of the whiskey traders arrested and tried in Helena, Montana. The next summer, the Fort Benton trade was limited to two licensed operations: the Northwest Company on the Teton River near present-day Choteau, Montana, who dealt with the Piegans; and I. G. Baker & Brother at Willow Round on the Marias River, who sold to the Blackfeet, Bloods, and North Piegan. The latter operation cleared $40,000 in the first winter.

As John Ewers notes, the cession of Rupert's Land to Canada by the Hudson's Bay Company in 1869 meant that there was no liquor law in place. That winter, American traders started crossing the line to exploit the new opportunity. Two of the foremost were John J. Healy and I. G. Baker's nephew, Alfred B. Hamilton. They carried a $25,000 outfit to the junction of the Oldman and St. Mary Rivers, which netted $50,000 for a six-month operation. Their log cabin at Fort Whoop-up was not quite forty miles north of the border, but there was no one to question their lubricating the Canadian Indians with fifty gallons of whiskey. Indians burned Fort Whoop-up after the first year, but a 50 percent profit ensured that the liquor traders would return.

In the next four years, more than a dozen stockaded stores sprouted U.S. flags and easy taps. Joe Kipp, the mixed-blood son of the Marias River post founder, planted Fort Standoff at the junction of the Belly and Waterton Rivers. Fort Slide-out was lower on the Belly. Some bands had withdrawn behind the medicine line to escape the ravages of liquor, but their old winter sanctuaries along the upper Bow and Oldman Rivers were now exposed to hell on wheels. Carts hauled in liquor and carried away the bulky packs.

Buffalo robes were valued according to color. White robes held superstitious meaning for the Indians; blue, or "silk," robes were valued for their long, fine hair; beaver-colored robes had fine, wavy hair; black or black-and-tan robes were common; and buckskin was the lightest color other than white. Two cups of whiskey and a blanket bought a silk robe; just two cups of the stuff with no blanket bought a common robe. The hunter who traded his prized buffalo runner for four gallons might have made it home on foot if he did not die of exposure along the trail.[352]

The North West Mounted Police arrived in 1874 to begin the difficult task of enforcing prohibition. In time, they contained the whiskey pedlars, but they could not dampen the Gens du Large desire for fire in the gut. It had been a hundred years since Edward Umfreville first comprehended the destructive potential of liquor for these communities. Eighty-eight Blackfeet were said to have died in drunken brawls in 1871, thirty-one Piegan in 1873, and forty-two North Blackfeet in 1873/74. In 1873, the U.S. commissioner of Indian Affairs believed that a quarter of the Blackfeet had died in the preceding six years from the effects of liquor.

In addition to alcohol, Healy and Hamilton sold repeating rifles at Fort Whoop-up. These deadly tools cost ten head-and-tail robes, and soon any self-respecting hunter or warrior had to have one. In 1870, Saskatchewan District chief trader William T. Christie claimed that his arms trade was limited to powder and ball for fusees. He did not sell percussion caps, but "Every other Blackfoot who trades at Rocky Mountain House now has a Revolver in his belt; and in our trade with them our lives are in great danger."[353]

Munitions kept the robe trade productive, even though guns weren't necessary in the hunting itself. While racing beside a running animal and blowing it away with a short-barrel fusee was the ultimate sport, bows were more efficient. Arms were for war, and the ability to kill enemies soared when repeating rifles, revolvers, and fast-reloading cartridges were introduced. The yarns of James Willard Schultz, often published in boy's magazines, were romanticized versions of the fatal final chapter of the old war games. The chivalrous myth of the mystic warriors of the plains was an imported construct that masked the reality of the self-destructive contest for a rapidly dwindling vital resource.

It was darkly symbolic that former travelers with the Indians like Jemmy Jock Bird and Hugh Munroe were reduced to driving carts around to collect hides. Their recollections, filtered through the pens of admiring outsiders like George Bird Grinnell and Schultz, were really images of a world in decline. The People were still playing the war games their grandfathers had invented, but with deadlier weaponry. This was no longer the mythic West, it was home on a range where fewer and fewer buffalo roamed.

In the relatively short span of 150 years, a mere blink in the steady stare of world history, a people were reduced by the very technology that had once seemed so attractive to their forebears. Increasingly sophisticated guns expanded the ability to kill, but alcohol was even more damaging because it killed more than flesh—it destroyed the spirit. The sale of munitions and liquor for robes was as reprehensible as the old triangular trade in molasses, rum, and slaves. Instead of selling each other to slave traders, the Gens du Large were annihilating themselves to provide lap robes for affluent outsiders, or factory pully belts.

While the whiskey trade kept the North Piegan and their neighbors anesthetized, their brethren to the south were being weaned away from the hunt and made dependent on United States annuities. Since there were only eleven bands calling themselves Piikani on the United States Blackfoot Reservation, on 15 April 1874, Congress reduced its area. It drew the new southern boundary north of Birch Creek and the Marias River. The duty of reconciling the Indians to the new line fell to a former Iowa lawman named John Wood.

On 20 April, Wood convinced the demoralized Blackfeet to elect chiefs and make laws to keep order. The head chief, who did not drink, was Little Plume. His subordinates were White Calf and Generous Woman. Three years later Little Plume died. The council of elders split the leadership between White Calf, who represented the conciliatory element, and Generous Woman, who stood with the traditionalists. Generous Woman died within a year, and the leadership of what was termed the "heathen element" passed to Three Suns of the Grease Melters band.

TWENTY

Shadows Passing

As the sun sets in the *niitsitapia'pii* part of the world, the lengthening shadows of the mountains stretch out east toward the Sand Hills. The sun drops behind the jagged horizon of the Rocky Mountains with impressive finality. At one moment the big-sky world is filled with light; the next moment it is very dark.

Although the buffalo seemed to disappear like the setting sun, it actually took fifty years to kill off those immense herds. Opening the robe trade to a world market accelerated the process. Barges from the upper Missouri floated away unbelievable numbers of robes. Demand was so great that the Indian processors had to work hard to keep up production. Between 1846 and 1870 the northern plainsmen delivered an average of twenty thousand buffalo robes a year to the upper Missouri receiving stations.

Transportation costs on the Missouri River had always been determined by the manpower necessary to row and portage against the stream to the upper posts. The expense of bucking 3,575 miles of current were offset by a virtually free ride downstream. After steamboats reached Fort Benton in 1860, however, transportation costs dropped so low that even the Hudson's Bay Company tried carting robes from Edmonton to Fort Benton.

The death of Pierre Chouteau Jr. in 1862 took the heart out of the Upper Missouri Outfit. Three years later, that interest was sold to an American company who had presumptuously appropriated the name Northwest Company. That operation had a lifespan of just ten years; then one of its former clerks, I. G. Baker, took it over. Baker and his brother had opened an earlier store at Fort Benton in 1866, just in time for the gold rush. I. G. Baker & Brother came to dominate the northern business. Their great bull trains full of robes wore out the Whoop-up Trail. After the robe trade played out, these same trains hauled coal to fuel riverboat boilers. But the prosperity of this private enterprise came at a considerable cost to others.

Canadian missionary Father Scollen saw the cloud rolling over the northern plains and reported his troubling observations to Lieutenant Governor David Laird at Winnipeg. "In the summer 1874 I was traveling amongst the Blackfeet. It was painful to me to see the state of poverty to which they had been reduced. Formerly they had been the most opulent Indians in the country, now they were clothed in rags without horses and without guns."[354]

In 1876, I. G. Baker & Company shipped 30,000 robes from Fort Macleod, while Fort Benton shipped 60,000 robes in 1875, 71,900 in 1876, and 50,500 in 1877, many of which came from the north.[355] Still there were animals left to hunt. In January 1876, missionary John McDougall saw buffalo moving up the Bow River into the foothills to escape the intense cold and snow. Fearing the consequences of the declining herds, however, the Queen's representatives encouraged conservation by prohibiting the practice of surrounds and drives.

At the height of the robe trade, other events coincided to increase pressure on the herds. Over five thousand Sioux fled across the Blackfoot medicine line after the destruction of blue-coats at the Little Bighorn, and most had reassembled around Sitting Bull by May 1877. Before the summer was out, hundreds of Nez Perce were also fleeing American troops and were headed for the medicine line. In October, after Joseph's people surrendered in the Bears Paw mountains, 104 Nez Perce, following White Bird, joined the Sioux camp. The Sioux and Nez Perce spent four years on the northwestern plains, contributing to the decline of the herds.

While the Fort Walsh mounted police detachment was preoccupied with the Sioux problem, their brothers in uniform from Fort Macleod and Fort Calgary escorted Lieutenant Governor Laird and his party to the Blackfoot Crossing of the Bow River. Coming to the treaty grounds, Laird noticed small herds with very few calves. Still, he told the Indians that there would be buffalo for at least another decade. The Gens du Large hunted buffalo between Fort Walsh and Fort Macleod from 1877 to 1879, and their local buyers sent out 30,000, 31,375, and 14,384 robes respectively in those years. In February 1879, an optimistic northern newspaper reported that buffalo were coming down from the mountains north of the medicine line.[356]

The heavy hunting by local plainsmen and the intruding Sioux thinned the northern herds or forced them south across the Musselshell River. The desperate hunting by starving Canadian Indians discouraged the buffalo's return. Of course there were small herds and pockets of bulls still grazing in obscure places until some hunter came upon them and, out of old habit, claimed the final kill. By then the Queen's hungry subjects were moving south to hunt in the United States.

The plains shimmered with heat rising from the baked grass. Hooves clacked over old skulls and bones. The horsemen rode hunched between the relentless sun and its reflected brilliance, squinting in hope of shade and pretending manly indifference. If Naapi revealed buffalo, it was likely a dusty, indigestible bull sulking in his solitude. Where were the herds?

White Calf, a Piikani head chief, led the winter hunt of 1878/79 and was pleased to find buffalo in the vicinity of the Bears Paw Mountains. Hunting across the medicine line and fires west of the Cypress Hills had caused these animals to cross the Milk River and the Missouri and move into the Judith Basin. While their kinsmen in the north were starving, some of White Calf's hunters took as many as seventy hides and left the meat to rot.

Hungry hunters from the north were also coming into the Judith Basin by the next winter. Some of those desperate fugitives, like Running Rabbit's northern Piikani, killed range cattle. Because the British were incapable of controlling the wandering bands, the United States Army was obliged to patrol the border and escort the Piikani back to the Badger Creek agency.

The last of the Sioux left the north in July 1881. No one could say why the summer hunt failed, but in December buffalo were found between the Sweetgrass Hills and the Bears Paw Mountains. In March, reservation Blackfeet were eating buffalo meat supplemented by government rations. But fewer hunters were willing to go after buffalo.

The number of Indians being fed on the reservation swelled from 605 in 1881 to 1,955 in 1882 to about 3,000 by 1883. In the spring of 1883, the agent had to supplement the beef and flour ration with potatoes, and reserved only a small stock of cattle for breeding. In July, Little Dog and Bull Shoe, ranging in the vicinity of the Sweetgrass Hills killed only six buffalo. The rightfully worried Three Suns told a visiting Congressional delegation that if nothing was done, many Indians would starve. The winter of 1883/84 was indeed haunted by a terrible hunger, and before relief finally came through, at least four hundred Piikani had starved to death.

The decline of the herds was naturally paralleled by that of robe shipments from Fort Benton. I. G. Baker sent down twenty thousand robes in 1880, five thousand in 1883, and none in 1884. Hides that didn't require conditioning began taking up the slack. The fatal effect of hide hunting was widespread and seen as far away as the eastern railhead at Bismarck, North Dakota. In 1880, as many as 34,901 robes and 4,570 hides had shipped from there. A year later, the balance had tipped, with 23,355 robes and 26,601 hides. In 1882, only 2,121 robes were shipped, compared to 15,464 hides. By 1884 there were no robes at all and only 529 hides. Similar totals elsewhere also suggest how the trade had shifted from Indian manufactured robes to the untreated hides taken by exploitative white hide-hunters with long-range guns.

There was an insane acceleration of buffalo killing. The number of robes shipped downstream seems beyond the production capacity of the Gens du Large. The capital that was generated was certainly beyond their capacity to sensibly absorb it. And it was hard work for the women who, according to John Ewers, took two days to hack at the stiff hides and work them soft. The shipment of 76,000 robes in 1876 represented 152,000 days of grueling labor for the women.

Why were the Gens du Large participating in their own destruction? Their contract with the devil had now been operative for half a century and had become a habit. By then the hunters included refugee Indians, Metis, white hide-hunters, wolfers, traders, soldiers, even grossly unrestrained sportsmen. The momentum that developed is difficult to blame on any particular group of participants. Who will be responsible when the last old-growth evergreen falls, or the last salmon is taken from the river?

When the robe trade started in 1831, the herds had been so immense that few could have foreseen any limit. Like the eternal seasons, buffalo always returned from their wintering places. When they didn't, that was attributable to some local condition, to a quirk of weather or inadequate grass. When hunters eventually located them, everyone feasted. Myths held that they came from a hole in the ground, and there was an endless supply. But the environmental debt that northwestern plains buffalo hunters were piling up grew from the average kill of twenty thousand animals a year previously to over one hundred thousand in 1875. On their own, the Indians might have gotten away with the unnatural exploitation. But the process was accelerated by professional hunters, visiting sportsmen, and, some say, an unstated federal policy. Eliminating the herds impeded Indian mobility and brought them sooner to the reservations. If roaming protein was a national problem, the Sharps rifle was Agent Orange. Although some recognized that extinguishing buffalo would subdue the Plains Indians, the effective impetus was economic rather than political. Eventually the deserted ranges were opened for ranching. It proved a fine irony that perfectly adapted creatures were cleared to make way for the breeds of domestic stock that were doomed to winterkill in 1886.

Fascination with the near loss of buffalo sometimes overlooks another animal casualty. The horse culture lasted about 150 years, but it disappeared with the buffalo. Oh, there were still ponies around to keep up the image, but by the end of the century they were being paraded in elaborately beaded gear and posed for photographs. The big horse herds dwindled; some went to the Great War and never returned, some went to the cannery. The wiry little animals were replaced by larger stock bred for farming. For the old-timers, it was a hard thing to see those wonderful creatures succeeded by characterless machines.

TWENTY-ONE

Manly-hearted Women

hen David Thompson noted the practice of polygamy among the Piegan in 1787, families still recovering from the smallpox epidemic averaged three or four wives. In 1833, Maximilian observed some families of eight wives. By 1840, British traders were exaggerating that even poor men were keeping six dependent women, while wealthy men supported from eight to a dozen. In 1860, the robe trader Charles Larpenteur penned an appreciation of those "big men" who might have two or three lodges, five or six wives, twenty or thirty children, and fifty to a hundred horses.

Horses were essentially idle capital while women, who prepared robes, turned families into mobile processing units. James Carnegie, the Earl of Southesk, may have stumbled on the real reason for the number of wives when talking with a northern plains chief. This man told Carnegie that one wife could produce only 10 or so robes a year, but his eight wives could dress as many as 150 robes a year. These lodge "factories" could generate upwards of $2,000 a year in finished robes.[357]

As the robe trade gathered momentum, this cottage industry, with multiple wives as the labor force, became firmly established. Much of the superintendence began passing to women. When her household changed from a family home into a sweatshop, the matron became foreman of a work crew chipping away at staked-down hides.

From observations made almost a hundred years later, Oscar Lewis wrote *The Effects of White Contact upon Blackfoot Culture*. His description of the "Manly-Hearted Women among the North Piegan" recognized the new responsibilities of a challenged sisterhood.[358] The women had taken over functions their liquor-eroded husbands had abdicated. Some remarkable parallels exist between the way the robe trade's intrusion in 1833 altered the lives of Indian women and Rosie the Riveter's contribution to the attitudes and lives of American women during and after World War II.

Lewis observed that some Piegan women went beyond the old status of *ninauake,* or sits-beside wife, to a fuller role as *ninauposkitzipxpe,* manly-hearted woman.[359] In their economic involvement, sexual independence, religious participation, and freedom of expression these women displayed attitudes that would have been unacceptable in other times. During the starvation winter, James Willard Schultz observed matrons who kept a few robes in reserve as a hedge against hard times, indicating that women had a hand in controlling the robe economy.

Portrait of a Piegan woman by Karl Bodmer —Courtesy Joslyn Art Museum

John Ewers wrote of the Piikani that "Young men enjoyed remarkable freedom in their sexual life. They accosted girls while they were alone gathering wood or water on the outskirts of camp. They bragged of their conquests, particularly if they had an affair with a married woman. Chastity before marriage was more an ideal than a reality for many girls. Yet a girl who earned a reputation for being too free with her favors might have to be satisfied with marrying a poor boy whose future prospects were equally poor."[360]

The implication is that girls could be as sexually adventuresome as lusty boys, yet they were inhibited by the possibility of disgracefully conceiving out of wedlock. Judging from the number of cut-nosed women seen in camps, wives occasionally ventured into extramarital affairs, but a double standard allowed the outraged husband to mutilate, even kill his unfaithful wife, while his own indiscretions were overlooked. On the other hand, women's easy relationships with the *naapiikoan* at the trading posts were sometimes condoned by husbands who were looking to gain special advantage. Athough these arrangements might have discomforted the trading-house journalists, their notes did show that the bourgeois and the engagees did not spend long winters without companionship.

What most of these women thought of their often temporary husbands is lost like the dying embers in a fireplace. It has been observed that Madame Culbertson, the Fort McKenzie trader's wife, was respected in her day and her name still carries a slightly exotic celebrity. Her Blood relatives enjoyed an inroad with the traders. But former trader Malcolm Clark's union with a Piikani woman from Mountain Chief's band was unfortunate not only for him but for others when the relationship became an unintentional catalyst for the massacre of Heavy Runner's camp.

The mixed-blood children resulting from casual or more permanent relationships grew up as involuntary intermediaries between the factions of their dual heritage. Jemmy Jock Bird, himself half-Cree, had several Piikani wives. Sally, the last of them, provided early ethnohistorical data about her people to the pioneer researcher Lewis Henry Morgan. When the government started a school on the Blackfoot reservation in 1874, six bilingual mixed-bloods translated lessons for their ten full-blood cousins. When the allotment system kicked in, marriage to Indian women became quite attractive to white men as a means of acquiring land on the reservation. In the 1910 census, mixed-bloods were already a majority of the population, and that increased to two-thirds in 1930 and to 85 percent by midcentury. But by then tribal enrollment had become a mathematical calculation subject to bureaucratic interpretation.

While unions between white men and Indian women were commonplace, Piikani men did not often go in search of non-Indian brides. More often they married Indian women captured from other tribes. The surviving term for this practice of taking a wife by force is *waahsowat*. There are stories of couples who never learned to speak each other's language but got along just fine. Because women generally needed someone to support them, they accepted husbands from outside their band.

Custom dictated that a husband could claim the unmarried and widowed sisters of his first wife, a practice that was supposed to lessen the chance of upsetting domestic tranquility. The sororate system was breached when outsiders were brought around the fire. The native term for a wife lower than third or fourth means slave wife, which accurately described the status of wives in that position.[361]

The competition for more workers also led to younger marriages for Piikani women. In the ruthless conversion from childhood to adult obligations, girls lost the brief beauty of adolescence. At the same time, with each new wife husbands had to work harder and take greater risks hunting to keep those growing households fed and clothed.

It took manly-hearted women to endure the changes that came upon their people. Perhaps the changes had already begun with the repeated shock of epidemics compounded with losses from the increasingly deadly war games. Certainly the increased demands of the robe trade and the resulting loss of the main food supply caused changes in the women's world. Declining herds forced the Piikani to fragment into ever smaller hunting bands. The seven or eight bands that Father Point noticed in 1846/47 were similar to the eight that Jemmy Jock Bird named in 1861. However, in 1911, in spite of severe population losses on the Blackfoot reservation, twenty-three bands were listed. Whether that indicated a decline in tribal and band unity or a changing pattern of individual residences, the once-close community of women had disintegrated.[362]

Some of the old polygamous relationships still survived after government agents began meddling with the true way of things. A few families still claimed more than one wife after the turn of the century. The official records, however, were careful to avoid drawing unnecessary attention to the potentially embarrassing residue of an outdated culture. The practice would have to die out with the other ones, the agents reasoned. And so it did.

As the new social constructs of reservation life overshadowed the old customs, the individual's sense of communal responsibility receded. Tribespeople began to see their obligations as limited to their own immediate families. With community went continuity. Their children were sent away to distant boarding schools. When the men went off on extended hunting trips in the mountains or traveled afar to take distant jobs, households were left for a long time without a male head.

The impact of the change from an active, positive role for men to that of nearly powerless dependence on government support can be seen in later photographs. In the eyes of these too-knowing men, the expression is one of sorrow but not total defeat. In the early decades of the twentieth century, white tourists and hunters came to see the wonders of the newly designated Glacier National Park. The Blackfoot Indians became a curiosity to be photographed posing in elaborately decorated costumes.[363] What must the women have felt as they patiently sewed and beaded those new artifacts?

Jemmy Jock Bird, who had traveled many years with the Piikani, finished off his last years in blindness, wandering across the northern plains with the last and most faithful of his several wives. Sally was the sister of the Blackfoot chief Three Suns, or Big Nose. After old Bird lost his teeth, Sally chewed her husband's meat for him until a sympathetic friend gave them a meat grinder. Sally died near Calgary as officials were leading the couple back to the American reservation. By then most of the old-time Piikani had been forgotten. It had happened as fast as the sunset shadows race across their graves.

TWENTY-TWO

Three Suns's War Record

Outsiders recorded the observations used to compile this history. Where is the Indian voice? Painted on a skin.

Petroglyphs, pictographs, winter counts, war records, and ledger-book drawings are the records of a largely nonliterate people. A number of Blackfoot winter counts note events that were significant in the record keeper's life or memory. The Blackfeet did not think in terms of the Julian calendar but compiled pictorial data in winter, when lodge-bound men had time for recollection and reflection. The pictographs were used like mnemonic wampum, to trigger recall of a significant tribal or personal event. Some accounts begin as early as 1764, and others continue into the middle of the twentieth century. There are no calendar dates, but a few better-known reference points include the smallpox epidemic of 1781/82, the meteor shower of 12 November 1833, the second visitation of smallpox in 1837, the first American treaty of 1855, and the British treaty of 1877. Less-recognized events can sometimes be cross-checked from other records. As a fuller appreciation of Indian history develops, the data from these winter counts will probably be merged into a complete chronological history.

Another type of record was a shirt, tipi, tipi liner, or skin robe painted with the achievements of a warrior's career. Those pictographs were mnemonic starting points as much as illustrations, helping to confirm the recounting necessary for some ceremonial occasions.[364] Proofs were important because truth stood beside bravery in the makeup of a leading man.

One day in August 1833, the Piikani were camped in the grove of trees near Fort McKenzie. When the Cree and Assiniboine attacked, young Three Suns got a vivid impression of his family's vulnerability. Later, during the Falling-leaves moon, his training as a warrior began with another thrill. Three Suns was hunting with his father, Bear Chief, when they bumped into fifty-three dangerous Crows. Realizing that the Crows meant to attack the Piikani's unsuspecting camp, Bear Chief, pretending to be unconcerned, tried to stall them. Feigning hospitality, he sent the boy ahead, ostensibly to prepare a proper welcome for their guests. Three Suns raced as his father's herald, calling for help to the three other winter camps nearby. Bear Chief had distracted the Crows until reinforcements arrived from Great Lake's camp.[365] Three Suns's training as a Piikani warrior began at an early age, but he did not count that adventure as a war honor.

During his career as a warrior, Three Suns—Ninokskatosi—participated in a total of thirty-six fights. He killed eleven men, several in hand-to-hand combat. Three Suns was wounded six times by gunshots and clubbed on three other occasions. His were the honorable scars of a Piikani warrior, and he recited the circumstances during ceremonies when it was appropriate to confirm his achievements. He also drew pictures commemorating those adventures on an elk skin.

The following notes on Three Suns's war count were written down by the unsympathetic Indian agent Captain Lorenzo W. Cooke. Cooke prohibited the sun dance on the reservation and ordered the old lodge to be torn down and the timbers used to build corrals. He also banned face paint, traditional costumes, and drumming. Anyone who cut off a finger in mourning was in danger of being jailed.[366] Cooke was not the sort to preserve Indian records of pointless bloodletting, but Three Suns's elk skin was a proper curiosity. Cooke recorded the meaning of the pictures. Later, Three Suns also explained his skin drawings to the sympathetic writer James Willard Schultz.[367] I have summarized and arranged Cooke's and Schultz's notes chronologically here to follow one man's martial career over the last days of the free-roaming raiders.[368]

In 1845, after the Black Robes had been in the country with the Flatheads, twelve Piikani went on a raid toward the Snake country. Along the Missouri River south of present-day Helena, Montana, they shot an elk for food. Going into the brush to find it, Three Suns was almost killed by a bear.

Two years later, three hundred lodges of Piikani were camped near the west butte of the Sweetgrass Hills when fifty-three Cree attacked during the night. The next morning the Piikani responded with a general charge against the attackers. Three Suns's horse was shot in the head and Three Suns fell. Though dismounted, he was able to kill one Cree with his gun and two with his knife. A Cree struck Three Suns with his flintlock gun and was then shot by another Piikani. Although all the Crees were finally killed, the attack cost the Piikani thirteen dead and five wounded.

Seven years passed without an incident that the maturing warrior could count as honorable. In 1854, the Americans came to Fort Benton to encourage intertribal peace. One hundred twenty-four Piikani marched on foot to raid in the Snake country, but the only damage they managed to inflict was on a luckless Shoshone family. The war party killed the father and two grown sons but spared the mother. Unsuccessful in obtaining horses, the Piikani took thirty-six days to trudge back to their own country.

The following year, the Gens du Large were greatly troubled by Sioux who were supposed to have been contained by the Fort Laramie treaty. Sixty lodges of Piikani and ten Pend d'Oreille, their former enemies, were camping together in the Sweetgrass Hills. During the night they were attacked by four hundred Sioux. Half the camp was overrun, and most of the horses inside the camp circle were killed or driven off. Three Suns managed to rally the rest of the camp and they held out until morning. The Piikani killed sixteen raiders but lost eleven of their own.[369] Perhaps those attackers were the same three hundred Sioux who had intercepted traders traveling from Fort Union in early May 1855 and who appeared at Fort Sarpy on 12 May. They had been out looking for Blackfeet.[370]

Later that year, two hundred Piikani lodges were still in the Cypress Hills. Pursuing two Sioux horse thieves, Three Suns overtook one of the running men and killed him with a knife. Later the camp grew to four hundred lodges of Piikani and Kainaa, and the size of the combined herd made it irresistible to raiders. Eight Sioux managed to steal six Piikani horses, but they were run down and all but one were killed. Three Suns exchanged shots with the Sioux leader and killed him.

In 1856, Three Suns was with another war party near the Great Falls. Going into a grove of trees he killed an elk. Surprised by a charging bear, the hunter felled it with his one shot when the animal *was almost upon him. The range was so close that the bear's fur smoldered from the powder burn.*

Two years later, five hundred Piikani lodges were camped on the Milk River, with almost as many Assiniboine and Crows planted just twenty miles away. The fight that developed in the morning took place midway between the camps. During the first charge, Three Suns almost captured a wounded black horse whose rider, the notable Crow Sitting Woman, disgraced himself by hiding in the brush.[371] In the second charge, Three Suns was lucky to catch a fat sorrel horse, whose rider got away by riding double with a comrade. Seven of the enemy were killed and ten wounded; one Piikani fell.

The next year, twenty-one Piikani went from their Badger Creek camp to the Prickly Pear Valley, near Helena. Three Suns and a companion crawled into a camp of sixty (Salish?) lodges to cut out fast buffalo runners. The other raider was killed, but Three Suns got away with one of the six horses that were finally taken.

In 1860, where the Tongue River empties into the Yellowstone, Three Suns and his party of forty-two Piikani were deep into dangerous country. In a fight with twelve Crows, the raiders drove their opponents into the brush. When the leading Crow stood his ground, Three Suns threw down his gun and grappled with him. Another Piikani shot the man in the stomach and cut his arm so badly that he dropped his knife. By stabbing him to death, Three Suns earned the name Crow Chief.

That same year, in the Judith Basin, thirteen Piikani raiders traveled a hundred miles to harry sixty lodges of Pend d'Oreille buffalo hunters. Again Three Suns risked crawling into the camp during the night to cut loose a picketed horse, but this time he was discovered. A shot went through Three Suns's coat without striking him.

In 1861, eleven Piikani ranging between the Big and Little Belt Mountains near White Sulphur Springs were surprised by sixty Pend d'Oreilles. Three Suns's brother was wounded and one of the attackers killed as the surprised Piikani retreated into the brush.

James Willard Schultz added another glimpse of Three Suns in 1865. At that time Hugh Munroe and his family were camped at St. Mary Lake when they were attacked by Assiniboine. They fled to Three Suns's camp on Two Medicine Creek. Raising eighty men, Three Suns ran down the Assiniboine.[372]

In 1865, the northern plains country was being overrun by miners. That fall, the Bloods who followed Calf Shirt killed ten white woodcutters at the mouth of the Marias River and fled north across the border. On

16 November, agent Gad E. Upson assembled the principal Blackfoot reservation men in council. Little Dog, Great Lake, Mountain Chief, Bear Chief, and Heavy Runner agreed to cede the lands south of the Teton River to the United States. There was not much else they could have done since, in the ten years after Lame Bull's treaty, the mining towns of Helena, Virginia City, and Bannack had already begun tearing up that ground. The new paper failed, however, to prevent miners from stampeding to the Sun River. North Piegan led by Bull's Head retaliated with raids on the Sun River Agency farm and the recently established Jesuit mission. The following May, Little Dog and his son were overtaken by drunken Indians and killed. Some said that those murders reflected the views of traditionalists like Three Suns.

> *Three Suns continued to war with the Sioux in 1867. After a Piikani from the camp near Cypress Hills was killed by six Sioux raiders, thirty Piikani rallied behind Three Suns. The aging warrior claimed one of the five scalps.*

Because Three Suns's elk skin was a personal war record, not a winter count, it did not include the significant developments of the next three years. During that time, there was another attempt to revise the reservation boundary, smallpox struck again, and U.S. soldiers attacked and massacred Heavy Runner's people.

> *In 1870, Three Suns, who now wore a U.S. medal, intended to stop warring. When Piegan warriors surrounded eight incautious Pend d'Oreille raiders and were about to slay them, Three Suns interceded and saved their lives. They were allowed to go home with the understanding that the old warrior was now committed to keeping the peace.*
>
> *After the Sioux fought the bluecoats on the Little Bighorn, they headed for the medicine line. Two hundred lodges of Piikani were camped near the Cypress Hills when some of the men discovered four Sioux horse thieves and surrounded them in a thicket. Throwing off his wife's attempt to restrain him, Three Suns crawled into the brush until he could see the breastwork they'd put up. Heavily armed with Winchester rifles, cartridge belts, and knives, they were ready to sell their lives dearly. Risking death, Three Suns spoke with them, displayed his medal and his pipe, and assured them that they would not be harmed. When their leader softened, Three Suns leaped inside the barricade and immobilized him. Three Suns's wife, Kris-tuck-ah-ke (Beaver Woman) grabbed another of the raiders and the other two*

surrendered. Sending advance notice by a herald known to the whites as Jack the Ripper, Three Suns turned the Sioux over to the astonished commander of the mounted police at Fort Walsh.

On 21 October 1878, the death of Generous Woman thrust Three Suns into the leadership of the Grease Melters band. According to another Schultz story, Three Suns was with the great Piegan camp on the Arrow River the next summer when he was named in a council of twelve leaders. His associates included the head chief White Calf, Running Crane, Fast Buffalo Horse, Little Dog, and others, including several important mystery (medicine) men.[373] Unfortunately, his traditionalist views were at odds with the more conciliatory views of White Calf.

It was discouraging to be a Piikani leader during those trying times. Each year there were fewer buffalo for his people to hunt. The last great herds seemed to be concentrated in the Judith Basin. The twenty-two hundred American Blackfeet counted in 1880 were increasingly dependent on government food. The agency ration for each person was supposed to be a pound and a half of meat, a pound of flour, a few beans, and some bacon, salt, soda, and coffee each week. But all too often, the people who were now penned in the creek bottoms near the Old Agency on Badger Creek waited for food that never came.

In 1881 forty lodges of Piikani were hunting there when three Sioux were discovered making an attempt on their horses. Three Suns charged one of the raiders and took his gun from him when it failed to fire. That was the greatest war honor that a Piikani could claim; it was of secondary consequence that it was Under Bull and Young Bear Chief who finished the raider off.

Within a few years, Three Suns had given up the hunt and settled his followers in ten cabins on Two Medicine Creek. Cree horse raids in spring 1883 forced them to move closer to the Old Agency, which had grown into a settlement of around two hundred houses. By September, it was apparent that the weekly ration the agency issued was insufficient to feed all the hungry people. Three Suns predicted in council that they would soon be starving unless something was done.

That winter, James Willard Schultz came to survey the hungry Blackfoot camps then reported to George Bird Grinnell on their condition. He found Little Dog's people camped on Badger Creek where

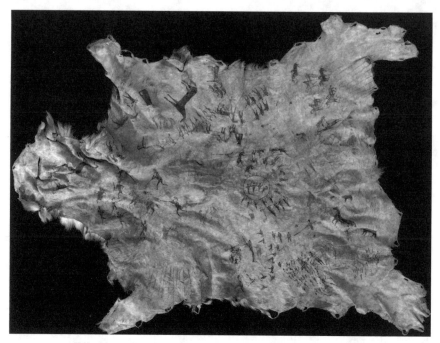

Elk skin painted with war record of Ninokskatosi (Three Suns or Big Nose) —Courtesy Minnesota Historical Society

the desperately hungry Black Antelope ate taboo trout, and died.[374] The camps of White Calf and Three Suns were on Two Medicine Creek, and Red Paint's one hundred lodges were on Birch Creek. When they could get them, the Indians wore blankets stamped USID (United States Indian Department). There were some who believed that the Methodist Indian agent, Major Young, withheld food that he could have issued.[375] During that starving time, Joe Kipp's Mandan mother, Earth Woman, and the adopted captive Crow Woman sold a hundred of their last buffalo robes to buy $900 worth of groceries from Fort Benton. It was not until February that soldiers from Fort Shaw broke through the snow with cattle and wagons of food. By then, Schultz believed that nearly five hundred of the eighteen hundred Indians had died of starvation.[376]

Another Piikani, Elk Horn, also kept a winter count, which was collected by Clark Wissler about 1909. It appeared to begin about 1845 but stopped after fifty-six entries. Most of the last entries recorded deaths of individuals. When Wissler questioned Elk Horn's preoccupation with mortality schedules, the old man answered that "since his people were confined to the limits of the reservation nothing else happened worth remembering."[377]

Three Suns's painted war count recorded the changes that had taken place in his once expansive world. When he rode into the Beaverhead country in 1845, the old trails along the Snake River were already being ground to dust under the wagon wheels of overlanders going to Oregon. The beaver contest was over, and hunters were fighting over access to the buffalo.[378] The Black Robes' promise of new spirit power to the Salish and the Gens du Large had little lasting consequence. After the Black Robes spread their message, there were times when Flathead, Pend d'Oreille, and Kutenai camped peacefully with the Piikani. But those truces were always broken and war parties continued to range afar.

The introduction of Christian concepts failed to keep young men like Three Suns from seeking fights with the Cree, Assiniboine, Crows, and intrusive Sioux. During the first sixteen years of his thirty-six-year record, Three Suns made seven notable war expeditions and withstood four raids. His personal body count of eighty-two enemies had to be set against the deaths of twenty-five of his tribesmen. The restraint of the experienced warrior was terribly tested when bluecoat soldiers killed the 174 smallpox-stricken Piikani on Two Medicine Creek in 1865, but he did not organize any retaliation. That tragedy was beyond redemption.

Moving easily back and forth across the medicine line, Three Suns and his people followed the thinning herds while trying to keep clear of the obnoxious gold miners swarming over their former ranges. Significant defeats of the Gros Ventre and Crow in 1866 and of the Cree and their Assiniboine allies three years later ruptured a fragile peace.[379] By then the distant Sioux had also come to the Cypress Hills to rustle Piikani horses. The agents encouraged the Piikani to turn the other cheek until the United States could corral those intruders on their own reservations.

By 1870, at age forty-seven, Three Suns had mellowed to where he could release Pend d'Oreille horse raiders and turn captured Sioux over to the Mounties. When old enemies attacked his camp on the Judith River, the old warrior took a gun and charged but left it to younger men to spill blood.

A couple of years after the starvation winter of 1883, the Great Northern Railway was blowing smoke along the reservation border. And

behind that iron expression of eminent domain panted a tribe of specula-
tors and developers lusting for Indian lands. Even remembering how
President Grant had taken away land with a pen in 1873 and 1874,
and how the Canadians had tied up the northern tribes in 1877, 222
chiefs and principal men of the Piikani, Kainaa, and Siksika came to
council. During five cold days in February 1887, they gave away yet more
land and agreed to live on reservations. Onesta-poka (White Calf) and
Mokska-atose (Big Nose, Three Suns's new name) led the signing. What
good were empty buffalo plains when hungry people crowded around the
agency slaughterhouse begging for entrails?

As families accepted individual allotments and scattered to sheltered
places, cabins on cattle ranches made better sense than canvas lodges.
The unity of the bands was lost in a kind of ramshackle suburbanization.
In 1892, when the government began building a boarding school on
Willow Creek, west of present-day Browning, Montana, acting agent
Captain Lorenzo W. Cooke thought that the agency should also be moved
there because miners were pressing for access to the mountains behind
that dreary place.

During the winter of 1893/94, Big Nose was about seventy years
old. So much had passed that his war record no longer seemed as significant.
The warrior who had been Three Suns did not want to be just another
old man clinging to the past. After carefully recounting each of the
pictographs, the old warrior gave the soft document to Captain Cooke.[380]

On 25 January 1894, Captain Cooke told thirty-two Piikani leaders
that since so many white men were encroaching on the west side of the
reservation, it made no sense to keep it. Professing to have no personal
interest in the matter, Cooke recommended that they sell the land as a
way to solve the trespass. After Congress paved the way with the Indian
Appropriations Act of 2 March 1895, commissioners came in late September of that year to meet with thirty-five select members of the Blackfeet.
In a reversal of former positions, it was White Calf who proclaimed how
valuable that land was and tired old Big Nose who said, "We are to sell
some land that is of little use to us. . . . If you wish to give a good price,
we will be pleased."[381] When Little Dog emerged as the bargainer, the
old man supported the price the Indians tried to set of $3 million. On
25 September 1895, they agreed to accept $1.5 million for the land that
eventually became part of Glacier National Park.[382]

Two years after he gave his elk-skin war record to Cooke, the old warrior Big Nose died. He was buried with his powerful owl bonnet, which old Hugh Munroe had passed on to him.[383] Since Cooke discouraged the old ways, Big Nose was not buried in the sky in a traditional tree grave. He was carried to the top of a hill in a white man's box, and the things of his life were placed around it.

Although a coulee south of Browning recalls the name of Big Nose, his grave was actually on the hilltop. The isolation and serenity of the site have been intruded on by that most modern means of communication, a microwave relay tower. On the ground lies a disgraceful scattering of beer bottles and other trash. But someone in town has recovered a few things from the grave site and preserved them in a little tin box: a few shards of broken glass, some blue beads, pieces of corroded metal, and tacks used to decorate a knife sheath or saddle. One little nail still transfixes a bit of leather.

Notes

1 IN THE DOG DAYS

1   Taken broadly from Clark Wissler and D. C. Duvall, comps. and trans., *Mythology of the Blackfoot Indians* (1908; reprint, Lincoln: Univ. of Nebraska Press, 1995), 19–20.

Captions

1   James D. Keyser, "Writing-on-Stone: Rock Art on the Northwestern Plains," *Canadian Journal of Archaeology*, no. 1 (1977): 55, 69.

2 NAMES FOR THE PEOPLE

2   According to Donald Frantz, the similarity of the Cree terms with the name Piikani appears to be an unrelated coincidence. However, the traders' usage of Muddy River Indians seems at least to support that coincidence. Donald G. Frantz and Norma Jean Russell, *Blackfoot Dictionary of Stems, Roots, and Affixes* (Toronto: Univ. of Toronto Press, 1995).

3   Richard Glover, ed., *David Thompson's Narrative, 1784–1812* (Toronto: Champlain Society, 1962), 240–41. Compare the specific identification Peeagan or Peeganakoon to Anthony Henday's use in 1754/55 of the generalized Cree term Archithinue for all western tribes.

4   To resolve the complexities of spelling and definition, this work relies on Frantz and Russell, *Blackfoot Dictionary*. Accent marks have been omitted.

5   The generalization Blackfoot (in Canada) or Blackfeet (in the United States) confuses the identity of three very distinct groups. Applying the term to the Piikani living in the United States became fixed when it was written into the treaties, and those south of the line have largely resigned themselves to the usage. But it is a misnomer that suggests Siksika preeminence as well as the false concept of a confederacy.

6   In keeping with the focus on the Piikani, this work will generally use Blackfoot terms for their neighboring nations except when other native speakers or traders are quoted directly.

7   See Dale R. Russell, *Eighteenth-Century Western Cree and Their Neighbors* (Hull, Quebec: Canadian Museum of Civilization, 1991), 142–47.

8   The figure that the informant Saukamappee used was filtered through David Thompson, who quite often inflated numbers to dramatize his *Narrative*.

9   Glover, ed., *Thompson's Narrative*, 241–42.

10   Thompson wrote fifty, but five is probably closer.

11   In 1787 Edward Umfreville, the North West Company trader on the Saskatchewan, wrote the word as "pinnechometer." David Thompson soon wrote it as "ponokomita." John C. Ewers, *The Blackfeet: Raiders on the Northwestern Plains* (1958; reprint, Norman: Univ. of Oklahoma Press, 1985), 22. Frantz and Russell in the *Blackfoot Dictionary* write it as "ponokaomitaa," plural "ponokaomitaiksi."

3 HORSES

12   Click Relander, *Strangers on the Land* (Yakima: Franklin Press, for the Yakima Indian Nation, 1962), 77.

13   John C. Ewers, *The Horse in Blackfoot Indian Culture: With Comparative Material from Other Western Tribes* (1955; reprint, Washington, D.C.: Smithsonian Institution Press, 1985), 18.

14   Liz Bryan, *The Buffalo People: Prehistoric Archaeology on the Canadian Plains* (Edmonton: Univ. of Alberta Press, 1991), 133–36; Lethbridge Centre of the Archaeological Society of Alberta, *Story on Stone: A Photographic Record of Rock Art in the Southern Alberta Area Surrounding the City of Lethbridge* (Lethbridge: Archaeological Society of Alberta, 1995). The Snake continued to threaten the Hidatsa villages on the Missouri River until 1781.

15   Anthony Henday, "York Factory to the Blackfoot Country: The Journal of Anthony Hendry [*sic*], 1754–55," ed. Lawrence J. Burpee, *Proceedings and Transactions of the Royal Society of Canada*, 3d ser., vol. 1, no. 2: 335–39.

16   Ewers, *The Horse in Blackfoot Indian Culture*, 16–19.

17   Speculation, based largely on the suspect Saukamappee-Thompson codex, puts the time about 1730. In 1754, Anthony Henday met Archithinue with large herds and saw wild horses running on the northern plains.

18   This version of meat consumption is a composite of impressions based on the descriptions of John Ewers and the soaring interpretation of Bernard DeVoto in *Across the Wide Missouri* (Boston: Houghton Mifflin, 1947).

19   James Willard Schultz, *My Life as an Indian* (1907; reprint, New York: Fawcett Columbine, 1981), 96–99; Schultz, *Blackfeet and Buffalo: Memories of Life Among the Indians*, ed. Keith C. Seele (Norman: Univ. of Oklahoma Press, 1962), 30, 311–15.

20   Ewers, *The Blackfeet*, 88–95.

21   Data from James H. Bradley, Montana Historical Society MS, cited in Ewers, *The Horse in Blackfoot Indian Culture*, 20.

22   The large herds on the reservations were slaughtered and replaced by larger draft animals more suited to the plow. In 1994, mustangs were imported from Wyoming to Montana to restore an example of the elk-dogs.

23   Ewers, *The Horse in Blackfoot Indian Culture*, 24–28, 174–75.

24   "The Last Real War Party," as told by Last Gun in Adolf Hungry Wolf, *The Blood People: A Division of the Blackfoot Confederacy: An Illustrated Interpretation of the Old Ways* (New York: Harper & Row, 1977), 287–300.

Captions

2   All Bodmer prints in chapters 3, 8, 11, and 13 are from volume 25 of *Early Western Travels, 1748–1846* (Cleveland: Arthur H. Clark, 1906).

4 GETTING TO KNOW THE ARCHITHINUE

25   According to James Knight's interview with an old chief in 1715, the Mountain Indians had visited York Factory about 1700. Arthur J. Ray, *Indians in the Fur Trade: Their Role as Hunters, Trappers, and Middlemen in the Lands Southwest of Hudson Bay, 1660–1870* (Toronto: Univ. of Toronto Press, 1974), 55–56, believes they were Mandan, or more probably Hidatsa, because they referred to silver on the upper river (Missouri) and kept Crow slaves. But Russell, *Eighteenth-Century Western Cree,* 132–33 (Hull, Quebec: Canadian Museum of Civilization, 1991), identifies them as Cree living on the Manitoba escarpment.

26   Henry Kelsey, *The Kelsey Papers,* ed. Arthur G. Doughty and Chester Martin (Ottawa: Public Archives of Canada, 1929).

27   Ray, *Indians in the Fur Trade,* 53; Russell, *Eighteenth-Century Western Cree,* 191–92.

28   This raises the intriguing question of the extent of Snake expansion on the northern plains, which was probably the consequence of their earlier possession of horses.

29   E. E. Rich, ed. *James Isham's Observations on Hudson's Bay, 1743, and Notes and Observations on a Book Entitled "A Voyage to Hudson's Bay in the Dobbs Galley," 1749* (Toronto: Champlain Society, 1949); Glyndwr Williams, ed., *Andrew Graham's Observations on Hudson's Bay, 1767–91* (London: Hudson's Bay Record Society, 1969), xxxvii, 205–7. "Southward Indians" meant Cree living south of the Churchill River trade penetration.

30   Rich, ed., *Isham's Observations,* 112–14.

31   Cf. "Pikaraminiouach" to the Cree name *pikano wiyiniwak.* Russell *Eighteenth-Century Western Cree* states that *pikan* or *pikakamew* were terms for muddy or turbid water, but the Pegogamaw Cree were not mentioned until 1751.

32   "Carte contenant Les nouvelles dicouvertes de l'ouest En Canada, Mers, Rivieres, Lacs et Nations qui y habittent en L'annee 1737," in W. Raymond Wood, ed., *The Explorations of the La Verendryes in the Northern Plains, 1738–43* (Lincoln: Univ. of Nebraska Press, 1980), 38–39.

33   Antoine Champagne, *Les La Verendrye et Le Poste de L'Ouest* (Quebec: Les Presses de L'Universite Laval, 1968), 418–21.

34   York Factory Journal, 26 June 1754, Hudson's Bay Company Archives, B239/a/37, Provincial Archives of Manitoba, Winnipeg (hereafter cited as HBCA). Henday was instructed to go "to the Kesichachewon, Missinneepee, Earchithinue, Esinepoet, or any other Country Indians, that we have as yet any traffick with; and that you may converse with them, making them presents, perswading them to be at peace, and not to Warr . . . but to hunt and gett goods, and bring them to the fort."

35   Henday, "York Factory to the Blackfoot Country"; Glyndwr Williams, "The Puzzle of Anthony Henday's Journal, 1754–55," *The Beaver* 309, no. 3 (winter 1978): 41–56. Henday's fair-copied journal was sent to London in 1755 and is cataloged as HBCA, B239/a/140, fols. 1–45. According to Dale Russell (*Eighteenth-Century Western Cree*), three other versions were kept at York, or made there later, each a little different from the others as new information was added.

36   Russell, *Eighteenth-Century Western Cree,* 95, explains this nervousness as reluctance to hunt during the depth of winter.

37 Russell, *Eighteenth-Century Western Cree*, 91.

38 York Factory Journal, 13 November 1763, HBCA, B239/a/52. Russell (*Eighteenth-Century Western Cree*) suggests that the hostiles may have been Snakes.

39 Williams, ed., *Graham's Observations*, 18, 173.

40 York Factory Journal, HBCA, B239/a/59, fol. 114; HBCA, E2/4, fols. 44–45; Paul C. Thistle, *Indian-European Trade Relations in the Lower Saskatchewan River Region to 1840* (Winnipeg: Univ. of Manitoba Press, 1986), 25.

41 Russell, *Eighteenth-Century Western Cree*, 97–105; Lawrence J. Burpee, ed., "An Adventure from Hudson's Bay: Journal of Matthew Cocking, from York Factory to the Blackfoot Country, 1772–1773," *Proceedings and Transactions of the Royal Society of Canada*, 3d ser., vol. 2, no. 2 (1908): 103, 106.

42 See Elliott Coues, ed., *New Light on the Early History of the Greater Northwest: The Manuscript Journals of Alexander Henry . . . and of David Thompson . . . , 1799–1814* (1897; reprint, Minneapolis: Ross and Haines, 1965), 2:461–62 n. 20, for a description of this major river.

43 Burpee, ed., "Journal of Matthew Cocking," 110.

44 Alexander Henry, *Travels and Adventures in Canada and the Indian Territories between the Years 1760 and 1776* (1808; reprint, Ann Arbor: Univ. Microfilms, 1966), 273, 297–98, 306–7, 314.

45 E. E. Rich, ed., *Cumberland House Journals and Inland Journal, 1775–79*, 1st series. (London: Hudson's Bay Record Society, 1951), 14, 19, 45.

46 Rich, *Cumberland House Journals*, 1:94, 113, 354.

47 Ibid., 1:218, 287.

48 Ibid., 2:76–101.

49 Ibid., 2:111.

50 Ibid., 2:181–82.

5 INSIDE THE PIIKANI WORLD

51 Memoir of Donald Mackay, HBCA, E223/1, fol. 30.

52 Rich, ed., *Cumberland House Journals*, 258, 262.

53 Ibid., 246.

54 The statement of Saukamappee, as filtered through Thompson's memory, held that the disease broke out among the Piikani on the second day after they found a smallpox-decimated Snake camp. But the incubation period is from ten to twelve days. Ibid., 246.

55 Ibid., 235.

56 Ibid., 46–47, 237–38.

57 Alice M. Johnson, ed., *Saskatchewan Journals and Correspondence*, (London: Hudson's Bay Record Society, 1967), 264 n. 2, citing the journal of Peter Fidler.

58 Russell, *Eighteenth-Century Western Cree*, 144.

59 Rich, *Cumberland Journals*, 2:282. This is the first use of the name Blackfoot in these two house journals. The previous terms were Archithinue or Yachithinnee.

60 Glover, ed., *Thompson's Narrative*, 247. Thompson may have heard this story from his predecessor and mentor James Gaddy, who began going to the Piikani camps in 1785.

61   There is an outside possibility that James Mackay, who left his bourgeois (boss) Donald Mackay stranded at Nipawi, made a trip to the mountains with Holmes's men. Several years later Mackay described a journey along the east side of the mountains to the Spanish cartographer Antoine Soulard in St. Louis. Mackay is an overlooked but significant figure of western development. Thomas Danisi is preparing a definitive biography for publication.

62   Glover, ed., *Thompson's Narrative,* 45.

63   Edward Umfreville, *The Present State of Hudson's Bay* (London: Charles Stalker, 1790). This volume is frustrating for what it does not contain. Trained as a Bayman, Umfreville must have kept a journal or notes while he was on the Saskatchewan. He left the Saskatchewan in spring 1788 and reached London about December. When his expectation of being rehired by the company was disappointed, he completed a hasty little book that attacked the Hudson's Bay Company policies. Umfreville's notes, which may have been too extensive to be included in the book, apparently disappeared with the author. For a fuller consideration, see David H. Pentland, "In Defense of Edward Umfreville," *Papers of the Seventh Algonquian Conference 1975* (Ottawa: Carlton Univ. Press, 1976), 63–79.

64   Umfreville, *Present State,* 197–203.

65   Donald Mackay's unpublished memoir is now preserved in the Hudson's Bay Company Archives as E.223/1.3, 4, and the transcript as E.223/2. See John C. Jackson, "Mapping the Fur Trade: Inland from the Bay," *The Beaver* 72, no. 1 (February/March 1992): 37–42, for Donald Mackay's contribution to northwestern plains geography. See A. P. Nasatir, ed., *Before Lewis and Clark: Documents Illustrating the History of the Missouri, 1785–1804,* 2 vols. (St. Louis: St. Louis Historical Documents Foundation, 1952; reprint, Lincoln: Univ. of Nebraska Press, 1990), 96 and Soulard map (insert), for the contribution of James Mackay, who led Antoine Soulard to believe that he had made an exploration along the foot of the Rocky Mountains from the North West Company trading posts on the Qu'Appelle River.

66   Manchester House Journal, 10 April 1787, HBCA, B121/a/1, fol. 39.

67   Ibid., fols. 39, 50.

68   David Thompson's observations of the "Peeagans" are probably accurate, although these details are from a composite written later. Thompson compiled his experiences as a young initiate (1787/88), as a fledgling Nor'wester (1789/1801), and as a frustrated fur trader who felt that his later career accomplishment had been denied by them.

69   HBCA, E3/2, fol. 14. During the winter of 1789/90, Thompson and Fidler were together at Cumberland House. They both received instruction in surveying from Philip Turner and surely exchanged their impressions of the Indians.

70   Glover, ed., *Thompson's Narrative,* 48–49. Thompson's notes, amounting to nine field journals and seventy-seven revised notebooks, date from 1790. The story of the old Cree must have been reconstructed later, perhaps in the 1840s, when Thompson was an impoverished old man hoping to produce a bestseller from his dramatized experiences. Judging from comparative readings in the 1806–12 field journals, Thompson's narrative needs to be taken with a grain of salt.

71   Ibid., 51. It seems unlikely that an animal would have been grazing fully saddled with the Snake herd, but Spanish gear is also described around the Hidatsa villages on the Missouri River about the same time.

72   Ibid., 50–51; Manchester House Journals, HBCA B121/a/2, fols. 29d–30.

73 Coues, ed., *Journals of Henry and Thompson,* 2:530, 722.

74 Manchester House Journals, HBCA, B121/a/2, fols. 29d–30.

75 Manchester House Journals, HBCA, B121/a/6, fols. 10d, 30, 31. Contrary to the usual belief, Indian hunters took beaver by digging them out of their dens rather than setting traps.

76 The northern herds crossed the Saskatchewan to winter in the shelter of the northern forests. The southern herds headed north from the Missouri and Milk River pastures but may have taken shelter in the foothills. Glover, ed., *Thompson's Narrative,* 48.

77 The journey of Peter Fidler and John Ward is recorded in Peter Fidler, "Journal of a Journey over Land from Buckingham House to the Rocky Mountains in 1792 & 3 by Peter Fidler," HBCA, E3/2. This has been published in a limited edition of five hundred copies as Bruce Haig, ed., *Journal of a Journey over Land from Buckingham House to the Rocky Mountains in 1792 & 3* (Lethbridge, Alberta: Historical Research Centre, 1990).

78 David G. Mandelbaum, *The Plains Cree: An Ethnographic, Historical and Comparative Study* (Regina, Saskatchewan: Canadian Plains Research Center, 1979), 36–37 and map 13.

6 EXPANSION AND RIPOSTE

79 James Willard Schultz, "Gros Ventre Slaughter (Told by Big Brave)," *Blackfeet and Buffalo,* 271. Like other data drawn from Schultz's fictionalized tales, this is risky information. Although he pretended to repeat Indian lodge tales verbatim, Schultz was also well read in the available Indian history of the last quarter of the nineteenth century and sometimes distorted facts to suit his artistic purposes.

80 Johnson, ed., *Saskatchewan Journals,* xvii, n. 2.

81 Arthur S. Morton, ed., *The Journal of Duncan M'Gillivray of the North West Company at Fort George on the Saskatchewan, 1794–5* (1929; reprint, Fairfield, Wash.: Ye Galleon Press, 1989), 62–64.

82 Johnson, *Saskatchewan Journals,* xvii n, xxvi, 9 n, 75 n, 76 n, 316. The shocked traders never forgave the Atsiina, as is shown in Maximilian, Prince of Wied-Neuwied, *Travels in the Interior of North America,* vols. 22–25 of *Early Western Travels, 1748–1846,* ed. Reuben Gold Thwaites (Cleveland: Arthur H. Clark, 1906), 23:90–92.

83 The foregoing statements were taken from Morton, ed., *Journal of Duncan M'Gillivray,* 41–42, 69, 70–76.

84 Nor'westers at Fort George believed that the Cree had attacked and massacred sixteen lodges of Atsiina on the South Branch in summer 1793, and that their kinsmen, fearing to attack the culprits in the wooded country, vented their frustration on the Pine Island houses.

85 Morton, ed., *Journal of Duncan M'Gillivray,* 41.

86 Ibid., 32, 34, 41.

87 Ibid., 56.

88 Johnson, ed., *Saskatchewan Journals,* xxvii.

89 Morton, ed., *Journal of Duncan M'Gillivray,* 28–29.

90 Raymond W. Wood and Thomas D. Thiessan, eds., *Early Fur Trade on the Northern Plains* (Norman: Univ. of Oklahoma Press, 1985), 62–67.

91 Edmonton Correspondence, HBCA, B60/c/1, 1.

92 Edmonton House Journal, HBCA, B60/a/27, 11.

93 Johnson, ed., *Saskatchewan Journals,* 19–20.

94 Ibid., 112.

95 Bird returned to Edmonton, leaving Gilbert Laughton, an experienced canoe builder, in charge of Acton House. Laughton sent down 2,289 MB in the spring.

7 ACTION AT ACTON HOUSE

96 Barbara Belyea, ed., *Columbia Journals: David Thompson* (Montreal: McGill-Queen's Univ. Press, 1994), 181.

97 David Thompson field journal 13, Archives of Ontario, in ibid., 7–11, 188–92.

98 Taken broadly from Jack Nisbet, *Sources of the River: Tracking David Thompson across Western North America* (Seattle: Sasquatch Books, 1994), 57–61.

99 James Bird to William Tomison, Nelson House, 14 February 1801, HBCA, B49/c/1, fols. 1–4.

100 Nisbet, *Sources of the River,* 66.

101 Johnson, ed., *Saskatchewan Journals,* xci–xcii, 130.

102 Ibid., 293, 317 n. 1; Daniel Williams Harmon, *Sixteen Years in the Indian Country: The Journal of Daniel Williams Harmon, 1800–1816,* ed. W. Kaye Lamb (Toronto: Macmillan Company of Canada, 1957), 48, 51.

103 HBCA, B39/a/2, 13.

104 Peter Fidler, 19 March 1802 list of Muddy River Indians who came to visit Chesterfield House, HBCA, B39/a/2, fol. 94 (Fidler's phonetic spellings): Sin ne pow pin now, Sheeks kin a kn, Oo nis stay akow pe, Imme tow, Ax e pee ta, Sech kin now, Mat ta-pe ow tit che ow (or Mangy Leather), Oo nis stay ma teo ye (or Beaver), Pee tay peet ta, She keech in now, Nin nay pee kos in, Nin now nis tow (or Old Man's Son, Beaver Chief), Sow ke kin ape pre (or Chief), Oo nis tay kut ta, Na pin oo iso, Sin ne pow too can, Tatche kis stommich's wife, E Man ne tow's wife, Is sag oo mok con (or Old Man Leather), Cuo quy it to pe, E tam ya pe, and, on 20 March, Toby.

On 19 March a Blood named Oo to can a poo also arrived, as well as a number of Blackfeet: Ka ap pe pus, Tache kow pe, In noo too mox, Stommix a kew, A pouch kin, Stommix is chis, Nestow oo tan, Ne tan ni, Oo too can a hews, Stommix is chee, Ki oo six num, Ol nis stew sum, A pee nis stow, and On nis tay tachche kay poy.

105 Chesterfield House Journal, HBCA, B39/a/2, 27.

106 Harmon, *Sixteen Years,* 96. The editor indicates that the location was actually about seventy miles above the forks.

107 John McDonald of Garth, "Autobiographical Notes," in *Les Bourgeois de la Compagnie du Nord-ouest: Recits de voyages, lettres, et rapports inedits relatifs au Nord-ouest canadien,* ed. Louis F. A. Masson (1889/90; reprint, New York: Antiquarian Press, 1960), 2:31–32, 34.

108 Wood and Thiessen, *Early Fur Trade,* 256–59.

109 Harmon, *Sixteen Years,* 100.

110 Edmonton House Journal, HBCA, B60/a/6, fol. 1.

111 Ibid., fol. 2.

112 Robert G. Ferris, ed., *Lewis and Clark: Historic Places Associated with Their Trans-continental Exploration (1804–06)* (Washington, D.C.: United States Department of the Interior, National Park Service, 1975), 216–20.

113 Ibid., 220.

114 Edmonton House Journal, HBCA, B60/a/6, fol. 6. This contemporary detail is interesting in that it calls into question the recollection of the incident that an aging Piikani named Wolf Calf told to George Bird Grinnell decades later. Wolf Calf claimed to have been a youthful member of the party, but his memory that two of them were killed suggests that he may have repeated the prevailing under-standing rather than that of an eyewitness. Distortion of memories by outside sources is a danger in oral history.

8 OVER THE STONEY MOUNTAINS

115 "Report of the Archives of British Columbia" (1913), in Arthur S. Morton, "Did Duncan M'Gillivray and David Thompson Cross the Rockies in 1801?" *Canadian Historical Review* 18, no. 2 (June 1937): 123.

116 David Thompson, Rocky Mountain House Journal, notebook no. 18, Archives of Ontario, microfilm reel no. 2; Irene M. Spry, "Routes through the Rockies," *The Beaver* (autumn 1963): 27–29.

117 Thompson was so upset by his experience on the trail that he recommended that Jacco Finlay be sacked, thereby creating another freeman. Finlay may have been the man who had already wintered in the "Cootaias lands" when he came to James Bird in October 1807. He had taken six hundred beaver that year and was outfitted to return across the mountains the next summer on the condition that he bring his catch to the Hudson's Bay Company (HBCA, B60/a/7, 4d). In return, the Bayman got a map of the West, which came into the hands of Peter Fidler and is reproduced in Spry, "Routes through the Rockies," 29. Thompson later recognized his impru-dence and rehired Finley as a clerk on 28 March 1810.

118 This is the first of two communications from the enigmatic Captain Zackery Perch.

119 Nisbet, *Sources of the River,* 106. The manuscript of the discovery book is in the collection of the Vancouver, British Columbia, public library.

120 There has been speculation on the identity of the Poltito paltons, also known as the Blue Mud Indians, but as early as February 1801 the Siksika informant Akomaki had correctly placed them north of the Clark Fork River and west of the Salish territory.

121 Salish hunters might depart for the buffalo country as early as February and trappers would want to begin the spring hunt by then.

122 The 21 December 1810 letter from Thompson to his Montreal friend refers to "an American officer and 8 soldiers" killed by the Piegan. Masson, ed., *Les Bourgeois de la Compaigne du Nord-ouest,* 2:41. Thompson was aware of the death of American trader and trapper Charles Courtin, who does not fit the description.

123 Draft of a letter to an unidentified recipient, found in the back of Thompson field journal. Rocky Mountain House Journal, notebook no. 18, Archives of Ontario, Toronto.

124 Thomas James, *Three Years among the Indians and Mexicans* (1846; reprint, Lincoln: Univ. of Nebraska Press, 1984), 26.

125 Edmonton House Journal, HBCA, B60/a/8, fols. 4–4d.

126 Theodore Binnema, "Old Swan, Big Man, and the Siksika Bands, 1794–1815," *Canadian Historical Review* 77, no. 1 (March 1996): 1–32.

127 Coues, ed., *Journals of Henry and Thompson,* 2:495.

128 Edmonton House Journal, HBCA, B60/a/8, fols. 4–4d.

129 Ibid., fol. 12.

130 Compare these to the statements being made by the downstream management, e.g., by John Ogilvy and Thomas Thain, agents of the North West Company, and by McTavish, McGillivrays & Company of Montreal, 3 October 1808, in Harold A. Innes, *The Fur Trade in Canada* (1930; reprint, New Haven: Yale Univ. Press, 1964), 235–36.

131 Coues, ed., *Journals of Henry and Thompson,* 2:568.

132 From a later letter to a friend it appears that Thompson was interested in making a more economical schooling arrangement for his oldest daughter, who had been sent east for education.

133 Much has been made of the Indians' shock of facing guns for the first time, but firearms had been available to the western peoples since before the turn of the century. Guns were traded from the Kutenai or passed along the Yellowstone trade channel from the Hidatsa-Mandan villages on the Missouri.

134 Joseph Howse to James Bird, Cootenaes R., 20 August 1810, HBCA, B60/a/9, fol. 2. The party they stopped was the first Hudson's Bay Company venture led by Joseph Howse.

135 Thompson may have anticipated this and reengaged Jacco Finlay to deny the competition a valuable asset among the western tribes.

136 Howse to Bird, 20 August 1810, HBCA, B60/a/9, fol. 2; H. Christoph Wolfart, "Joseph Howse," in *Dictionary of Canadian Biography,* vol. 8 (Toronto, Buffalo, London: University of Toronto Press, n.d.). Alexander Ross, a later observer, puts Howse's winter camp on the Finlay Creek branch of Jacques Fork (Jocko Creek); see Kenneth A. Spaulding, ed., *Alexander Ross: The Fur Hunters of the Far West* (Norman: Univ. of Oklahoma Press, 1956), 210–11.

137 Coues, ed., *Journals of Henry and Thompson,* 2:643.

138 Edmonton House Journal, HBCA, B60/a/9, fols. 13–13d.

139 Edmonton House Journal, HBCA, B60/a/9, 2, 8d, 11d, 13.

Captions

3 Hudson's Bay Company Archives, Provincial Archives of Manitoba, E3/2 fol. 103d, N4797. Judith Hudson Beattie, "The Indian Maps Recorded by Peter Fidler, 1801–1810," a paper presented at the Eleventh International Conference on the History of Cartography, Ottawa, Ontario, July 1985; Beattie, "Indian Maps in the Hudson's Bay Company Archives: A Comparison of Five Area Maps Recorded by Peter Fidler, 1801-1802," *Archivaria* 21 (winter 1985/86); Theodore Binnema, "Indian Maps as Ethnohistorical Sources," a paper presented to the Thirtieth Annual Northern Great Plains History Conference, Brandon, Manitoba, September 1995.

9 BLOWING THE PIEGAN CONNECTION

140 James Bird confirmed the North West partners' intention to take a third interest in the American enterprise. Edmonton House Journal, HBCA, B60/a/9, fol. 2d.

141 Coues, ed., *Journals of Henry and Thompson,* 2:666, 732. The Crows meant the Missouri Fur Company's Fort Remon on the Yellowstone at the mouth of the Bighorn.

142 Ibid., 2:718–19.

143 Ibid., 2:720–22.

144 Ibid., 2:719, 723.

145 For background, see Walter McClintock, *The Old North Trail: Life, Legends, and Religion of the Blackfeet Indians* (1910; reprint, Lincoln: Univ. of Nebraska Press, 1968). For a modern update, see Peter Stark, "The Old North Trail," *Smithsonian* 28, no. 4 (July 1997): 54–66.

146 Coues, ed., *Journals of Henry and Thompson*, 2:735; James, *Three Years*, 46. Note that these killings of intruding Indians resemble the firm rejection of the Iroquois on the South Branch of the Saskatchewan in 1802.

147 Edmonton House Journal, HBCA, B60/a/10, fols. 11d, 14. Perhaps Whitway accompanied the beaver-hunting Inuk'sik band.

148 The Missouri Company Trappers probably traveled via the Wind River valley, the logical route.

149 Alexander Ross, *Adventures of the First Settlers on the Oregon or Columbia River*, ed. Milo Milton Quaife (1849; reprint, New York: Citadel Press, 1969), 235; Edmonton House Journal, HBCA, B60/a/11, 4d.

150 Glover, ed., *Thompson's Narrative*, 393. Thompson's 350 slain freemen was an impossible overstatement.

151 Ross Cox, *The Columbia River*, ed. Edgar I. Stewart and Jane R. Steward (1831; reprint, Norman: Univ. of Oklahoma Press, 1957), 112.

152 M. Catharine White, ed. *David Thompson Journals Relating to Montana and Adjacent Regions 1808–12* (Missoula: Montana State Univ. Press, 1950), 210–12; Cox, *Columbia River*, 110–12.

153 Edmonton House Journal, HBCA, B60/a/12, 10d.

154 Ibid.

155 For a biography, see John C. Jackson, "Charles McKay," in *The Mountain Men and the Fur Trade of the Far West*, ed. Leroy Hafen (Glendale, Calif.: Arthur H. Clark, 1972), 9:251–58.

156 Edmonton House Journal, HBCA, B60/a/17 [1818/19] fols. 2, 23; B60/a/18 [1819/20].

157 Spaulding, ed., *Alexander Ross*, 138–39, 153.

158 Ibid., 151–52; HBCA, B34/a/4, fols. 13–13d, 15.

159 Spaulding, ed., *Alexander Ross*, 170.

160 Ibid., 186–7. A full record of McKenzie's adventures trapping on the Snake River would be of considerable historical interest, but Ross described his friend McKenzie as a leader who absolutely hated the pen. "To travel a day's journey on snowshoes was his delight; but he detested spending five minutes scribbling in a journal. His traveling notes were often kept on a beaver skin written with a piece of charcoal, and he would often complain of the drudgery of keeping accounts." Ross claims that McKenzie in retirement undertook to put together the account of his travels, but his Swiss wife found the effort so distressing to him—or to her—that she destroyed the partial manuscript and McKenzie never had the heart to start again. But McKenzie's letters to Governor George Simpson are something else—literate, witty, and stylish—quite out of keeping with Ross's story.

10 DRAWING THE LINE

161 Edmonton House Journal 1828/29, HBCA, B60/a/26, fols. 8, 13d, 29; George Bird Grinnell, "A White Blackfoot," *Masterkey: Quarterly of the Southwest Museum 47,* no. 1 (January/March 1973): 12–13; and less reliably Denton R. Bedford, "Lone Walker, the Small Robe Chief," *Indian Historian* 8, no. 3 (summer 1974): 41–54.

162 Grinnell, "A White Blackfoot," *Masterkey* 46, no. 4 (October/December 1972): 148–50. The memories of old Hugh Munroe were filtered through the ear and pen of eastern editor Grinnell, but details checked from other sources give credence to his yarns.

163 "Glossary of Geographical Names in English and Blackfeet," in Schultz, *Blackfeet and Buffalo,* 369–77. It is possible that those who informed the later observers had forgotten or put out of mind those places lost to them when the treaties were drawn.

164 Edmonton House Journal, 25 November 1822, HBCA, B60/a/21, fol. 7.

165 Spokane District Journal, 15 April 1822 to 20 April 1823, HBCA, B208/a/1.

166 Kennedy recommended withdrawing the freemen from the difficult Snake country and relocating them on the head of the Columbia River where "they would be more in our power and the furs of a better quality." Spokane District Report (1822/23), HBCA, B208/e/1.

167 John Edward Harriot, "Memoirs of Life and Adventures in Hudson's Bay Company Territories, 1819–1825" (written in 1860), Coe Collection, no. 90, no. 245, Yale University Library, New Haven.

168 Ibid.

169 Hiram Martin Chittenden, *The American Fur Trade of the Far West: A History of the Pioneer Trading Posts and Early Fur Companies of the Missouri Valley and the Rocky Mountains and of the Overland Commerce with Santa Fe* (1902; reprint, Lincoln: Univ. of Nebraska Press, 1986), 1:148.

170 The name Mehkskehme Sukahs (Iron Shirt) was heard by the Germanic ear of Prince Maximilian. Hugh Dempsey corrects that to Mexkemauastasn (Mikskim-auatawn), which means Iron Shield. Frantz and Russell's *Blackfoot Dictionary* has *mi'ksskimm,* having the property of a metal, and *awo'taan,* a shield. At one point James Bird requested that London send out metal shields or targets for trading. Iron Shield was at Fort McKenzie in 1833 when the artist Karl Bodmer took the portrait that shows a relatively young man looking out through a black mask with an oddly distant pensiveness. Having joined his first war raid at the age of fifteen, Iron Shield was still a young warrior when he encountered Immell and Jones.

171 "The paper contained a recommendation stating that he was one of the principal chiefs of his nation who was well disposed towards whites, and had a large quantity of furs, &c. The letter was written on the leaf of an account book, which seemed to have been headed, before it was taken from the book, 'Mountain Post, 1823' but was dated, at the bottom, '1820.'" Dale L. Morgan, ed., *The West of William H. Ashley* (Denver: Old West Publishing, 1964), 41. By another account this was a white man living with the Piikani. He may have been the Hudson's Bay Company's Hugh Munroe, who had been sent to live with the Indians and learn their language.

172 "19 May 1823 Jefferson's River 40 Miles above the 3 Forks. This instrument of writing is given the Iron Shirt, a Blackfoot Indian, in attestation of his good conduct while with us, and to the end that should the same be handed to any of the Missouri Fur Company Traders some tobacco and other small presents may be given the Bearer— He is a man of good repute among the N W Cos Traders, from whom he has credentials

to that effect, & also a man of some distinction among his nation.—[Signed] M:E:Immelle R:J:Jones C:Kermle Wm Gordon Partners & Clerks in the Missouri Fur Compy." Morgan, ed., *The West of William H. Ashley*, 42.

173 Iron Shield was the son of Little Mountain and was also known as Apesomuckka or Apiso-maken (Running Wolf) during much of his life. He had the power of Bear, and when he died on the Belly River about the middle of the century, he was the leader of the Grease Melters band and a medicine pipe owner. He had continued a winter count on a buffalo skin that was taken up by his son Natosia Nepe-e, or Brings Down the Sun, a spiritual leader who signed Treaty Number Seven in 1877. Paul M. Raczka, *Winter Count: A History of the Blackfoot People* (Brocket, Alberta: Oldman River Cultural Centre, 1979), 13–16. Arni Brownstone, *War Paint: Blackfoot and Sarcee Painted Buffalo Robes in the Royal Ontario Museum* (Toronto: Royal Ontario Museum, 1993), 68–69, has additional data drawn from records of Father Doucet.

174 Joshua Pilcher to Benjamin O'Fallon, 23 July 1823, in Morgan, ed., *The West of William H. Ashley*, 41, 48–50, 238 n. 121.

175 Statements and depositions in Morgan, ed., *The West of William H. Ashley*, 69–72; and see John C. Jackson, *Shadow on the Tetons: David E. Jackson and the Claiming of the American West* (Missoula, Mont.: Mountain Press, 1993), 54ff.

176 This often quoted statement is from Finan McDonald to John George McTavish, Spokane House, 5 April 1824, York Factory Correspondence, 1808–28, HBCA, B239/c/1, fols. 140–140d.

177 Edmonton House Journal, 28 November 1823, HBCA, B60/a/22, fol. 26d.

178 Edmonton Report, 1822–23, HBCA, B60/e/5, fols. 3d–4.

179 Edmonton House Journal, HBCA, B60/a/22, fols. 26–26d; Edmonton Report, HBCA, B60/e/6, fol. 2d.

180 Edmonton Report, 1824–25, HBCA, B60/e/8, fols. 1–1d.

181 Schultz, *My Life as an Indian*, 98. Schultz got his story from an old man who had mixed up his dates. However, some accounts, like Munroe's description of his first experience with the Small Robes, can be verified and adjusted for accuracy through comparison with Hudson's Bay Company records and other ethnohistorical data.

182 E. E. Rich, ed., *Peter Skene Ogden's Snake Country Journals, 1824–25 and 1825–26* (London: Hudson's Bay Record Society, 1950), 9, 19, 23.

183 Charles McKay to John Stuart, Missouri Forks, 11 July 1825, John Stuart Letterbook 4, microfilm no. 1502, Oregon Historical Society, Portland.

184 Rich, ed., *Ogden's Snake Country Journals*, 61–64.

185 "A Narrative of Col. Robert Campbell's Experiences in the Rocky Mountains Fur Trade from 1825 to 1835" (MS), pp. 14–18, Missouri Historical Society, St. Louis; T. D. Bonner, *The Life and Adventures of James P. Beckwourth* (1856; reprint, New York: Alfred A. Knopf, 1931), 74–79.

186 "Diary of Occurrences Transpiring at Edmonton House . . . by John Rowland, Chief Trader," HBCA, B60/a/24, fols. 2, 7.

187 "Extract of Occurrences, Summer 1827," HBCA, B60/a/25, fol. 18d, 25, 34d, 50d.

188 The slain Americans were with the Smith, Jackson & Sublette brigade led by Samuel Tullock. They were attacked after leaving their winter camp near Ogden's Snake brigade to join other Americans near Salt Lake. Ogden did not learn about the attack until his brigade encountered a party of Snakes returning from the Henry

Fork of the Snake River with gear recognized as Tullock's. About 8 May 1828, the Snakes attacked some Blackfeet driving thirty horses, some loaded with packs of furs. Two Blackfeet were killed in the ambush and fifteen horses captured. It is hard to believe Ogden's claim that the Snakes would have cut the packs loose and left the furs on the plain, or if they had, that Ogden would not have made an effort to recover a potentially valuable haul. Glyndwr Williams, ed., *Peter Skene Ogden's Snake Country Journals, 1827–28 and 1828–29* (London: Hudson's Bay Record Society, 1971), 71–72 n. 1, 81.

189 Rowand, "Diary of Occurrences at Edmonton House, Saskatchewan during the summer and winter 1828/29," HBCA, B60/a/26, fols. 8, 14d, 29.

11 "TEACH US TO LOVE ONE ANOTHER"

190 [George] Simpson's Correspondence, HBCA, D4/121, fol. 46d.

191 "Narrative of Campbell's Experiences," 20, 22–24, 26, 29.

192 Bernard DeVoto, *Across the Wide Missouri*; Don Berry, *A Majority of Scoundrels* (New York: Harper & Brothers, 1961).

193 Perhaps Onistaipokaa, or Calf Child?

194 Itsowaakiiyi, Be a Pretty Woman?

195 Cornelius M. Buckley, *Nicolas Point, S.J.: His Life and Northwest Indian Chronicles* (Chicago: Loyola Univ. Press, 1989), 386–88. Father Point based his account on contemporary statements taken from Berger and others at Fort Lewis.

196 Other accounts of this development are in Charles Larpenteur, *Forty Years a Fur Trader on the Upper Missouri: The Personal Narrative of Charles Larpenteur, 1833–1872*, ed. Milo Milton Quaife (1933; reprint, Lincoln: Univ. of Nebraska Press, 1989), 93–96; James H. Bradley, "Affairs at Fort Benton from 1831 to 1869 from Lieut. Bradley's Journal," *Contributions to the Historical Society of Montana* 3 (1900): 201–3. For backround on Berger, see David Smyth, "Jacques Berger, Fur Trader," *The Beaver* 69, no. 3 (June/July 1989): 39–50.

197 David Lavender, *The Fist in the Wilderness* (1964; reprint, Albuquerque: Univ. of New Mexico Press, 1979), 393, puts this figure at a precise ninety-two Piegan men and thirty-two Piegan women.

198 There are two printed versions of Kipp's statements to Lt. James Bradley, the more detailed being Bradley, "Establishment of Ft. Piegan as Told to Me by James Kipp," *Contributions to the Historical Society of Montana* 8 (1917): 244–50.

199 Maximilian, Prince of Wied, *Travels in the Interior of North America*. Vols. 22–25 of *Early Western Travels, 1748–1846*, ed. by Reuben Gold Thwaites (Cleveland: Arthur H. Clark, 1906), 22:317.

200 Mandan Indian agent J. F. A. Sandford to William Clark, 17 July 1832, confirms that the Indians also blamed the Hudson's Bay Company for inciting the Bloods to attack Kipp's post. Lavender, *Fist in the Wilderness,* 477 n. 8.

201 Charles DeLand and Doane Robinson, eds., "The Fort Tecumseh and Fort Pierre Journal and Letterbook," *South Dakota Historical Society Collections* 9 (1918): 155.

202 The Bloods seem to have preserved a garbled folk memory of those exchanges with the downstream tribes. In 1977, the Bloods still retained the Different-people Pipe, which is believed to date from spring 1833, when their chief, Seen from Afar, and his wife boarded the American Fur Company keelboat at Fort McKenzie and traveled to meet the Mandans. Prince Maximilian saw them in the Hidatsa

village when he arrived at Fort Clark but mentioned only two Piikani, Kiasax and his friend Matsokui. When Seen from Afar and his wife left, the Mandans gave him the pipe and his wife a buffalo headdress, which she later transferred to the Motokis woman's society. Seen from Afar made a second visit about twenty years later. Hungry Wolf, *Blood People*, 156–57.

203 W. A. Ferris, *Life in the Rocky Mountains: A Diary of Wanderings on the Sources of the Rivers Missouri, Columbia, and Colorado from February, 1830, to November, 1835*, ed. Paul C. Phillips (Denver: Old West Publishing, 1940), 133–38.

204 William S. Lewis and Paul C. Phillips, eds., *The Journal of John Work* (Cleveland: Arthur H. Clark, 1923), 62.

205 Ferris, *Life in the Rocky Mountains*, 146–7.

206 Ibid., 147.

207 "Journal of Occurrences at Fort Sanspariel from 23rd May 1832," HBCA, B60/a27, fols. 1d, 2d.

208 Edmonton House Journal, HBCA, B60/a/27, fols. 1d, 2d, 10, 10d–11.

209 If Hugh Munroe's memory can be trusted, he and his wife may have been left on the Missouri to spy on the American Fur Company's activities and later to keep the Kutenai at arm's distance from the traders. Anne McDonnell, ed., "The Fort Benton Journal, 1854–56, and the Fort Sarpy Journal, 1855–56," *Contributions to the Historical Society of Montana* 10 (1940): 255 n. 22.

210 "Journal of Occurrences at Fort Sanspariel," HBCA, B60/a/27, fol. 11.

12 PETOHPEKIS AND THE BLOOD BARRIER

211 "Bug's Boys" was a trapper term for the Blackfeet repeated by Joe Meek in Francis Fuller Victor, *The River of the West* (1870; reprint, Columbus Ohio: Long's College Book Company, 1950), 61. Meek's biographer later rendered the expression as "the Devil's own."

212 In the perception of abused trappers, distinctions between Blackfeet, Bloods, Gros Ventre, and Piegan were never clear. Blackfoot was a general term, used just as the northern traders spoke of the Slave or Meadow Indians.

213 The 1832 oil portrait identified as Eagle Ribs, a Piegan Blackfoot warrior, is in the Smithsonian Institution. It has been reproduced in John C. Ewers, *Artists of the Old West* (Garden City, N.Y.: Doubleday, 1965), 78; a version of the same is also in George Catlin, *Letters and Notes on the Manners, Customs, and Conditions of North American Indians* (1844; reprint, New York: Dover, 1973), vol. 1, plate 14.

214 See McDonnell, ed., "Fort Benton Journal and Fort Sarpy Journal," 243 n. 3. Indian genealogy, however, is difficult, and the name Eagle Ribs was also used by the Piikani. Hugh Dempsey obtained his identification from Blood informants. A younger man named Eagle Ribs was given a horse by young Red Crow between 1845 and 1850. See Hugh A. Dempsey, *Red Crow: Warrior Chief* (Lincoln: Univ. of Nebraska Press, 1980).

215 Catlin noticed that the Blackfeet were at odds with Cree from the north. Catlin, *Letters and Notes*, 1:38.

216 Catlin, *Letters and Notes*, 1:29–34.

217 Stomick-sosack's 1832 portrait is in Catlin, *Letters and Notes*, 1:30; and the 1833 study is in David C. Hunt and Marsha V. Gallagher, eds., *Karl Bodmer's America* (Lincoln, Nebr.: Joslyn Art Museum, 1984), 261.

218 DeLand and Robinson, eds., "Fort Tecumseh and Fort Pierre," 155–57. This was Fontanelle's brigade from St. Louis, who finally connected with the mountain hunters on 7 August.

219 Lavender, *Fist in the Wilderness,* 392.

220 Davis Thomas and Karin Ronnefeldt, eds., *People of the First Man: Life Among the Plains Indians in Their Final Days of Glory, the Firsthand Account of Prince Maximilian's Expedition up the Missouri River, 1833–34* (New York: E. P. Dutton, 1976), 75.

221 The events of these years of the mountain hunt have been treated in two fine studies: DeVoto, *Across the Wide Missouri,* and Berry, *A Majority of Scoundrels.*

222 Ferris, *Life in the Rocky Mountains,* 321–24.

223 This statement was made years after the fact by the trader Joseph Brazeau, who was then working for the Hudson's Bay Company at Fort Edmonton. See the Earl of Southesk, *Saskatchewan and the Rocky Mountains . . . in 1859 and 1860* (1875; reprint, Rutland, Vt.: Charles E. Tuttle, 1969), 160–61.

224 Claude E. Schaeffer, "Echoes of the Past on the Blackfoot Reservation: Loretto, the Young Mexican Trapper," *Montana* 2, no. 2 (April 1952): 19 n. 27. In 1843, Alexander Culbertson presented a John James Audubon associate, the ornithologist Edward Harris, with a quillwork- and scalplock-decorated shirt that had belonged to Woman Moccasin. Schaeffer later equates that person with the Mountain Chief who signed the 1855 treaty.

225 Ferris, *Life in the Rocky Mountains,* 183–84.

226 The Piikani woman Kit Fox Woman (or Kills on Both Sides), of the Fat Roasters band, had been a prisoner of the Crows. Traded by them to the trapper Lorento, she left her baby with the father. During the melee between the trappers and the Bloods, she was retaken by her own people and the Crow father had to ride into the enemy camp to deliver the child to her. Schaeffer, "Echoes," 21.

227 This story was picked up by Washington Irving; see his *Adventures of Captain Bonneville* (1868; reprint, Portland, Ore.: Bidford & Mort, n.d.), 83–85. In Joe Meek's version (told in Victor, *River of the West*), 132–34, Bridger responded to a friend's question "What's the matter?" with "Only a few feathers in my [ass]." One of the arrowheads was later removed, sans anesthesia, by the medical missionary Marcus Whitman. Another version came from Petohpekis through the trader J. E. Brazeau, who told it to the Earl of Southesk at Edmonton in 1859.

228 Mitchell went on to a career in the Indian service. William Clark's old job as St. Louis superintendent passed to Joshua Pilcher, and then to Mitchell on 13 September 1841. He yielded it to Thomas H. Harvey in 1843 but took over again on 30 March 1849. In the reorganization of 13 March 1851, that position became the central superintendency, but Mitchell kept his headquarters in St. Louis. Mitchell went to Fort Laramie that fall for the treaty being negotiated with the Sioux, Cheyenne, Arapaho, Crows, Assiniboine, Gros Ventre, Mandan, and Arikara. An active advocate of clearing a central passageway through the Indian country, Mitchell was prepared to be generous with annuities because he realized it was going to be costly to redirect the ill-fated tribes into agriculture. Francis Paul Prucha, *The Great Father* (Lincoln: Univ. of Nebraska Press, 1984), 1:343.

229 Earl of Southesk, *Saskatchewan and the Rocky Mountains,* 161.

230 Chittenden, *American Fur Trade,* 1:366.

231 HBCA, D4/126, fols. 13d, 62. If the Blood tribal memory is trustworthy, by autumn 1833 they were also jealous of the offers being made to the Piegan by the Hudson's Bay Company to build a trading station for them on the upper Bow River; the Bloods and Blackfeet would still be expected to go to Edmonton to trade. The Buffalo Followers band, who led the Bloods, advised the Piegan to boycott this new outpost. When the admonition was ignored, Blood chiefs intercepted the southern tribesmen at Badger Creek, and in the resulting fight a number of Piegan were killed. See also Dempsey, *Red Crow*, 13.

232 Edmonton House Journal, HBCA, B60/a/27.

233 Ibid., fol. 19d.

234 Ibid., fol. 28.

235 Fort Carlton Journal, 1833–34, and Fort Pelly Journal, 1834–35, 1837, in Susan R. Sharrock, "Crees, Cree-Assiniboines, and Assiniboines: Interethnic Social Organization on the Far Northern Plains," *Ethnohistory* 21, no. 2 (1974): 110–11.

13 SKIN GAMES

236 James Hamilton to Alexander Culbertson, Fort Union, 5 May 1835, Fort Union Letterbook, Choteau Collection, Missouri Historical Society, St. Louis, Missouri.

237 In his 1830 report at York Factory, governor George Simpson wrote that the peltry traded from the Blackfeet was taken in theft from other tribes, as they rarely hunted themselves. Simpson to Hudson's Bay Company, York Factory, 26 August 1830, HBCA, D4/97, fols. 37–39; Marcel Giraud, *The Metis of the Canadian West*, trans. George Woodcock, 2 vols. (1945; reprint, Lincoln: Univ. of Nebraska Press, 1986), 32–33, 509 n. 89.

238 The report of the Blood seige and the resulting shift to a trade in robes had arrived downstream by July 1832, when the U.S. Indian Agent at Fort Clark, J. A. Sanford, wrote to superintendent of Indians William Clark that the British had incited the Bloods. Lavender, *Fist in the Wilderness*, 477. The news undoubtedly arrived with the pirogues that brought McKenzie, Kipp, and the former Hudson's Bay confidential servant James Bird Jr.

239 Robes also made good return cargo for the wagons on the Santa Fe trail, where a robe trade developed after 1821. John Jacob Astor authorized his agent Ramsay Crooks to begin purchasing robes in 1827, perhaps because the commodity represented half the business of the rival Columbia Fur Company. In 1831, the former mountain trader William Sublette hauled eight hundred buffalo robes overland in wagons from Santa Fe to the St. Louis market. Jackson, *Shadow on the Tetons*, 173.

240 In 1854, the cost of a robe to the seller was about $1.35 in goods plus $1.20 in the trader's expenses, for a total of $2.55; it sold for $3.00, a profit of 45 cents a robe. According to Maximilian, the American Fur Company took in 25,000 robes in 1830 and 40,000 to 50,000 in 1833. J. B. Sanford told Fremont in 1845 that U.S. and Canadian companies traded 90,000 robes a year. Chittenden claims there were 110,000 robes traded in 1848. The American Fur Company took 100,000 in 1850. T. Lindsay Baker, "Beaver to Buffalo Robes: Transition in the Fur Trade," *Museum of the Fur Trade Quarterly*, vol. 23, no. 1 (spring 1987) and no. 2 (summer 1987).

241 Ibid.

242 Rowand to Hudson's Bay Company, Edmonton, 10 January 1834, HBCA, D4/126, fol. 61, reports that a Piegan war party killed forty-four Flatheads and two white men across the mountains the previous summer and returned with a great number of horses.

243   Thomas and Ronnefeldt, eds., *People of the First Man*, 100. Although it is not a complete record of Maximilian's observations, this work is cited because it uses excerpts from the unpublished field journals.

244   In 1833 at Fort McKenzie, Bodmer painted portraits of Ninock-kiau (Bear Chief) previously known as Ketsepenn-nuka (Spotted Elk); Natoie-poochsen (Word of Life), his uncle; Tatsicki-stomick (Middle Bull), a principal Piegan chief; Mehskehme-sukahs (Iron Shirt); Hotokaueh-hoh (Head of Buffalo Skin); Pioch-kiaiu (Distant Bear); Homachseh-katatohs (Great Star); Pachkaab-sachkoma-poh (Mean or Wicked Boy); and others.

245   For observations on Bear Chief, see Thomas and Ronnefeldt, eds., *People of the First Man*, 100–102; for the events of 28 August in the field journal, see 108–10.

246   Maria R. Audubon, *Audubon and His Journals*, annotated by Elliott Coues (New York: Dover, 1960), 133–36.

247   Piegan Post Accounts Outfit, 1833, HBCA, B21/d/2.

248   Lavender, *Fist in the Wilderness*, 478 n. 1, cites conflicting accounts of the length of the seige.

249   Audubon, ed., *Audubon and His Journals*, 178–80; Edwin Thompson Denig, *Five Indian Tribes of the Upper Missouri: Sioux, Arickaras, Assiniboines, Crees, Crows*, ed. John C. Ewers (1961; reprint, Norman: Univ. of Oklahoma Press, 1985), 177–78.

250   Denig, *Five Indian Tribes*, 185.

14 SMALL ROBES, BIG HEARTS

251   Fidler, "Journal of a Journey," HBCA, E3/2, fols. 2–39.

252   This "fused" relationship may have been similar to that between Cree and Assiniboine bands as discussed in Sharrock, "Crees, Cree-Assiniboines, and Assiniboines," 95–122.

253   John C. Ewers, "Identification and History of the Small Robes Band of the Piegan Indians," *Journal of Washington Academy of Sciences* 36, no. 12, (15 December 1946): 397–98. Catlin's estimate of ten persons to a lodge would come to a total of about twenty-five hundred Small Robes, not far off from John Rowand's 1824/25 count of twenty-four hundred hunters on the headwaters of the Missouri.

254   Edmonton House Journal, HBCA, B60/a/22, fol. 26.

255   Grinnell, "A White Blackfoot," *Masterkey* 46, no. 4 (October/December 1972): 148. The most extensive speculation on the identity of this puzzling character is in Bedford, "Lone Walker," 41–54.

256   Munroe repeated this story to several journalists in his later years and may have combined two experiences into one adventure. See the *Plevna Herald* (unidentified new article, n.p., n.d.); John W. Hanney story in *Holiday River Press*, 28 December 1881, 3; *Fort Benton River Press*, 19 February 1890; *Chinook Opinion*, 29 October 1891, 1; and of course Schultz.

257   The story needs to be taken with caution, as Schultz used the same locations for other war stories. On the other hand, Munroe told the same yarn to others.

258   "Saskatchewan Report for 1824 and 25 by John Rowland, dated Edmonton, 14 May 1825," HBCA, B60/e/8, 1–1d.

259   Ibid., fols. 1d–2.

260 Ogden's Journal, 20 and 28 June 1825, and Kittson's Journal, 27–29 June 1825, in Rich, ed., *Ogden's Snake Country Journals*, 62–65, 240–41; Charles McKay to John Stuart, Missouri Forks, 11 July 1825, John Stuart Letterbook 4, microfilm 1502, Oregon Historical Society, Portland; Grinnell, "A White Blackfoot," *Masterkey* 46, no. 4 (October/December 1972): 142–51, and *Masterkey* 47, no. 1 (January/March 1973): 12–22.

261 Edmonton House Journal, HBCA, B60/a/23, 3, 10d; B60/a/26, 8, 29.

262 This is based on a statement of risky credibility from James Beckwourth: see T. D. Bonner, *The Life and Adventures of James P. Beckwourth*, 75. For background from the American perspective, see John C. Jackson, *Shadow on the Tetons*.

263 For an example of an adoption that must have taken place about this time, see Joseph P. Donnelly, trans., *Wilderness Kingdom: Indian Life in the Rocky Mountains, 1840–1847: The Journals & Paintings of Nicolas Point, S.J.* (New York: Holt, Rinehart & Winston, 1967), 193.

264 This Small Robe–Flathead marriage connection resurfaced in the summer of 1831, when Warren Ferris mentioned the "Blackfoot" chief who had deserted his people to live with the Flatheads. Phillips, ed., *W. A. Ferris*, 115.

265 Jackson, *Shadow on the Tetons*, 151, 155.

266 Donald R. Johnson, ed., *William H. Gray: Journal of His Journey East, 1836–1837* (Fairfield, Wash.: Ye Galleon Press, 1980), 33. Gray had traveled to Fort Vancouver and arranged to accompany Ermatinger to the Salish country so he could find a way to return east.

267 Ibid., 29. It is a bit of a stretch to guess that the "Sqashin, or a Pagona, or a Blackfoot" who joined the party on 7 May in the Bitterroot Valley may have been Wolf's Son, whom Ferris observed in 1831 and Bodmer painted in 1833, and who later assumed the role of mediator for the Jesuits between the Salish and Piikani.

268 Hunt and Gallagher, *Bodmer's America*, 253, 257, 258.

269 Buckley, ed., *Nicolas Point*, 250, 260 n. 3.

270 The latest compilation of her career is in Nisbet, *Sources of the River*, 134–37, 251.

271 Johnson, ed., *William H. Gray*, 48.

272 Ibid., 46.

273 For an intrepretation of those developments, see DeVoto, *Across the Wide Missouri*, 327–33.

274 Johnson, ed., *William H. Gray*, 74.

275 T. C. Tessendorf, "Red Death on the Missouri," *The American West* 14, no. 1 (January/February 1977): 48–53. Original sources are in Abel, *Cardon's Journal at Fort Clark*, and Denig, *Five Indian Tribes;* a general analysis is in DeVoto, *Across the Wide Missouri*.

276 Fathers De Smet and Point mention passing the same site in late summer 1846.

277 Victor, *The River of the West*, 231–32; Osborne Russell, *Journal of a Trapper, 1834–1843*, ed. Aubrey L. Haines (Lincoln: Univ. of Nebraska Press, 1965), 86, 89.

278 Ewers, "Identification and History of the Small Robes Band," 398, 402.

279 John Rowand to James Hargrave, Edmonton, 31 December 1838, in G. P. de T. Glazebrook, ed., *The Hargrave Correspondence, 1821–43* (Toronto: Champlain Society, 1938).

Captions

4 The artist Gustav Sohon, traveling with the United States Peace Commission, made this portrait on 15 October 1855, two days before the conclusion of the Judith River treaty. The name of Nen-na-i-poh-sy does not appear on the document.

15 A BLACK ROBE DECADE

280 Hiram Martin Chittenden and Alfred Talbot Richardson, eds., *Life, Letters and Travels of Father Pierre-Jean De Smet, S.J. 1801–1873* (New York: Francis P. Harper, 1905), 1:220.

281 Curiously, each time he repeated this account, De Smet inflated the numbers. He later has seventy Flatheads holding off a thousand Blackfeet, and finally they're defeating fifteen hundred.

282 Buckley, ed., *Nicolas Point*, 249.

283 Chittenden and Richardson, eds., *Life, Letters, and Travels*, 1:318–19; De Smet to Rev. Father, St. Mary's, 18 October 1841, in Reuben Gold Thwaites, ed., "P. J. De Smet, S.J., Letters and Sketches, with a Narrative of a Year's Residence Among the Indian Tribes of the Rocky Mountains," in *Early Western Travels 1748–1846* (1906; reprint, New York: AMS Press, 1966), 27:284–85.

284 Chittenden and Richardson, eds., *Life, Letters, and Travels*, 1:233.

285 Hugh Dempsey, ed., *The Rundle Journals, 1840–1848* (Calgary: Historical Society of Alberta, 1977), 54–56, 84.

286 De Smet, "Oregon Missions," 27:137, 147, 178, 251–52, 318–19.

287 Albert J. Partoll, ed., "Mengarini's Narrative of the Rockies," in *Frontier Omnibus* (Missoula: Montana State Univ. Press, 1962), 145.

288 Donnelly, ed., *Wilderness Kingdom*, 64.

289 Buckley, ed., *Nicolas Point*, 250. The "letters" that make up the original material by Father Point in this study are sixty-five manuscript pages that he had written, corrected, and annotated before his death in 1869. They are on permanent loan to the Gleeson Library, University of San Francisco. Apparently Point was reworking his original journals.

290 The description of the hunt that follows is taken from Donnelly, ed., *Wilderness Kingdom*, 145–63. Point apparently rewrote it from his field notes at Sault-au-Recollet near Montreal after 1859, when the aging priest was composing his *Souvenirs des Montagnes Rocheuses* and embellished his beautiful line drawings with innocent coloring. Father De Smet also had access to Point's notes and confirmed them in his journals and letters.

291 Buckley, ed., *Nicolas Point*, 252. Point wrote that the Pend d'Oreille attack was led by a red-coated woman named Kuilix.

292 Donnelly, ed., *Wilderness Kingdom*, 47.

293 Ibid., 115. James D. Keyser, in his presentation "Reading the Ambrose Ledger: A Blind Test," American Society for Ethnohistory annual meeting, 7 November 1996 in Portland, Oregon, suggests that this document may have been produced by the Salish convert Ambrose. Nicolas (Wolf's Son), who had returned to the Piikani, is another possibility.

294 Donnelly, ed., *Wilderness Kingdom*, 184.

295 Buckley transcribes this name as Itchetles Melakas, which may have been the Salish translation. Niookska-mai'stoiksi might approximate the Blackfoot.

296 Wheeler, William F., "Personal History of Mr. George Weippert, Choteau County, Montana," *Contributions to the Historical Society of Montana* 10 (1940; reprint, Boston: J. S. Canner, and Company, 1966), 247–49. The Bradley MS cited by Ewers, *The Blackfeet*, 66–67, has a somewhat more extravagant version of this episode.

297 Donnelly, ed., *Wilderness Kingdom*, 188.

298 Dempsey, ed., *Rundle Journals*, 162.

299 Ibid., 199.

300 Chittenden and Richardson, eds. *Life, Letters, and Travels*, 2:524, and Denig, *Five Indian Tribes*, both cited in Ewers, "Identification and History of the Small Robes Band," 398.

301 Denig, *Five Indian Tribes*, 148, 163–64. Denig may have merged this episode with an earlier exploit of the war leader Rotten Belly, who was killed in 1834. Denig's account of that event described the double envelopment of a camp of eighty Blackfoot lodges on the Musselshell River in which 100 men were killed, 230 women captured, and 500 horses taken.

302 Buckley, ed., *Nicolas Point*, 271–72.

303 Thwaites, ed., *Oregon Missions*, 29:341–43.

304 Ibid., 29:359–60.

305 The Jesuits baptized ninety-six children and two old men at Big Lake's camp on 20 September 1846, but those records have not been traced. However, the Jesuit Archives at Gonzaga University in Spokane, Washington, has the "Registre des baptemes et Mariages administres sur la terre des Pied-noirs. N. Point missionnaire S. J. Depuis le 29 Septembre 1846 jusque [1847]."

306 McDonnell, ed., "Fort Benton Journal and Fort Sarpy Journal," 239 n. 1, 240 n. 2, 292 n. 205; Larpenteur, *Forty Years*, 207, 225.

307 Thwaites, ed., *Oregon Missions*, 29:364–65.

308 Buckley, ed., *Nicolas Point*, 326.

309 Donnelly, ed., *Wilderness Kingdom*, 114–17. Perhaps Panarkuinimaki is also the medicine man in Donnelly's book (p. 187) whose headdress includes a small bird.

310 This trader was probably Robert Meldrum at Fort Cass, located below the mouth of the Bighorn on the Yellowstone River.

311 Jacqueline Peterson, who recently mounted the De Smet exhibition "Sacred Encounters," located the originals in the Archives des Jesuites, St. Jerome, Quebec. Eleven pages are reproduced in Donnelly, ed., *Wilderness Kingdom*, 96–115.

312 Dempsey, ed., *Rundle Journals*, 264.

313 Ibid., 276–78.

314 Larpenteur, *Forty Years*, 274.

315 Sata performed the role of broker as his father, Wolf's Son, had done and as his grandfather, Kootenai Man, had tried to do from Fort McKenzie in 1833.

316 Larpenteur, *Forty Years*, 234–39.

317 James Teit, "Salishan Tribes of the Western Plateau," *Forty-fifth Annual Report of the United States Bureau of Ethnology* (Washington, D.C.: Government Printing Office, 1930), 364.

318 Ewers, "Identification and History of the Small Robes Band," 398–99.

16 "OUR WOMEN FLATTERED US TO WAR"

319 The phrase "we were fond of war, even our women flattered us to war" originally appeared in J. B. Tyrrell, ed., *David Thompson's Narrative of His Explorations in Western America 1784–1813* (Toronto: Champlain Society, 1916), 339; it was repeated in Oscar Lewis, *The Effects of White Contact upon the Blackfoot Culture, with Special Reference to the Role of the Fur Trade,* Monographs of the American Ethnological Society, no. 6, ed. A. Irving Hallowell (New York: J. J. Augustin, 1939), 50. Reprinted as *The Effects of White Contact upon the Blackfoot Culture, with Special Reference to the Role of the Fur Trade* (Seattle: University of Washington Press, 1973).

320 It was not entirely the marvelous combination of man and horse that brought the native peoples to war games. Archaeologists have unearthed fractured skulls and hacked bones showing how tribal wars roiled in North America long before horses or imported European technology escalated the violence.

321 Frantz and Russell, *Blackfoot Dictionary.*

322 Napoleon A. Chagnon, "Life Histories, Blood Revenge, and Warfare in a Tribal Population," *Science Magazine,* 26 February 1988. The studies of this University of California at Santa Barbara anthropologist show that about half the male Yanomamo Indians of Venezuela have killed someone, and that 70 percent of their people past the age of forty have had a close relative—a parent, child, or sibling—slain.

323 Theodore Binnema, "Old Swan, Big Man, and the Siksika Bands, 1794–1815," *Canadian Historical Review* 77, no. 1 (March 1996): 1–32.

324 Schultz, *Blackfeet and Buffalo,* ix–x, 229–30, 347–50.

325 Donnelly, ed., *Wilderness Kingdom,* 192. The French term means "mock warfare."

326 Buckley, ed., *Nicolas Point,* 288–89.

327 Kane's picture of this war party is now in the National Gallery of Canada. J. Russell Harper, ed., *Paul Kane's Frontier, Including Wanderings of an Artist among the Indians of North America, by Paul Kane* (Austin: Univ. of Texas Press, 1971), 146, 149–51.

Captions

5 There is an interesting question as to the origin of the painted war robe that Prince Maximilian copied at Fort Union on 30 June 1833. It could have belonged to the slain Matsokui or to his companion Kiasax, Blackfeet who were at the post then, but there is a possibility that it was collected the previous year from the delegations that visited during that eventful traveling season. See Davis and Ronnefeldt, *People of the First Man,* 17.

17 PAPER BOUNDARIES

328 Thaddeus A. Culbertson, *Journal of an Expedition to the Mauvais Terres and the Upper Missouri in 1850,* ed., John Francis McDermott (1952; reprint, Fairfield, Wash.: Ye Galleon Press, 1986), 111–12, 115, 134, 137.

329 Doty to Stevens, Fort Benton, 28 December 1853, Indian office records, in Ewers, *The Blackfeet,* 213; McDonnell, ed., "Fort Benton Journal and Fort Sarpy Journal," 2–48.

330 D. D. Mitchell to H. R. Schoolcraft, St. Louis, 26 January 1854, in Henry Rowe Schoolcraft, ed., *Information Respecting the History, Condition, and Prospects of the Indian Tribes of the United States* (Philadelphia: Lippincott, Grambo, 1851–57), 685–87.

331 Department of the Interior, Office of Indian Affairs, Secretary of the Interior Rept. 105, 3 May 1855, in 34th Cong., 1st sess., 1855/56, 530–31.

332 Former captain John McClallen attempted in 1807 to effect the suggestions made by Lewis and Clark for promoting peace among the tribes.

333 Ewers, *The Blackfeet*, 215–21; *Treaties and Agreements of the Indian Tribes of the Pacific Northwest* (Washington, D.C.: Institute for the Development of Indian Law, n.d.), 51–55.

334 Father Adrian Hoeken to Rev. Father, Flathead Mission, 15 April 1857 in De Smet, *Oregon Missions*, 311, 317; *Report of the Commissioner of Indian Affairs for 1856*, 75–76, cited in Ewers, *The Blackfeet*, 227.

335 Wilfred P. Schoenberg, *Jesuits in Montana: 1840–1960* (Portland, Ore.: Oregon-Jesuit, 1960), 35–36. The Ulm mission had to be abandoned after the disturbances from the Sun River miners' stampede.

336 Albert J. Partoll, ed., "The Blackfoot Indian Peace Council," in *Frontier Omnibus* (Missoula: Montana State University Press, 1962), 200 n. 15.

337 See Ben Bennet, *Death Too, for the Heavy Runner* (Missoula, Mont.: Mountain Press, 1982). Due to the focus on the Indian wars of the central plains, this—the most tragic of military actions against an unsuspecting community—has been largely overlooked.

338 The epidemic was felt as far north as Edmonton.

339 Hugh A. Dempsey, ed., "Alexander Culbertson's Journey to Bow River," *Alberta Historical Review* 19, no. 4 (autumn 1971): 14.

340 Gerald Friesen, *The Canadian Prairies: A History* (Toronto: Univ. of Toronto Press, 1984), 132–33 n. 6.

341 For an overview of the Canadian treaty process, see Friesen, *Canadian Prairies*.

342 Hugh Dempsey, ed., "The Starvation Year: Edgar Dewdney's Diary for 1879," *Alberta History* 31, no. 1 (winter 1983): 9–12; and 31, no. 2 (spring 1983): 12–15.

343 Hugh A. Dempsey, "Story of the Blood Reserve," in *The Pioneer West*, no. 2 (1920): 1–2 (reprint from *Alberta Historical Review*). The number was 3,300 when they returned in 1881.

Captions

6 Note that the subject is missing three fingers of his right hand, which could be accidental but might represent typical mourning mutilation.

18 JACKALS AND HIDES

344 David A. Dary, *The Buffalo Book: The Full Saga of the American Animal* (Chicago: Swallow Tail Press, 1974).

345 To the consternation of the protein industrialists, many of the cattle that replaced the buffalo died in the winter of 1885.

19 WHITE MAN'S WATER

346 Lavender, *Fist in the Wilderness*, 395–96.

347 John E. Sunder, *Bill Sublette: Mountain Man* (Norman: Univ. of Oklahoma Press, 1959), 124, 132–33.

348 McDonnell, ed., "Fort Benton Journal and Fort Sarpy Journal," 302 n. 281; Donnelly, ed., *Wilderness Kingdom*, 104.

349 The distilling equipment that created problems at Fort Union in 1834 eventually went on to the Red River settlement.

350 Paul E. Sharp, *Whoop-up Country: The Canadian-American West, 1865–1885* (1955; reprint, Norman: Univ. of Oklahoma Press, 1978), 35.

351 Ewers, *The Blackfeet*, 70, 238.

352 Gerald L. Berry, *The Whoop-up Trail* (Lethbridge, Alberta: Lethbridge Historical Society, 1995), 24.

353 W. T. Christie to Hudson's Bay Company Secretary W. G. Smith, Fort Edmonton, 29 June 1870, cited in Ewers, *The Blackfeet*, 255.

20 SHADOWS PASSING

354 Sharp, *Whoop-up Country*, 50.

355 Berry, *Whoop-up Trail*, 14.

356 Frank Gilbert Roe, *The North American Buffalo: A Critical Study of the Species in Its Wild State* (1951; reprint, Toronto: Univ. of Toronto Press, 1970), 309 nn. 135, 137.

21 MANLY-HEARTED WOMEN

357 Southesk, *Saskatchewan and the Rocky Mountains*, 155; Ewers, *The Blackfeet*, 95–96.

358 Oscar Lewis, "Manly-hearted Women among the North Piegan," *American Anthropologist* 3, no. 2 (April/June 1941); Lewis, *Effects of White Contact*, 38–40. Both works are available in Oscar Lewis, *Anthropological Essays* (New York: Random House, 1970).

359 Perhaps the same as *niinawaaki* (queen), *niitaakaopiiwa* (she is living on her own), or *niita'pawooka'pssiwa* (she is truly independent).

360 Ewers, *The Blackfoot*, 98.

361 Lewis, *Anthropological Essays*, 176.

362 Ewers, *The Horse in Blackfoot Indian Culture*, 97, 298–99, 307.

363 Ann Regan of the Minnesota Historical Society examined aspects of the Blackfeet and tourism in a paper, "The Blackfeet and the Bureaucrats," delivered at the twenty-sixth annual conference of the Western History Association in Billings, Montana, 17 October 1986.

22 THREE SUN'S WAR RECORD

364 Brownstone, *War Paint*, examines "the traditional role of pictographic robes in Blackfoot culture," based on the five war histories of eight veteran chiefs of the Blackfeet and Sarcee, collected by the artist Edmund Morris between 1907 and 1911.

365 Schultz, *Blackfeet and Buffalo*, 252–63.

366 Ewers, *The Blackfeet*, 310–11.

367 "Three Suns's War Record (Told by Three Suns)," in Schultz, *Blackfeet and Buffalo*, 264–70.

368 According to Schultz, Three Suns recalled that the Piegans went to winter on the Sun River in autumn 1833. Bear Chief took his forty lodges to Milk (Teton) River, Calf Looking and Big Skunk camped on the Sun River, while Big Lake and Heavy Shield's people lived on the banks of the Missouri. A war party also crossed the mountains to raid the Kalispel and Kutenai.

Most of Bear Chief's band had gone to the Dearborn River to hunt when the fifty-three Crows appeared. The hunters led the Crows to Calf Looking's camp of ten lodges, who spent a long night in terror until Big Lake arrived with two hundred warriors and killed the Crows. The event was believed to have taken place after the Piikani traded on the Big North River (Saskatchewan), but Maximilian keeps the Piikani at Fort McKenzie through August. Hudson's Bay Company records in the north do not show a substantial increase in trade that would confirm this.

369 "Events in the Life of 'Three Suns' (Otherwise Known as Big Nose), Last War Chief of the Piegan Indians, as Portrayed by Him on an Elk Skin," file 8151, Minnesota Historical Society, St. Paul.

370 McDonnell, "Fort Benton Journal and Fort Sarpy Journal," 125, 288 n. 178.

371 McDonnell, "Fort Benton Journal and Fort Sarpy Journal," 274 n. 102, identifies Sitting Woman as a Gros Ventre chief, but this may not be the same individual.

372 Gleaned from Schultz's various retellings of the attack on the family.

373 Schultz, *Blackfeet and Buffalo*, 226–27, 238. It is interesting that the marital incident that required this council was generated by a visiting Blood named Low Horn. His appearance caused him to be known as Handsome Man, and he could not resist meddling with the Piikani women.

374 Schultz's "Starvation Winter (1883–84)" was published in the *Great Falls Tribune*, 18 November 1936, and reprinted in Schultz, *Blackfeet and Buffalo*, 76–81.

375 John Ewers, *The Blackfeet*, 294–95, believes this account grew from Schultz's personal prejudice.

376 Schultz, *Blackfeet and Buffalo*, 76–81.

377 Clark Wissler, "Blackfoot Social Life," in Daniel Hurst Thomas, ed., *Blackfoot Source Book: Papers of Clark Wissler* (New York: Garland Publishing, 1986), 47.

378 The Blackfeet killed two Metis beaver trappers from Fort Union on the Milk River in the fall of 1835. During the winter of 1848/49, they told Charles Larpenteur at Fort Benton that they would kill any beaver trappers they found in the western mountains.

379 Ewers, *The Blackfeet*, 242–43.

380 This impressive record is preserved in the collection of the Minnesota Historical Society, which provided the photograph that illustrates the life of Three Suns. John Ewers kindly provided the information about its location.

381 Gerald A. Diettert, *Grinnell's Glacier: George Bird Grinnell and Glacier National Park* (Missoula, Mont.: Mountain Press, 1992), 61, 67.

382 William E. Farr, *The Reservation Blackfeet 1882–1945: A Photographic History of Cultural Survival* (Seattle: Univ. of Washington Press, 1984); "Agreement with the Indians of the Blackfeet Indian Reservation in Montana [28 September 1895]," in *Treaties and Agreements*, 138–42.

383 Bedford, "Lone Walker," 49.

APPENDIX A

Names of the People

According to Walter McClintock in *The Old North Trail*, Blackfeet did not have names denoting ancestry or family but might pass distinguished names from father to son.[1] Parents asked elders to name children based on physical characteristics, dreams, or medicine animals. It was bad luck to have a young person name a child and bad luck to tell the name. When a boy reached manhood he might change his name to celebrate a valorous deed or notable event. Fathers often named a daughter to commemorate a notable event of the parent's life.

As an example, Kinaksitaki (Little Mountain) had a son named Apesomuckka (Running Wolf), who was later known as Mikskimiksohas (Iron Shirt) and was a member of the Grease Melter's band of the North Piegan. The name Iron Shirt passed to one brother and the name Running Wolf was given to the man known in later life as Natosinnepee (Brings Down the Sun). His son continued the name Running Wolf into the third generation.[2]

Tracking individuals is difficult due to the shifting composition and creation of bands. The Small Robes were once almost large enough to be a separate division. Some bands apparently separated after social or political arrangements became intolerable. The resulting band was sometimes not much bigger than an extended family. Quite likely, the later multiplication of bands reflected the social and cultural pressures on the Piikani. In the Piikani's world of fluid identity, it was easy for outsiders to mistake the name and affiliation of an individual. The Piikani world was not burdened with the absolutes of European culture.

James Gaddy, the earliest Hudson's Bay Company visitor to the Piikani, spent three winters with them. The young clerk David Thompson accompanied Gaddy in 1789. Gaddy did not or could not write, and Thompson mentions only three individuals by name: the old Cree Saukamappee, who was married to a Piegan woman; Sakatoo, the civil chief; and the war chief Kootenae-appe (Kutenai Man). It is disappointing that another Hudson's Bay Company traveler, Peter Fidler, names only two "Pekanow," or Muddy River Indians, during his travels with them from 8 November 1792 until 20 March 1793. These are his protector, Sakatoo, an aging former warrior of about forty-five, and his functionary, A-win. Fidler also mentions the old Cree who had been living with the Muddy River Indians for about twenty-five years.[3] Names are probably missing in these accounts because the traders did not have much command of the language of their hosts. Later accounts, listed here in chronological order, include more names and increasingly detailed descriptions of tribal affiliation, family relationships, and age.

When Duncan McGillivray and David Thompson traveled to the Bow River winter camps between 17 November and 3 December 1800, Thompson noted "Sac-o-tow-wow" as the Piikani principal chief and Old Bear as a useful functionary. Another individual who was mentioned is "Fox Head."[4]

On 19 March 1802, Peter Fidler used his phonetic spelling in making a list of Indians who visited Chesterfield House:[5]

Muddy River Indians
Sin ne pow pin now
Sheeks kin a kn
Oo nis stay akow pe
Imme tow
Ax e pee ta
Sech kin now
Mat ta-pe ow tit che ow, or Mangy Leather
Oo nis stay ma teo ye, or Beaver
Pee tay peet ta
She keech in now
Nin nay pee kos in
Nin now nis tow, or Old Man's Son, Beaver Chieff
Sow ke kin ape pre, or Chief

Oo nis tay kut ta
Na pin oo iso
Sin ne pow too can
Tatche kis stommich's wife
E Man ne tow's wife
Is sag oo mok con, or Old Man Leather
Cuo quy it to pe
E tam ya pe

On 20 March, Fidler added the intermediary called Toby.

Kainaa
Oo to can a poo

Siksika
Ka ap pe pus
Tache kow pe
In noo too mox
Stommix a kew
A pouch kin
Stommix is chis
Nestow oo tan
Ne tan ni
Oo too can a hews,
Stommix is chee
Ki oo six num
Ol nis stew sum
A pee nis stow
On nis tay tachche kay poy

During his stay at Rocky Mountain House in 1806/07, David Thompson mentioned several Piikani:

The Black Bear and two other Peeagans
Tete qui Fleche
Little Iron
Nez Blanc and five others *[who died of the influenza-like disease]*
Kutenae Appe and fourteen family men

Alexander Henry named several Piikani during his stay at Rocky Mountain House in 1810/11:[6]

Black Bear and his brother
Big Throat
Le Borgne *[identified as a Piegan chief]*
Flat Ham
Shaved Head
Haranguer
White Buffalo Robe *[an old man]*
Fox Head
White Head

Names of Muddy River Indians mentioned by Francis Heron in the 1822/23 Chesterfield District Report:[7]

> The Muddy River Indian tribe amount
> to 600 tents and are directed by The Head.
> Chief Bird
> Middle Walker
> One Mountain
> Chief Mountain
> Black Mountain
> Spotted Buffalo
> Old Beaver
> Crow
> Tarrier
> Doctor
> Shield
> White Buffalo
> White Wolf
> Crooked Legs
> Sitting Bear
> Little Horn
> Middle Sitter

Names of Indians who traded at Edmonton House, with dates:

> Man e cape (The Young Man) *[7 November 1826]*[8]
> Parflesh Pasant *[4 August 1828]*[9]
> Stommach-sopeteh (Buffalo Robes Head) *[4 August 1828]*
> Tete que Leve *[4 February 1829]*[10]
> Kot-o-kyai-yu *[a Kutenai]*

Names of individual Piikani whom Karl Bodmer painted at Fort McKenzie between 9 August and 14 September 1833:[11]

> Ninoch-Kiaia (Chief of the Bears)
> *[formerly Ketsepenn-nuka (Spotted Elk)]*
> Natoie-Poochse (Word of Life)
> Tatsicki-Stomick (Middle Bull) *[principal Piegan chief]*
> Mehkskehme-Sukahs (Iron Shirt)
> Hotokaueh-Hoh (Head of Buffalo Skin)
> Pioch-Kiaia (Distant Bear) *[coifed as a medicine-pipe bearer]*
> Homachseh-Katatohs (Great Star) *[implied by Maximilian
> to be Siksika]*
> Homach-Ksachkun (The Great Earth) *[Kutenai; probable
> father of Makuie-Poka]*
> Makuie-Poka (Child of the Wolf) *[Piikani and Kutenai; he
> married a Salish woman]*
> Packkaab-Sachkoma-Poh (Mean or Wicked Boy)
> Kiasax (Bear on the Left) *[married a Hidatsa woman]*
> Matsokui *[killed at Fort Union]*

Bodmer's employer, Prince Maximilian, mentions these "Piekans" either in his field journal, as translated by Dr. Emery Szmrecsanyi, or in his published book:

> Kutonapi [called Blackfoot]
> Tomeksih-Siksinam (The White Buffalo)
> Otsequa-Stomik, an old man
> Natag-Otann, a young man
> Haisikat (The Stiff Foot)
> Little Robe and his horde

The Reverend Robert Rundel baptised nineteen people during his visit to the Highwood, Sly-shooting, and Bow Rivers from 30 May until 6 July 1846. It is impossible to determine their tribal affiliation.

The following is a list of people baptised by Father Nicolas Point during the fall and winter of 1846/47 in the vicinity of Fort Lewis. While there, Father Point baptised 330 boys, 295 girls, 4 men, and 22 women, totaling 651 persons out of a population of over 2,000.

On 20 September, Father Point baptised ninety-six children and two old men in the Big Lake camp. Unfortunately those names were not recorded. Two days later he baptised an old Piikani and renamed him Ignatius Xavier. Baptisms on St. Michel's Day, 29 September 1846, include Pied-noir (Blackfoot) and Gens du Sang (Blood) families, demonstrating the mixture of tribes when the priest first arrived. Thereafter only names of Piegan families are listed. The baptisms at Fort Lewis on and after 29 September generally list, in order, the Christian name of the child, the age, the parents and their tribal affiliation, and, when appropriate, the interpreter or godparent.

The spellings here reflect Father Point's version of the names he heard or my own imperfect reading of those marvelous pages.[12]

Baptisms on 29 September 1846 at Fort Lewis [ages not recorded]:

Nicolas, of Naponsta and Starsits, Pied-noir, Jean Baptiste
    Champaigne, parrain [godparent]
Paul, of Manikapiatos and Nimiske, Pied-noir
Marcel, of Parraskomapi and Sepapiaki, Pieds-noir
Felix, of Sarsky and Arsoiaki, [Gens] du Sang
Jules, of Kaetsawe and Memeskaki, du Sang
Honore, of Starsisekach and Sedski, du Sang
Charles, of Kaetsawa and Nametspicks, du Sang
Michel, of Napensta and Nafarse Ketskah, du Sang
Joseph, of Stominamark and Maeae, Pegane

Alexandre, of Snawarka and Arsewaiaki, du Sang
Pierre, of Kiaessemakay and Matisine, Pegane
Marie and Lucie of Mainkapialos and Natokini, Peid-noir,
    Honore Arnold, parrain
Francoise, of Kaetsekoke and Nametspiks, du Sang
Adele, of Napensta and Aponi, Pied-noir
Adelaide, of Kaetseioke and Nametspiki, du Sang
Agathe, of Kaetseioke and Sinosisaki, du Sang
Julie, of Kaetseoke and Sinosisaki, du Sang
Josephine, of Kaetseoke and Sinosisaki, du Sang
Augustine, of Sikapishe and Saiotekini, Pied-noir
Felicite, of Kaetseloke and Netkosin, du Sang

Father Point baptised 104 Gros Ventre children at Fort Lewis on 13, 14, 15, 17, and 18 October with Jean Baptiste Champaigne and Honore Arnold acting as interpreters/parrains.

Baptisms on 1 November at the Camp de Chasse of the Pied-noir:

Sabas [age] 3, of Stamasorkinas and Nastortopi, Pegane-
    G[reat]. Lac, Gervais Sata, parrain
Justin 1, of Stamasorkinas and Nastortopi
Pierre 1, of Iksoa and Matokisini
Marcellin 2, of Mikaniki and Kitorksini
Lucia 3, of Arsenamarqua and Natokis
Marie Paulina 2, of Arsenamarqua and Pikanaqui
Lucie Marie 2, of Kitsipinnoka and Akoene
Honore 5, of Iksoa and Matokisi
Romain 6, of Mikannima and Kakseka
Aubin 8 mois, of Mastorsealse and Atsenike
Charles 3, of Mikannina and Kaksoaki
Casimir 7, of sans pere connu and Matissini
Thomas 5, of Neksiena and Skorpchini
Eulsgi 6, of Naskapotamiso and Naama
Gregoire 5, of Kotenapi and Kitosksinigue
Longin 5, of Onesta and Skitoisahi
Patrice [specifics not recorded]
Cyrille 5, of Kitepaki and Inoquone

On 8 November at Fort Lewis, Father Point baptised two Gens du Sang and nine Mangeurs de Poisson (Fish Eaters, a Blood band), with Jean Baptiste Deschamps as parrain. The next day at Fort Lewis Isle, at the Fish Eaters camp, he baptised another six children, with Augustine Hamelle assisting him. On the same day at the Fish Eaters camp, Francois Sata also assisted Father Point in baptising a number of children.

Baptisms on 9 November at the Camp des Mangers de Poisson, with Francois Sata:

Jeanne 7, of Sokaiomarqua and Nakamani, Pegane
Francoise 3, of Mikanina and Mokaki
Adele 5, of Kokuitapi and Makakuina
Adeline 6, of Kokuitapi and Matitso
Adelaide 8 mois, of Mikanina and Kaksaquin
Louise 4 mois, of Kotenapi and Itsortssenique
Pauline 5, of Mokuiapokse and Kaetsepenique
Augustine 60, belle mere de Michel Champagne
Marie Baptisee 25, a l'article de la mort, Peganne

Between 8 and 12 December at Fort Lewis Isle, Father Point baptised twenty-one Gens du Sang, thirty-seven Mangers de Poisson, and eighty-one Gros Ventre. He baptised six more children on 20 December at Fort Lewis.

Baptisms on 20 December at Fort Lewis:

Angelique 5 mois, of Augustin Hamel and Sartoxaki, Pegane, called Canadienne, with Pierre Mathieu as parrain

Jacques 4, of Alexandre Culbertson and Natoesepina, du Sang, called Americaine, with Augustin Hamel as parrain

Edouard 8, of Augustin Hamel and Sartoxaki, Pegane, called Canadien, with Joseph Aord as parrain

Etienne 3, of the same parents, with Charles Norke as parrain

Godefroid 3, of the same parents, with Charles Landry as parrain

Julie 2, of Alex. Colberston and Natoesixina, du Sang, called Americaine, with Augustin Hamel as parrain

On 23 December at Fort Lewis, Father Point baptised one child of Pied-noir parents and four of Gens du Sang parentage.

Victoire 1 jour, pere inconu and Somapina

On 27 December, Father Point recorded marriages between fort personnel and native women.

Marriages on 27 December at Fort Lewis:

Marie Nitchetoaka 30, daughter of an infidele homme du sang Le boeuf le long de lecorre and Augustine Caphisee Pegane. She was then married with Michel Champagne, the son of Simon Champagne and Lisette de Makinan of Lachine. Witnesses were Etienne Chauvin and Jacques Berger, Canadiens.

Helene Atoxaki 29, daughter of Pegane parents Scham and Seienike, was married with Augustine Hamel, the son of Augustin Hamel and Marie Louise Lamotte. Witnesses Michel Champagne and Charles Landry, Canadiens.

Helene 18, daughter of Konika and Nemeskie Peganes, was married with Expedien Denoyer, son of Joseph Denoyer and Helene Hunot. Witnesses were Louis Matte and Louis Vachard, Creoles of St. Louis.

Therese Sepsenike 19, daughter of Sonopapine and Senosisaki Peganes, was married to Louis Matte, the son of Ambroise Matte and Therese Robillard, ne a St. Joseph district de Montreal. Witnesses Malken Clark and Louis Vachard.

Veronique Sikitsine 18, daughter of Mistepoko and Matiekistaki Peganes, was married to John Oregon, son of Jacques Oregon and Raphele Martins, Mexicains. Witness Jos. Aord and Carpentier.

Marriage on 30 December:

Marie Louise Stomisses 20, daughter of Sistawana, homme du sang and Anaski Sikane, Pegane, was married with Henri Saulette Aubert, son of Saulette Aubert and [illegible] Cote of Widesoche, Missouri. Witnesses were Michel Champagne and Louis Grangieo.

Marriage on 10 January 1847:

Angelique Apeksistinani, daughter of [illegible] and Spamesepi Peganes, was married to Charles [Moitie]. Witnesses were Louis Matte and Augustin Hamel.

Baptisms on 16 January at Fort Lewis:

Louise, daughter of Lacorn basse chef and Matoisnisque Peganes, Michel Champagne parrain

Jacques 21, son of pere inconnu and Veronique Pika Metif, Joseph Manuel parrain

Baptisms and marriages on 24 January at Fort Lewis:

Michel 4, son CocWatchess and [illegible] Pegane, Michel Champagne parrain

Louise Marie 18, daughter of Mixtaxsmita and Tetes Gros Ventre, married with Jacques Berger, son of Jean Baptise Berger and Lisette Rousselle Canadians. Witnesses Michel Champagne and Henri Sauielle Creole.

Martin 1, son of Oppas and Sata Peganes

Magdeleine Kaemike 27, daughter of Stomixatos and Kokana, Pegane [was apparently baptised and the godparents were Charles Moitie and Angelique Apeksistinani. Magdeleine was then married to Denysvard, the legitimate son of Denysvard and Marie Ignatio-trouhirr, Mexican. The witnesses were Charles Moitie, of St. Louis, and John Manuel, Mexican.]

Louis 2, Koiepoarce and Nomia*[?]* Peganes
Stanislas 2, Snespita and Akokua Peganes
Pierre 2, Sakakina and Korskue Peganes
Marie 1, Koiepaora and Namina Peganes
Louis 6 mos., Saokakine and Sana Peganes
Rosalie 1, Saokakine and Korsakoue Peganes

From 1 to 9 February 1847 at Fort Lewis and in the camps of Depouille de Boeuf and Collieu de Feu, Father Point baptised forty-six Gens du Sang children.

Baptism on 8 February at Fort Lewis:
Isidore 8, Eskimisokasi and *[illegible]* Pegane du Nord

On the same day in the camp of Depouille de Boeuf, Father Point baptised sixteen Gens du Sang.

Baptisms on 9 February at the camp of Collier du Feu:
Jules 6 and Hubert 11, sons of Kishimurquel and Ankasatos, Pegane

Father Point also baptised five more Gens du Sang that day.

Baptism on 10 February at Fort Lewis:
Adelaide 2, Nakomotarke and Arsenic Peganes

On 11 February at the Camp du Chef, Father Point baptised five Gens du Sang children. The next day at the camp of Immoposta[?], he baptised two Pied-noir. On 13 February in the camp of Imasarce, he baptised ten Pied-noir children and one seventy-year-old woman. In total, between 10 and 15 February he baptised thirty-four Pied-noir and Gens du Sang children.

Baptism on 15 February at Sarkakimopi [camp?]:
Marc 2, of Inesteniate and Natsenike, Pegan,
J. B. Champagne parain

Baptisms on 16 February in the camp of Chemise de Fer:
Marcellin 1 and Felix 7, of Chemise de fer
and Nustaps Pegan
Jules 2, of Arsenamarka and Etseptisinai Pegan
Adolphe 3, of Kaeniss and Sepiomosta Pegan
Henry 3, of Kinakokia and Atkospotoanis Pegan
Leopold 6 and Ferdinand 5, of Inarkiae
and Wotkeniskie Pegan
Joseph 1, of Otsekna and Kehistimi Pegan
Lucien 1, of Inarkia and Arsawaia Pegan
Michel 2, of Nepusatos and Akassemmi, Pegan

Gabriel 7, of Maksiepoiss and Xepi, Pegan
Bernard 1 and Sue 5, of Nitenamuka and Sinopetpitaki
Bernardini 1, of Nitenamua and Iniskimi
Lue 5, of Nitenamuka and Sinapapita

On 17 February at Fort Lewis, Father Point baptised four Gens du Sang.

Baptism on 17 February at the camp of the Mangers de Poisson:
Jean 4, of Kassisso and Aessoaki, Pegane

Baptisms on 20 February at Fort Lewis:
Sylvain 6, of Nixistaki and Natoeniskue, Pegane
Paul 1, of Maburkiai and Arsine, Pegane

Baptisms on 22 February at Fort Lewis:
Helene 1, of Aketsike and Mastake, Pegane
Angelique 1, Ninestako and Nistorsis, Pegane

On 23 February at the camp of Cornetane, Gens du Sang chief, Father Point baptised seven Blood children.

Baptism on 26 February at Fort Lewis:
Vincent 3, of Minaesk and Kikiapotta, Pegane

Baptisms on 28 February at Fort Lewis:
Pauline 7, of Soina and Estsepi, Pegane
Julie 1, of Ninaesta and Nekaposte, Pegane

On 1 March at the Fish Eaters camp, Father Point baptised twelve young Gens du Sang.

Baptisms on 7 March at Fort Lewis:
Pierre 3, of Cametsetseca and Sakoechine,
    Pegane. J. B. Deschamp parain
Paul 2, of Cametsetseca and Setski, Pegane
Jean 2, of Omanketsenekue and Natokisa, Pegane
Pauline 4, of Parseniske and Ksistaki, Pegane,
    J. B. Deschamp parain
Josephine 2, of Ktasmksipouarse and Sakoisis, Pegane
Therese 2, of Sipisto and Pitaski, Pegane
Adele 1, of Satsekoski and Naskisi, Pegane
Adeline 2, of Matokampo and Msxiniski, Pegane
Adelaide 3, of Matokampo and Kotsekue, Pegane

Baptisms on 8 March at Fort Lewis:
Maurice 4, of Pitastamike and Essisatos, Pegane
Placide 2, of Pitastamike and Essisatos, Pegane
Julien 3, of Akaetsike and Apetsiorse, Pegane
Joseph 3, of Ninatistamarka and Paiekscnike, Pagane

Baptism on 10 March at Fort Lewis:
Joseph 72, of Ineomarka and Sakoarsina, Pegane de Lecor

Baptisms on 16 March at Fort Lewis:
Nicolas 6, le nom napas ete donne, Pagane
Antoine 7, Sepistokosi and Akekoa, Pegane
Pierre 6, of Sepistokosi and Akuekakate, Pegane
Marie 1, of Aspane and Atsoteaki, Pegane
Therese 3, of Makoiena and Nepsoki, Pegane

Baptisms and marriages on 17 March at Fort Lewis:
Saul 6, of Sepistokosi and Natorkuene, Pegane
Jacques 3, of Sepistokosi and Natorkuene, Pegane
Nicolas Matistena 25, of Natosiste and Nikasse, Pegane,
    mari le meme jour avec Agnes Sako, Pegane, fille
    Nitapaiapi and Soietex, Pegane, baptise cher les bete
    [illegible] en presence de Jean Bte Deschamps et de Jn.
    Bte Champagne.

Baptisms on 19 March at Fort Lewis:
Pierre 3, of Nikotsistami and Nakesis, Pegane, Francise
    Kutpe parain
Paul 2, of Tsikomarkue and Natokine, Pagane
Jean 3, of Omarksipi and Omartakaiaki, Pegane
Nicolas 1, of Omarksipi and Omartakaiaki, Pegane
Jacques, of Nakoiena and Nepissaki,
    Jn. Bte Champagne Parain
Antoine 2, of Apixtimani Skitapi and Ksipsenike, Pagane
Jacques 2, of Kitseponesta and Kspiaoake, Petite tete grise
Andre 5, of Ninastakoie and Akekona, Pegane

Baptisms and marriages on 24 March at Fort Lewis:
Joseph Snepta 35, of Stamitsitkipo and Matista, Pegane du
    Nord, Honore Arnande, parain, and
Marie Sakoesisa 30, of Atsomita and Sika, Pegane du Nord,
    marie le meme jour, witnesses Honore Arnaud et Jn. Bte.
    Champagne, metif.
Pierre 12, of Snepita and Sapapitsoitsaki, Pegane du Nord
Paul 2, of Kaerkinas and Nitsetoaki, Pegane

The following is a list of Piegan leaders who signed the 17 October
1855 treaty at the mouth of the Judith River.[13] Only the English interpretations of these names were published. I have taken the Blackfoot
names from the labels of Gustav Sohon's drawings of the leaders.[14]

Nee-ti-nee, or Ne-tannay (The Only Chief),
    later Stam-yehk-sas-ci-cay (Lame Bull)
Nen-ne-as-ta-cui (Chief Mountain)
In-hus-cay-stamy (Low Horn)

Po-nu-cay-ci-nen-nou (Little Gray Head)
Ou-mah-sis-tsek-se-na-cou (Big Snake)
Ap-ye-cay-e (The Skunk)
Pah-ca-poa-tu-can (The Bad Head)
Kitch-eepone-istah, or Keh-ci-pu-nis-taw (White Buffalo
on a Sidehill)
Su-cou-yaw-u-tany (Heavy Shield), or Ih-ta-tsek-yo-pew
(Middle Cold Sitter)

In another grouping on the treaty:

Running Rabbit
Chief Bear
The Little White Buffalo
The Big Straw

Sohon also made portraits of the following:

Mek-yapy (Red Dye)
Nen-na-i-poh-sy (Chief Talker) [chief of the
Little Robes band]
O-nes-tah-stam-mek (White Bull) [his hairdress shows he
was a medicine-pipe owner]

Two others also pictured by Sohon:

Sakuistan (Heavy Shield) [a Blood warrior]
Cut-te-na-pay [identified as an old Blackfoot chief]

The following is a list of Piegans who, in addition to several Gros
Ventres and Bloods, signed the treaty between the United States and the
Blackfoot Nation of Indians on 16 November 1865 (unratified):[15]

Little Dog
Big Lake
Mountain Chief
White Elk
Bird Chief
Little Wolf
Boy Chief
Heavy Runner
Almost a Dog
Hump of White Cow
Bear Chief
Under Bull
Child of the White Cow
War Eagle Bear
Rising Head
Strangled Wolf
Blackfoot
The Fish Child

There were 222 signers of the treaty at the Blackfoot Agency on 11 February 1887.[16] Agent George Steel attested that the adult male population at the time was 381.[17] The interpretations of these names of chiefs and principal men of the Piegan, Blood, and Blackfoot Nation were made by Will Russell, U.S. Interpreter, and Joseph Kipp, Special Interpreter. James Willard Schultz certified that he wrote the names of these full-blood Indians and mixed-bloods:

Onesta-poka, White Calf
Moksak-atoes, Big Nose
Penoke-moiase, Tearing Lodge
Em-ki-o-toss, Fast Buffalo
Soquee-omuce, Brocky
Si-ee, Crazy Wolf
Kyes-iskee, Curly Bear
Natose-onesta, Big Brave
Nis-atskina, Four Horns
Ap-kichomake, Skunk Cap
Epe-toyese, Shortie
Enouc-kiys, Four Bears
Machee-tometah, Almost a Dog
Nina-kije, Bear Chief Number Two
Kipi-tosorcuts, Kicking Woman
Stoye-ka, Cold Feet
Onesta-pika, White Calf Number Two
Es-suker-kin, Heavy Collar
Ape-cotoye, Hat Tail
Mix-so-atsus, Red Bird Tail
Pa-cops-in-copy, Lazy Man
Ah-co-to-mack, Running in the Road
Ma-qua-is-to-mack, Strangling Wolf
Mo-quee-ma-con, Running Wolf
Ima-ta-oot-a-kan, Dog's Head
Es-soka-a-pish, Heavy Roller
Espi-cooma, Shooting Up
Ah-pas-to-ki, Behind the Ears' Tack
Na-mok-saco-pe, Man Mooring
Ah-cats-e-men, Many Guts
Ah-chista-omue, Running Rabbit
E-sick-katock-a-nacash,
    Chief of the Prairie
Frank Pearson, Pete
Frank Pearson, One Horn
Ne-toot-skenah, Jack
Co-chuck-sin, Fancy Jim
Omuck-emucka, Big Elk

Pone, Paul
Sa-kop-oo-cee, Good Robe Out
Nama, Cross Gun
Heachoa, Left Hand
Aso-kenac, Old Doctor
Ah-ko-su-nats, Many Tail Feathers
Ke-nuck-we-uish-tah, John Power
Stomech-chokos, Bull Calf
Onesta-paka, Jim White Calf
Sepes-tokini, Old Top
Atiopan, Rye Grass
Mash-tana, Crow Chief
Ena-coocum, Chief Coward
Aneshtashlowootan, Calf Shield
Motina, Chief All Over
Emu-ch-konash-ketope,
    Roan Horse Rider
Oo-muck-ootakan, Big Head
Okaneport, Talked About
Keeschicum, Thunder
Six-tux, Bite
Muckaw, Mack
Mik-kimaston, Iron Crow
Upuny, Butterfly
Sah-que-na-mah-ka, Dick
Jack Miller
Passhee, Visitor
Na-makon, Takes a Gun
Alex. Kys
Dick Sandervice
Frank Gardipee
George Star
Alex. Kyo, Junior
John White Calf
Louis Kiyo
Oliver Sanderville
Will Russell
Horace J. Clarke

Tom Kiya
Pete Champagn
Frank Spearson
Apakeok, Spread Out
Spi-yo-quon, Apache Pete
Secuks-stomacks, Proud Bull
Ma-stow-apini, Crow Eyes
Isk-scena, Worm
Kemmuteque, Unlucky
Maginnio
Apashish, Weasel Fat
Akkai, Old Thing
Mexican Joe
Enucsapo, Little Plume
Ah-nis-ta-yee, White Calf Robe
Sap-po-po, Packing Meat
Oc-api-otoss, Many White Horse
Umuk-kikimi, Big Top
Kayotses, Bear's Hand
Sak-potin, Short Hair Robe Out
Nina-stocks, Mountain Chief
Emuc-stomicks, Small Bull
Enua-ota-supse-suk, Buffalo Adviser
Api-si-inum, Black Weasel
Appatappi, Blood Person
Eddie Jack
Anthony
Joe Shorty
Sape-na-machai, Talking Gun at Night
Pa-ute-ta-set-se-co, Billy Kipp
Eneshtonas, Buffalo Shape
Puitianos, Catch One Another
Ock-she-muk, Good Stabber
Slok-to-pochin, Under Swimmer
Piscon, Pound
Mia-apoa-ksis, Drags Blanket
Mexisaspe, Brave Old Man
Stomichhs-quon, Bull Child
Manecupeatush, Bush Medicine
Pete-pepepimi, Spotted Eagle
Essokquaoma-kon, Heavy Runner
E-co-me, Billy Ellis
Si-ichikin, Bear Shoes
Shuatoin-ena, Feather Tail Chief
Men-nase, Berry Carrier
Ma-sum-a-katoosh, Lone Star
Siccim-pistacon, Man Loves Tobacco
Batiste Rondin
See-coor-copatose, Last Star

Peta-ootacon, Eagle Head
Se-coxina, Black Cayote
O-ne-cus-omuch, Antelope Running
Omok-shoqua, Big Road
Nina-emuka, Chief Elk
Peek-shawin, Bird Flies
Peta-peckshina, Poor Eagle
Oksh-ah-wootan, Good Shield
Ne-tana, Lone Chief
Mooe-su-kash, Hairy Goat
Ne-tut-skina, Lone Horn
Ape-naka-peta, Morning Eagle
Espi-cooma, Man Shoot in Air
Enuc-k'yo, Small Bear
E-sta-opata, Man Sits from Them
Six-i-ki-po-ka, Black Foot Child
Stomichs-oopush, Bull's Son
Sick-sucksa, Black Sousee
Shoks-maim, Heavy Gun
Me-ta-nah, Second Lone Chief
Pe-tah, Eagle
Petah-epu, Eagle Talk
Esci-ste-quan, Wolverine
Shut-is-to-pit-qua, Split Ear
Ata-kapis, Yellow Wolf
Abpo-nishta, White Weasel
Na-ta-coo-ce-me-ka, Double Gun
Ah-kutsa, Gambler
Neti-num-echa, Lone Medicine Man
Egosi-petah, Red Eagle
Etos-otocon, Red Head
Sheko-kia, Black Bear
Sepish-loo-atoash, Owl Medicine
Apts-kina, Weasel Horn
Tor-ke-pis, Ear Ring
Moqui-chickin, Wolf Shoe
Kesh-sip-poo-nish-ta,
  Cow Running on Side Hill
Mamck-cupeena, Buck Chief
Mashlanauo-ck, Crow Feather
Sapo-chini, Crow Gut
Lecam-omue, Running Crane Three
Slach-listomik, Under Ball
Mequid-se-sapoop, Red Plume
Apixis, Scabby
Ockshisho, Good Warrior
Ashenasham, Cree Medicine
Petah-pickish, Eagle Rib
Nina-instom, Lodge Pole Chief

Natooup, Medicine Weasel
Ienaquishapoop, Morning Plume
Kishekiw, Sharp
Piutes-ena-mukum,
  Take Guns from Both Sides
Ech-to-ko-pa,
  Man Rides Horse in a Day
Socots, Coat
Acotoka, Side and Side
Es-ta-sha-ko, White Cow Looking
Pin-ti-ah-cocoma, About to Shoot
Su-natsis, Tail Feathers
Na-to-kes-cenupa, Two Fox
Chaco-coomi, Last Shot
Upsha-kini, Arrow Top
Esto-pes-to-muk,
  Wears Hat on Side
Sepiapo, Night Walker
Sumovquotoke, Old Rock
Che-nawape, Old Kayote
Apuk, Broad Back
Nichitap, The Lone Man
Nape-quon, White Man
Cho-que-iscum, Big Spring
Ma-que-apeti, Wolf Eagle
Ochequon, Grebs

Ope-kina, Brain Head
Me-ca-peape, Bad Old Man
Nop-ourcush, White Antelope
Mashtane, Chief Crow
Keapetoon, Temporary Married
Enapitze, Bones
Manashto, Young Crow
Necha-pope, Chief Standing Alone
Estomich-atoosh, Bull Medicine
Spio, Mexican
Massuua, Red Paint
Kutto-macon, Man Who Don't Run
Cava-chish, Bear Leggings
Enucksee, Small Robe
Omucksinstom, Big Pole
Cotta-sucks, Man Don't Go Out
Acadmmon, Man Takes Plenty Arms
Echo-ka-mix, Man Holds a Pipe
Kut-ta-nah, Top Chief
Skikenna-kema, Pities People
She-pe-na-muk, Night Gunman
Pena-tuya-a-muk, Running Fisher
A-cokeya, Plenty Bears
Ma-que-a-koopah, Wolf Child
Oke-shema, Mean Drinker
Meko-kim-namoke, Iron Gun

Only O-nis-tai-po-kah (White Calf) is listed on the Agreement with the Indians of the Blackfoot Indian Reservation in Montana, 26 September 1895.

For an interpretation of the names of the individuals named in the 1907/8 reservation census who received allotments, see Roxanne DeMarce, ed., *Blackfeet Heritage, 1907–1908*.[18]

NOTES

1   Walter McClintock, *The Old North Trail: Life, Legends, and Religion of the Blackfeet Indians* (1910; reprint, Lincoln: Univ. of Nebraska Press, 1968), 395.

2   Ibid., 395–405, 532.

3   Richard Glover, ed., *David Thompson's Narrative, 1784–1813* (Toronto: Champlain Society, 1962), 240, 252; Peter Fidler, *Journal of a Journey over Land from Buckingham House to the Rocky Mountains in 1792 & 3*, ed. Bruce Haig (Lethbridge, Alberta: Historical Research Centre, 1990), 30. The protector is identified by name only in the Buckingham House Journal.

4 Barbara Belyea, ed., *Columbia Journals: David Thompson* (Montreal: McGill-Queen's University Press, 1994), 3, 14–15.

5 Hudson's Bay Company Archives (HBCA), B39/a/2, fol. 94. Provincial Archives of Manitoba, Winnepeg.

6 Elliott Coues, ed., *New Light on the Early History of the Greater Northwest: The Manuscript Journals of Alexander Henry . . . and of David Thompson . . . , 1799–1814* (1897; reprint, Minneapolis: Ross & Haines, 1965), vol. 2, passem.

7 Chesterfield District Report, HBCA, B34/e/4, fol. 2.

8 HBCA, B60/a/24, fol. 7.

9 HBCA, B60/a/26, fol. 8.

10 Ibid., fol. 29.

11 David C. Hunt and Marsha V. Gallagher, annts., *Karl Bodmer's America* (Lincoln: University of Nebraska Press, 1984).

12 Extracted from "Registre des baptemes et Mariages adminsitres Sur la terre des Pied-noirs Par le P. N. Point missionnaire S. J. Depuis le 29 Septembre 1846 jusqua 1847," vol. 1, Fascio X, nos. 1–5, Jesuit Archives, Gonzaga University, Spokane, Wash. Much more work needs to be done in the correction and interpretation of this invaluable insight into the families of the Piikani on the lip of a great change.

13 *Treaties and Agreements of the Indian Tribes of the Pacific Northwest* (Washington: Institute for the Development of Indian Law, n.d.), 54–55.

14 David L. Nicandri, *Northwest Chiefs: Gustav Sohon's Views of the 1855 Stevens Treaty Councils* (Tacoma: Washington State Historical Society, 1986).

15 *Treaties and Agreements*, 73.

16 "Public No. 73, Act to ratify and confirm agreement with Gros Ventre, Piegans, Blood, Blackfoot and River Crow Indians in Montana, 28, 31 December 1886, 21 January 1887, Treaty with 1887 of the above by John V. Wright, Jared W. Daniels and Charles F. Larabee, Commissioners," Report of Negotiations of the Commissioners, February 11, 1887, Special Case no. 144, Indian Official Records, probably in *Reports of the Commissioner of Indian Affairs, 1888*.

17 *Treaties and Agreements*, 138–42.

18 Roxanne DeMarce, ed., *Blackfeet Heritage, 1907–1908* (Browning: Blackfeet Heritage Program, 1980).

APPENDIX B

Counting the Winters of Discontent

In this light brushing of the intensely interesting Piikani winter counts—
personal histories painted on animal hides—I hope to demonstrate
how historians might use surviving records to gain a fuller understanding
of this distant people.

The oldest count represented here is the recollection of the third
son of Little Mountain, who was known as Apisio makan (Running Wolf)
for most of his life but historically as Mehkskehme Sukahs (Iron Shirt).
He died in the 1850s as a leader of the Grease Melters and a medicine-
pipe owner. His son, born about 1831, was known as Running Wolf, and
later as Natosi-nepe-e (Brings Down the Sun) when Walter McClintock
met him in about 1911. Later the count was taken over by Bull Plume
(BP), who passed his interpretation of the painted buffalo hide to the
North Piegan missionary Reverend Cannon William Haynes. Haynes's
journal record of Bull Plume's count was preserved at the Fort McLeod
museum, then published by the Oldman River Cultural Centre in 1979.[1]

Another winter count comes from the Piegan Elk Horn (EH). It
begins about 1845 and was collected by David Duvall and Clark Wisler

around 1903. They also published the count of Big Brave (BB), whose recollection spanned sixty-one years.² These two Piikani accounts are compared to one by the Kainaa Bad Head (BH), as published by Hugh Dempsey.³

Winter counts began in October and continued to the next summer. Spring and autumn were white men's concepts that the count keepers seem to have adopted. Remarkably, the emphasis of the counts is less on great matters such as battles, epidemics, and extreme weather than on the experience of the individual. These counts represent personal time, an individual's recollection of his world unburdened by the necessity to mesh with those of others. We modern historians strain, perhaps pointlessly, to fit those lives into our own rigid calendars.

1830/31. When the whites from the south and north met. BP. *[Jacques Berger contacted the Piikani at the mouth of the Bear River.]*

Itsenipitsop: When we were freezing. BH.

1831/32. Kipp/otsitsitawpipi/etotoartay: Kipp/when he lived there/where the rivers meet. BH. *[In October James Kipp established a post at the confluence of the Missouri and Maria Rivers, and the Bloods and Blackfeet began trading robes.]*

1832/33. Otsitsitorkkanipi/omarxistowan/itstoyemix: When he was camped there/Big Knife/where he wintered. BH. *[In July 1832, David Mitchell came to Kipp's old post to build Fort McKenzie.]*

1833/34. When lots of stars fell. BP. *[Brilliant display of meteorites and total eclipse of the sun observed at Fort McKenzie.]*

Kakatosen/otsitsenisipi: Stars/when they fell. BH. *[On the night of 12 November 1833 the Bloods were camped on the Highwood River.]*

1837/38. Year of smallpox. BP.

Apixosin/itspsow/stoyew: Smallpox/when it ended/winter. BH. *[Infection of smallpox brought by the steamer* St. Peters *began in June; about two-thirds of the People (6,000) died. Cold weather helped control it and by spring it had run its course.]*

1838/39. Onistena/otsenitarpi: Calf Chief/when he was killed. BH. *[In spring 1838 at Fort McKenzie, Alexander Culbertson killed a Blood called Big Road.]*

When Bear Moving was bitten by a bear. BP.

1839/40. When Eagle was killed. BP.

1840/41. When Calf Falling was killed. BP.

1841/42. When Crow Moving *[Walking Crow]* and his band were killed by Crows. BP.

1842/43. When many horses died of starvation. BP.

1843/44. Sorkoyenamay/sixika/iteskunakatarpi/napelwam: Big-mouthed gun/ Blackfoot/hunted by/white men. BH.

When the white men shot at Old Sun. BP.

[In spring 1844, Fort McKenzie was abandoned and operations moved to Fort Chardon, near the mouth of the Judith River.]

1844/45. When we fought at the Belly River. BP.

Itayak/etorpommaop: Separated/when we went to trade. BH. *[One party of Bloods went to the British at Rocky Mountain House and the other to the Americans on the Missouri River.]*

1845/46. Gambler killed on war excursion in fall. Piikani wintered on Bear River. BB.

Camped at mouth of river. Gambler killed. Sun dance at Crow Garden. EH.

When the Piegan's line of march was broken by the Sioux *[Crows].* BP. *[This appears to be the attack on the Small Robes band.]*

[In fall 1845, Alexander Culbertson burned Fort Chardon and moved up the Missouri to a place later named Fort Lewis. In May 1846, Fort Lewis was moved to the other side of the river and renamed Fort Benton.]

1846/47. Big Lake of Don't Laugh Band died in fall. Piikani on Bear River where their camps were flooded. Summer sun dance in Sweet Grass Hills. BB.

The Horse *[a prisoner]* slipped out of tent and ran away. BP.

1847/48. Leaves Big Lodge Camp Marks clubbed a Flathead. In summer Piikani kill Sioux on Bear River. BB

The year of stealing horses while they were busy buying in the store *[at Edmonton].* BP.

1848/49. Black Tattoo becomes crazy. In spring Goose killed by Sioux and his father goes on war path and kills Crows. BB.

When the Sioux *[Assiniboine?]* stole many of our horses. BP.

On Bear River, Goose killed. Hunted south of Fort Benton in autumn and traded at the fort. EH.

Nitsto/matapistotsim: Winter/started to move with our camps. BH. *[Bad Head left winter camps and took large band of Bloods to winter near the new Fort Benton.]*

1849/50. Still Smoking killed. Piikani steal sorrel racehorse from Flatheads. Piikani raid south of Missouri and kill a Sioux woman with some whites. BB.

When the Piegans killed fifty Crees *[Assiniboines?]* down in the bottom near Old Agency. BP

Nisitsippi/otsenotsaw/assinay: Fifty/when they were killed/Assiniboines. BH. *[By December 1849, fifty-two Assiniboines had been killed by Blackfeet on the Marias, while the latter lost twenty-five.]*

1850/51. When the Bloods stole many horses from the states. BP.

1851/52. When the river flooded in winter. BP.

1852/53. When Wolf Chief died suddenly. BP.

Itapatorstoyemiw/manistokos: Went north where he wintered/Father of Many Children. BH. *[Bad Head wintered in the northern part of the hunting grounds while the rest of the Bloods and Piegans went to Fort Benton.]*

1854/55. Itaomitaohoyop: When we ate dogs. BH.

1855/56. Fall treaty at mouth of Yellow River. Mountain Chief wintered on Belly River where one of his daughters is burned and died. In summer Mountain Chief has hiccoughs. BB.

When the treaty was first paid. BP.

Nitsitsitorkotspi/ennakex: When we were first paid/soldiers. BH.

1856/57. When the whole prairie was covered with ice. BP.

Itestskarkoy: When we were slipping. BH.

1857/58. Prairie White Man committed murder. BP.

Sawkiapekwan/enitsiw/neetarta-tapekwan: Prairie White Man/killed/Pend d'Oreille Indian *[near present-day Shelby, Montana]*. BH.

1858/59. Lazy Boy killed. Bloods in summer camp at Yellow Mountains quarrel. Calf Shirt killed by his own people. BB.

When the Piegans broke the Kutenai Indian's gun. BP. *[An eleven-day running fight from the foothills near Pincher Creek to the Tobacco Plain described by William T. Hamilton.]*

Itomarkitseskaop: We made a big sweat lodge. BH.

1859/60. South of Missouri, Bloods fight among themselves. First steamboat comes to Fort Benton *[2 July 1860]*. EH.

When Fish Child and Hind Bull, two brothers *[Blackfeet]*, were drunk and killed each other. BP.

1860/61. When Four Horns' scalp was taken off by his own people by mistake. Assiniboine attack on Pend d'Oreille hunting camp driven off by Piikani from nearby camp. BP.

1862/63. When Tattoo *[Tartowa]* went crazy and had to be killed by his two brothers. BP.

Tartowa/otsenitarpi: Tartowa/when he was killed. BH.

1863/64. Eclipse in summer. BP.

1864/65. Smallpox *[sikpixosin: black smallpox or scarlet fever]* killed 1,100 Blackfeet. BP

1865/66. When we sold lots of buffalo hides. BP.

1866/67. When there was a great massacre of Crees. BP. *[A Gros Ventre and Crow army moving toward Cypress Hills ran into Piikani gathering for the sun dance.]*

1867/68. When the Sioux came into camp. BP. *[This event was also recorded on Big Nose's elk skin.]*

1868/69. When all the tribes last made a corral for buffaloes *[near Gleichen, Alberta]*. Smallpox. BP.

1869/70. Piikani have smallpox. Soldiers attack camp of Heavy Runner, killing old men, women, and children. BB.

1870/71. Piikani fight Cree on Belly River, killing a hundred. In summer battle with Assiniboine, Big Brave and his horse are wounded. BB.

When we beat the Crees at Lethbridge. BP.

1875/76. When there were many buffaloes. BP. *[I. G. Baker Company shipped 75,000 robes in the spring.]*

1876/77. Year when all the horses *[of Grease Melters and Bloods]* were frozen to death *[in camp near Sweet Grass Hills].* BP.

1877/78. Treaty Blackfoot Crossing. BP.

1878/79. Mild winter. BP.

1879/80. Deep snow. When they move camp. When the buffalo disappeared. BP.

1880/81. When they built the first houses *[on North Piegan reserve at Brocket, Alberta].* BP.

1881/82. Mange among the horses. BP.

1882/83. When the ration house burned. BP.

NOTES

1   Paul M. Raczka, *Winter Count: A History of the Blackfoot People* (Brocket, Alberta: Oldman River Cultural Centre, 1979).

2   David Hurst Thomas, ed., *A Blackfoot Source Book: Papers by Clark Wissler* (New York: Garland Publishing Inc., 1986), 45-49.

3   "A Blackfoot Winter Count," *Glenbow-Alberta Institute Occasional Paper No. 1* (Calgary: Glenbow-Alberta Institute, 1965), 6-19.

Bibliography

BOOKS

Arima, Eugene Y. *Blackfeet and Palefaces: The Pikani and Rocky Mountain House: A Commemorative History from the Upper Saskatchewan and Missouri Fur Trade.* Ottawa: Golden Dog Press, 1995.

Audubon, Maria R. *Audubon and His Journals.* Vol. 2. Annotated by Elliott Coues. New York: Dover, 1960.

Axtell, James. *The European and the Indian: Essays in the Ethnohistory of Colonial North America.* New York: Oxford University Press, 1981.

Belyea, Barbara, ed. *Columbia Journals: David Thompson.* Montreal: McGill-Queen's University Press, 1994.

Bennet, Ben. *Death Too, for the Heavy Runner.* Missoula, Mont.: Mountain Press, 1982.

Berry, Don. *A Majority of Scoundrels.* New York: Harper & Brothers, 1961.

Berry, Gerald L. *The Whoop-up Trail.* Lethbridge, Alberta: Lethbridge Historical Society, 1995.

Bonner, T. D. *The Life and Adventures of James P. Beckwourth.* 1856. Reprint, New York: Alfred A. Knopf, 1931.

Brownstone, Arni. *War Paint: Blackfoot and Sarcee Painted Buffalo Robes in the Royal Ontario Museum.* Toronto: Royal Ontario Museum, 1993.

Bryan, Liz. *The Buffalo People: Prehistoric Archaeology on the Canadian Plains.* Edmonton: University of Alberta Press, 1991.

Buckley, Cornelius M. *Nicolas Point, S.J.: His Life and Northwest Indian Chronicles.* Chicago: Loyola University Press, 1989.

Camp, Charles L., ed. *James Clyman: Frontiersman.* . . . Portland, Ore.: Champoeg Press, 1960.

Catlin, George. *Letters and Notes on the Manners, Customs, and Condition of the North American Indians.* 2 vols. 1844. Reprint, New York: Dover, 1973.

Champagne, Antoine. *Les La Verendrye et Le Poste de L'Ouest.* Quebec: Les Presses de L'Universite Laval, 1968.

Chittenden, Hiram Martin. *The American Fur Trade of the Far West: A History of the Pioneer Trading Posts and Early Fur Companies of the Missouri Valley and the Rocky Mountains and of the Overland Commerce with Santa Fe.* 2 vols. 1902. Reprint, Lincoln: University of Nebraska Press, 1986.

Chittenden, Hiram Martin, and Alfred Talbot Richardson, eds. *Life, Letters, and Travels of Father Pierre-Jean De Smet, S.J., 1801–1873.* 4 vols. New York: Francis P. Harper, 1905.

Coues, Elliott, ed. *New Light on the Early History of the Greater Northwest: The Manuscript Journals of Alexander Henry . . . and of David Thompson . . . , 1799–1814.* 1897. Reprint, Minneapolis: Ross & Haines, 1965.

Cowie, Isaac. *The Company of Adventurers: A Narrative of Seven Years in the Service of the Hudson's Bay Company during 1867–1874 on the Great Buffalo Plains, with Historical and Biographical Notes and Comments.* Toronto: William Briggs, 1913.

Cox, Ross. *The Columbia River.* Ed. Edgar I. Stewart and Jane R. Stewart. 1831. Reprint, Norman: University of Oklahoma Press, 1957.

Culbertson, Thaddeus A. *Journal of an Expedition to the Mauvais Terres and the Upper Missouri in 1850.* Ed. John Francis McDermott. 1952. Reprint, Fairfield, Wash.: Ye Galleon Press, 1986.

Dary, David A. *The Buffalo Book: The Full Saga of the American Animal.* Chicago: Swallow Tail Press, 1974.

DeMarce, Roxanne, ed. *Blackfoot Heritage, 1907–1908.* Browning, Mont.: Blackfoot Heritage Program, n.d.

Dempsey, Hugh A. "History . . . of Blood Bands." In *Plains Indian Studies: A Collection of Essays in Honor of John C. Ewers and Waldo R. Wedel.* Vol. 30 of *Smithsonian Contributions to Anthropology.* Washington, D.C.: Smithsonian Institution Press, 1982.

———. *Red Crow: Warrior Chief.* Lincoln: University of Nebraska Press, 1980.

———, ed. *The Rundle Journals, 1840–1848.* Calgary: Historical Society of Alberta, 1977.

Denig, Edwin Thompson. *Five Indian Tribes of the Upper Missouri: Sioux, Arickaras, Assiniboines, Crees, Crows.* Ed. John C. Ewers. 1961. Reprint, Norman: University of Oklahoma Press, 1985.

De Smet, P. J. *Oregon Missions and Travels over the Rocky Mountains in 1845-46.* Vols. 27–29 of *Early Western Travels, 1748-1846.* Ed. Reuben Gold Twaites. Cleveland: Arthur H. Clark, 1906.

DeVoto, Bernard. *Across the Wide Missouri.* Boston: Houghton Mifflin, 1947.

Donnelly, Joseph P., trans. *Wilderness Kingdom: Indian Life in the Rocky Mountains, 1840–1847: The Journals and Paintings of Nicolas Point, S.J.* New York: Holt, Rinehart & Winston, 1967.

Elders and Tribal Council, with Walter Hildebrandt, Dorothy First Rider, and Sarah Carter. *The True Spirit and Original Intent of Treaty Seven.* Montreal and Kingston, Ontario: McGill-Queen's University Press, 1996.

Ellison, William Henry, ed. *The Life and Adventures of George Nidever.* Berkeley: University of California Press, 1937.

Ewers, John C. *Artists of the Old West.* Garden City, N.Y.: Doubleday, 1965.

———. *The Blackfeet: Raiders on the Northwestern Plains.* 1958. Reprint, Norman: University of Oklahoma Press, 1985.

———. *Blackfoot Indians: Ethnological Report on the Blackfoot and Gros Ventre Tribes of Indians.* New York: Garland Publishing, 1974.

———. *The Horse in Blackfoot Indian Culture: With Comparative Material from Other Western Tribes.* 1955. Reprint, Washington, D.C.: Smithsonian Institution Press, 1985.

———, ed. *Adventures of Zenas Leonard, Fur Trapper*. Norman: University of Oklahoma Press, 1959.

Farr, William E. *The Reservation Blackfeet, 1882–1945: A Photographic History of Cultural Survival*. Seattle: University of Washington Press, 1984.

Ferris, Robert G., ed. *Lewis and Clark: Historic Places Associated with Their Transcontinental Exploration (1804–06)*. Washington, D.C.: United States Department of the Interior, National Park Service, 1975.

Ferris, W. A. *Life in the Rocky Mountains: A Diary of Wanderings on the Sources of the Rivers Missouri, Columbia, and Colorado from February, 1830, to November, 1835*. Ed. Paul C. Phillips. Denver: Old West Publishing, 1940.

Fidler, Peter. *Journal of a Journey over Land from Buckingham House to the Rocky Mountains in 1792 & 3*. Ed. Bruce Haig. Lethbridge, Alberta: Historical Research Centre, 1990.

Franchere, Hoyt C., ed. and trans. *The Overland Journal Diary of Wilson Price Hunt*. Ashland, Ore.: Oregon Book Society, 1973.

Frantz, Donald G., and Norma Jean Russell. *Blackfoot Dictionary of Stems, Roots, and Affixes*. 2d ed. Toronto: University of Toronto Press, 1995.

Friesen, Gerald. *The Canadian Prairies: A History*. Toronto: University of Toronto Press, 1984.

Frost, Donald Mckay, ed. *Notes on General Ashley, the Overland Trail and South Pass*. Worcester Mass.: American Antiquarian Society, 1945.

Giraud, Marcel. *The Metis of the Canadian West*. Trans. George Woodcock. 2 vols. 1945. Reprint, Lincoln: University of Nebraska Press, 1986.

Glover, Richard, ed. *David Thompson's Narrative, 1784–1813*. Toronto: Champlain Society, 1962.

Gregg, Josiah. *The Commerce of the Prairies*. Ed. Milo Milton Quaife. 1926. Reprint, Lincoln: University of Nebraska Press, 1967.

Grinnell, George Bird. *Blackfoot Lodge Tales*. 1892. Reprint, Lincoln: University of Nebraska Press, 1966.

Harmon, Daniel Williams. *Sixteen Years in the Indian Country: The Journal of Daniel Williams Harmon, 1800–1816*. Ed. W. Kaye Lamb. Toronto: Macmillan Company of Canada, 1957.

Harper, J. Russell, ed. *Paul Kane's Frontier, Including Wanderings of an Artist among the Indians of North America, by Paul Kane*. Austin: University of Texas Press, 1971.

Harrod, Howard L. *Mission among the Blackfeet*. Norman: University of Oklahoma Press, 1971.

Hays, Carl D. W. "David E. Jackson." In *The Mountain Men and the Fur Trade of the Far West*. Vol. 9. Ed. Leroy H. Hafen. Glendale, Calif.: Arthur H. Clark, 1975.

Henry, Alexander. *Travels and Adventures in Canada and the Indian Territories between the Years 1760 and 1776*. 1808. Reprint, Ann Arbor: University Microfilms, 1966.

Hodge, Frederick Webb, ed. *Handbook of Indians of Canada*. 1913. Reprint, New York: Kraus Reprint Company, 1969.

Humfreville, James Lee. *Twenty Years among our Hostile Indians*. New York: Hunter & Company, 1899.

Hungry Wolf, Adolf. *The Blood People: A Division of the Blackfoot Confederacy: An Illustrated Interpretation of the Old Ways*. New York: Harper & Row, 1977.

Hunt, David C., and Marsha V. Gallagher, annotators. *Karl Bodmer's America*. Lincoln, Nebr.: Joslyn Art Museum, 1984.

Innes, Harold A. *The Fur Trade in Canada*. 1930. Reprint, New Haven: Yale University Press, 1964.

Jackson, John C. *Shadow on the Tetons: David E. Jackson and the Claiming of the American West*. Missoula, Mont.: Mountain Press, 1993.

James, Thomas. *Three Years among the Indians and Mexicans*. 1846. Reprint, Lincoln: University of Nebraska Press, 1984.

Johansen, Dorothy O., ed. *Robert Newell's Memoranda: Travles in the Territory of Missourie; Travles to the Kayuse War; Together with a Report on the Indians South of the Columbia River*. Portland, Ore.: Champoeg Press, 1959.

Johnson, Alice M., ed. *Saskatchewan Journals and Correspondence*. London: Hudson's Bay Record Society, 1967.

Johnson, Donald R., ed. *William H. Gray: Journal of His Journey East, 1836–1837*. Fairfield, Wash.: Ye Galleon Press, 1980.

Josephy, Alvin M., Jr. *Five Hundred Nations: An Illustrated History of the North American Indians*. New York: Alfred A. Knopf, 1994.

———. *The Nez Perce Indians and the Opening of the Northwest*. New Haven: Yale University Press, 1965.

Kelsey, Henry. *The Kelsey Papers*. Ed. Arthur G. Doughty and Chester Martin. Ottawa: Public Archives of Canada, 1929.

Larpenteur, Charles. *Forty Years a Fur Trader on the Upper Missouri: The Personal Narrative of Charles Larpenteur, 1833–1872*. Ed. Milo Milton Quaife. 1933. Reprint, Lincoln: University of Nebraska Press, 1989.

Lavender, David. *The Fist in the Wilderness*. 1964. Reprint, Albuquerque: University of New Mexico Press, 1979.

Lewis, Oscar. *The Effects of White Contact upon the Blackfoot Culture, with Special Reference to the Role of the Fur Trade*. Monographs of the American Ethnological Society, no. 6. Ed. A. Irving Hallowell. New York: J. J. Augustin, 1939.

Lewis, William S., and Paul C. Phillips, eds. *The Journal of John Work*. Cleveland: Arthur H. Clark, 1923.

Linderman, Frank B., and Winold Reiss. *Blackfeet Indians*. St. Paul: Great Northern Railway, 1935.

Mandelbaum, David G. *The Plains Cree: An Ethnographic, Historical, and Comparative Study*. Regina, Saskatchewan: Canadian Plains Research Center, 1979.

Maximilian, Prince of Wied-Neuwied. *Travels in the Interior of North America*. Vols. 22–25 of *Early Western Travels, 1748–1846*. Ed. Reuben Gold Thwaites. Cleveland: Arthur H. Clark, 1906.

McClintock, Walter. *The Old North Trail: Life, Legends, and Religion of the Blackfeet Indians*. 1910. Reprint, Lincoln: University of Nebraska Press, 1968.

McDonald of Garth, John. "Autobiographical Notes." In *Les Bourgeois de la Companie du Nord-ouest: Recits de voyages, lettres, et rapports inedits relatifs au Nord-ouest canadien*. Vol. 2. Ed. Louis F. A. Masson. New York: Antiquarian Press, 1960.

Mengarinni, Gregory. *Recollections of the Flathead Mission. . . .* Ed. and trans. Gloria Ricci Lothrop. Glendale, Calif.: Arthur H. Clark, 1977.

Morgan, Dale L., ed. *The West of William H. Ashley*. Denver: Old West Publishing, 1964.

Morgan, Lewis Henry. *The Indian Journals, 1859–62*. Ed. Leslie A. White. Ann Arbor: University of Michigan Press, 1959.

———. *Systems of Consanguinity and Affinity of the Human Family*. Smithsonian Contributions to Knowledge. Oosterhout N. B., the Netherlands: Anthropological Publications, 1970.

Morton, Arthur S., ed. *The Journal of Duncan M'Gillivray of the North West Company at Fort George on the Saskatchewan, 1794–95*. 1929. Reprint, Fairfield, Wash.: Ye Galleon Press, 1989.

Nasatir, A. P., ed. *Before Lewis and Clark: Documents Illustrating the History of the Missouri, 1785–1804*. 2 vols. 1952. Reprint, Lincoln: University of Nebraska Press, 1990.

Nisbet, Jack. *Sources of the River: Tracking David Thompson across Western North America*. Seattle: Sasquatch Books, 1994.

Oglesby, Richard Edward. *Manuel Lisa and the Opening of the Missouri Fur Trade*. Norman: University of Oklahoma Press, 1984.

Partoll, Albert J., ed. "The Blackfoot Indian Peace Council" and "Mengarinni's Narrative of the Rockies." In *Frontier Omnibus*. Ed. John W. Hakola. Missoula: Montana State University Press, 1962.

Patterson, E. Palmer, II. *The Canadian Indian: A History Since 1500*. Don Mills, Ontario: Collier-Macmillan Canada, 1972.

Peterson, Jacqueline, with Laura Peers. *Sacred Encounters: Father De Smet and the Indians of the Rocky Mountain West*. Norman: University of Oklahoma Press, 1993.

Raczka, Paul M. *Winter Count: A History of the Blackfoot People*. Brocket, Alberta: Oldman River Cultural Centre, 1979.

Ray, Arthur J. *Indians in the Fur Trade: Their Role as Hunters, Trappers, and Middlemen in the Lands Southwest of Hudson Bay, 1660–1870*. Toronto: University of Toronto Press, 1974.

Rich, E. E., ed. *Cumberland House Journals and Inland Journal, 1775–82*. 2 vols. London: Hudson's Bay Record Society, 1951/52.

———, ed. *James Isham's Observations on Hudson's Bay, 1743, and Notes and Observations on a Book Entitled "A Voyage to Hudson's Bay in the Dobbs Galley," 1749*. Toronto: Champlain Society, 1949.

———, ed. *Peter Skene Ogden's Snake Country Journals, 1824–25 and 1825-26*. London: Hudson's Bay Record Society, 1950.

Roe, Frank Gilbert. *The North American Buffalo: A Critical Study of the Species in Its Wild State*. 1951. Reprint, Toronto: University of Toronto Press, 1970.

Rollins, Philip Ashton, ed. *The Discovery of the Oregon Trail: Robert Stuart's Narratives*. New York: Charles Scribner's Sons, 1935.

Ross, Alexander. *Adventures of the First Settlers on the Oregon or Columbia River*. Ed. Milo Milton Quaife. 1849. Reprint, New York: Citadel Press, 1969.

———. *The Fur Hunters of the Far West*. Ed. Kenneth A. Spaulding. Norman: University of Oklahoma Press, 1956.

Russell, Dale R. *Eighteenth-Century Western Cree and Their Neighbors*. Hull, Quebec: Canadian Museum of Civilization, 1991.

Russell, Osborne. *Journal of a Trapper, 1834–1843*. Ed. Aubrey L. Haines. Lincoln: University of Nebraska Press, 1965.

Samek, Han. *The Blackfoot Confederacy, 1880–1920*. Albuquerque: University of New Mexico Press, 1987.

Sanderson, James Francis. *Indian Tales of the Canadian Prairies*. Calgary: Historical Society of Alberta, 1965.

Schoenberg, Wilfred P. *A History of the Catholic Church in the Pacific Northwest*. Washington, D.C.: Pastoral Press, 1987.

Schoolcraft, Henry Rowe, ed. *Information Respecting the History, Condition, and Prospects of the Indian Tribes of the United States*. 6 vols. Philadelphia: Lippincott, Grambo & Co., 1851–57.

Schultz, James Willard. *Blackfeet and Buffalo: Memories of Life among the Indians*. Ed. Keith C. Seele. Norman: University of Oklahoma Press, 1962.

———. *Friends of My Life as an Indian*. Boston: Houghton Mifflin, 1923.

———. *My Life as an Indian*. 1907. Reprint, New York: Fawcett Columbine, 1981.

————. *Why Gone Those Times? Blackfoot Tales.* Ed. Eugene Lee Silliman. Norman: University of Oklahoma Press, 1974.

Sharp, Paul E. *Whoop-up Country: The Canadian-American West, 1865–1885.* 1955. Reprint, Norman: University of Oklahoma Press, 1978.

Shimkin, Demetri B. "Eastern Shoshone." *Handbook of North American Indians: Great Basin.* Vol. 10. Washington, D.C.: Smithsonian Institution, 1986.

Smith, G. Hubert. *The Explorations of the La Verendryes in the Northern Plains, 1738–43.* Ed. W. Raymond Wood. Lincoln: University of Nebraska Press, 1980.

Southesk, Earl of (James Carnegie). *Saskatchewan and the Rocky Mountains in 1859 and 1860.* 1875. Reprint, Rutland, Vt.: Charles E. Tuttle, 1969.

Sunder, John E. *Bill Sublette: Mountain Man.* Norman: University of Oklahoma Press, 1959.

Thistle, Paul C. *Indian-European Trade Relations in the Lower Saskatchewan River Region to 1840.* Winnipeg: University of Manitoba Press, 1986.

Thomas, Daniel Hurst, ed. *A Blackfoot Source Book: Papers of Clark Wissler.* New York: Garland Publishing, 1986.

Thomas, Davis, and Karin Ronnefeldt, eds. *People of the First Man: Life among the Plains Indians in Their Final Days of Glory, the Firsthand Account of Prince Maximilian's Expedition up the Missouri River, 1833–34.* New York: E. P. Dutton, 1976.

Thwaites, Reuben Gold, ed. *The Original Journals of Lewis and Clark.* 1904/5. Reprint, New York: Antiquarian Press, 1959.

Townsend, John K. *Narrative of a Journey across the Rocky Mountains, to the Columbia River (1834).* Vol. 21 of *Early Western Travels, 1748–1846.* Ed. Reuben Gold Thwaites. Cleveland: Arthur H. Clark, 1906.

Treaties and Agreements of the Indian Tribes of the Pacific Northwest. Washington, D.C.: Institute for the Development of Indian Law, n.d.

Tyrrell, J. B., ed. *David Thompson's Narrative of His Explorations in Western America, 1784–1813.* Toronto: Champlain Society, 1916.

————, ed. *Journals of Samuel Hearne and Phillip Turnor.* Toronto: Champlain Society, 1934.

Umfreville, Edward. *The Present State of Hudson's Bay.* London: Charles Stalker, 1790.

Victor, Francis Fuller. *The River of the West.* 1870. Reprint, Columbus, Ohio: Long's College Book Company, 1950.

Wessel, Thomas R. "Political Assimilation on the Blackfoot Indian Reservation, 1887–1934." In *Plains Indian Studies: A Collection of Essays in Honor of John C. Ewers and Waldo R. Wedel.* Vol. 30 of *Smithsonian Contributions to Anthropology.* Washington, D.C.: Smithsonian Institution Press, 1982.

White, M. Catharine, ed. *David Thompson Journals Relating to Montana and Adjacent Regions, 1808–12.* Missoula: Montana State University Press, 1950.

Williams, Glyndwr, ed. *Andrew Graham's Observations on Hudson's Bay, 1767–91.* London: Hudson's Bay Record Society, 1969.

Wissler, Clark, and D. C. Duvall, comps. and trans. *Mythology of the Blackfoot Indians.* 1908. Reprint, with an intro. by Alice Beck Kehoe, Lincoln: University of Nebraska Press, 1995.

Wood, W. Raymond, ed. *The Explorations of the La Verendryes in the Northern Plains, 1738–43* Lincoln: University of Nebraska Press, 1980.

Wood, W. Raymond, and Thomas D. Thiessen, eds. *Early Fur Trade on the Northern Plains.* Norman: University of Oklahoma Press, 1985.

PERIODICALS AND PUBLISHED PAPERS

Baker, T. Lindsay. "Beaver to Buffalo Robes: Transition in the Fur Trade." Parts 1 and 2. *Museum of the Fur Trade Quarterly* 23, no. 1 (spring 1987); no. 2 (summer 1987).

Beattie, Judith Hudson. "Indian Maps in the Hudson's Bay Company Archives: A Comparison of Five Area Maps Recorded by Peter Fidler, 1801–1802." *Archivaria* 21 (winter 1985/86).

Bedford, Denton R. "The Fight at Mountains on Both Sides." *The Indian Historian* 8, no. 2 (spring 1975).

———. "Lone Walker, the Small Robe Chief." *The Indian Historian* 8, no. 3 (summer 1974).

Bell, Charles N., ed. "The Journal of Henry Kelsey (1691–1692), the First White Man to Reach the Saskatchewan from Hudson's Bay." *Historical and Scientific Society of Manitoba Transactions*, no. 4 (1928).

Binnema, Theodore. "Old Swan, Big Man, and the Siksika Bands, 1794–1815." *Canadian Historical Review* 77, no. 1 (March 1996).

Bradley, James H. "Affairs at Fort Benton from 1831 to 1869 from Lieut. Bradley's Journal." *Contributions to the Historical Society of Montana* 3 (1900).

———. "Blackfoot War with Whites." *Contributions to the Historical Society of Montana* 9 (1923).

———. "Characteristics, Habits, and Customs of the Blackfoot Indians." *Contributions to the Historical Society of Montana* 9 (1923).

———. "Establishment of Ft. Piegan as Told to Me by James Kipp." *Contributions to the Historical Society of Montana* 8 (1917).

Burpee, Lawrence J., ed. "An Adventure from Hudson's Bay: The Journal of Matthew Cocking, from York Factory to the Blackfoot Country, 1772-1773." *Proceedings and Transactions of the Royal Society of Canada*, 3d ser., vol. 2, no. 2.

Chagnon, Napoleon A. "Life Histories, Blood Revenge, and Warfare in a Tribal Population." *Science* 239 (26 February 1988).

DeLand, Charles, and Doane Robinson, eds. "The Fort Tecumseh and Fort Pierre Journal and Letterbook." *South Dakota Historical Society Collections* 9 (1918).

Dempsey, Hugh A. "Alexander Culbertson's Journey to Bow River." *Alberta Historical Review* 19, no. 4 (autumn 1971).

———. "A Blackfoot Winter Count." *Glenbow-Alberta Institute Occasional Paper*, no. 1 (1965).

———. "The Starvation Year: Edgar Dewdney's Diary for 1879." Parts 1 and 2. *Alberta History* 31, no. 1 (winter 1983); no. 2 (spring 1983).

———. "Story of the Blood Reserve." *The Pioneer West*, no. 2: 1–2 (1920). Reprint, *Alberta Historical Review* 2, no. 2.

Dunwiddie, Peter W. "The Nature of the Relationship between the Blackfeet Indians and the Men of the Fur Trade." *Annals of Wyoming* 46 (spring 1974).

Edmunds, David. "Blackfoot Military Ascendency on the Northern Plains." *Papers in Anthropology* (University of Oklahoma) 10 (1969).

Ewers, John C. "Food Rationing Is Nothing New to the Blackfeet." *The Masterkey: Quarterly of the Southwest Museum* 18, no. 3 (May 1944).

———. "Identification and History of the Small Robes Band of the Piegan Indians." *Journal of the Washington Academy of Sciences* 36 (15 December 1946).

———. "The Nicolas Point Drawings: A Pictorial Record of Plains and Rocky Mountain Indian Life 150 Years Ago." *Columbia* (fall 1996).

———. "A Unique Pictorial Interpretation Blackfoot Religion in 1846–1847." *Ethnohistory* 18, no. 3 (1971).

———. "Were the Blackfeet Rich in Horses?" *American Anthropologist* 45 (1943).

Flannery, Regina. "The Gros Ventres of Montana." Part 1. *Catholic University of America Anthropological Series* 15 (1953).

Giannettino, Susan. "The Middleman Role in the Fur Trade: Its Influence on Interethnic Relations on the Saskatchewan-Missouri Plains." *Western Canadian Journal of Anthropology* 7, no. 4 (1977).

Grinnell, George Bird. "A White Blackfoot." Parts 1 and 2. *The Masterkey: Quarterly of the Southwest Museum* 46, no. 4 (October-December 1972); 47, no. 1 (January/March, 1973).

Henday, Anthony. "York Factory to the Blackfoot Country: The Journal of Anthony Hendry [sic], 1754–55." Ed. Lawrence J. Burpee. *Proceedings and Transactions of the Royal Society of Canada*, 3d ser., 1, no. 2.

Jackson, John C. "Mapping the Fur Trade: Inland from the Bay." *The Beaver* 72, no. 1 (February/March 1992).

Jenness, Diamond. "The Sarsi Indians of Alberta." *National Museum of Canada Bulletin* 90. Anthropological Series 23 (1938).

Keyser, James D. "A Lexicon for Historic Plains Indian Rock Art: Increasing Interpretive Potential." *Plains Anthropologist: Journal of the Plains Anthropological Society* 32-115 (1987).

———. "The Plains Indian War Complex and the Rock Art of Writing-on-Stone, Alberta, Canada." *Journal of Field Archaeology* 6, no. 1 (1979).

———. "Rock Art of North American Northwestern Plains: An Overview." *Bollettino de Centro Camuno di Studi Preistorici* 25, no. 26 (1990).

———. "Writing-on-Stone: Rock Art on the Northwestern Plains." *Canadian Journal of Archaeology* 1 (1977).

Kroeber, Alfred L. "The Arapaho." Parts 1 and 2. *Bulletin of the American Museum of Natural History* (1902/04).

Lewis, Oscar. "Manly-hearted Women among the North Piegan." *American Anthropologist* 3, no. 2 (April/June 1941).

McClintock, Walter. "Blackfoot Warrior Societies." *Southwest Museum Leaflets* 8.

———. "Painted Tipis and Picture Writing of the Blackfoot Indians." *The Masterkey: Quarterly of the Southwest Museum* 10, no. 59 (July/September 1936).

McDonnell, Anne, ed. "The Fort Benton Journal, 1854–1856, and the Fort Sarpy Journal, 1855–56," *Contributions to the Historical Society of Montana* 10 (1940).

MacLean, John. "Social Organization of the Blackfoot Indians." *Transactions of the Canadian Institute, 1892–93* 4 (1895).

Moodie, D.W., and Barry Kaye. "The Ac Ko Mok Ki Map." *The Beaver* 307, no. 4 (spring 1977).

"More Reports on the Fur Trade." *Missouri Historical Society Glimpses of the Past.* 9, no. 3 (July/September 1942).

Schaeffer, Claude E. "Echoes of the Past on the Blackfoot Reservation: Loretto, the Young Mexican Trapper." *Montana* 2, no. 2 (April 1952).

Sharrock, Susan R. "Crees, Cree-Assiniboines, and Assiniboines: Interethnic Social Organization on the Far Northern Plains." *Ethnohistory* 21, no. 2 (1974).

Smith, Marian W. "War Complex of the Plains Indians." *Proceedings of the American Philosophical Society* 78, no. 3 (1938).

Smyth, David. "Jacques Berger, Fur Trader." *The Beaver* 69, no. 3 (June/July 1989).

———. "The Struggle for the Piegan Trade: The Saskatchewan versus the Missouri." *Montana: The Magazine of Western History* 34, vol. 2 (spring 1984).

Spry, Irene M. "Routes through the Rockies." *The Beaver* (autumn 1963).

Tessendorf, T. C. "Red Death on the Missouri." *The American West* 14, no. 1 (January/February 1977).

Williams, Glyndwr. "The Puzzle of Anthony Henday's Journal, 1754–55." *The Beaver* 309, no. 3 (winter 1978).

Wilson, R. N. "Report on the Blackfoot Tribes." *Report of the 57th Meeting of the British Association for the Advancement of Science,* 1887.

Wissler, Clark. "Ethnographic Problems of the Missouri-Saskatchewan Area." *American Anthropologist* 10 (April 1908).

———. "Material Culture of the Blackfoot Indians." *American Museum of Natural History Anthropological Papers* 5, no. 1.

———. "The Sun Dance of the Blackfoot Indians." *American Museum of Natural History Anthropological Papers* 16, no. 3.

Wood, W. Raymond. "The John Evans 1796–97 Map of the Missouri River." *Great Plains Quarterly* 1, no. 1 (winter 1981).

PUBLIC DOCUMENTS AND UNPUBLISHED SOURCES

Blackfoot Indian Agency records, 1875–1952. Census rolls, 1891/92. RG75, M595, roll 3. National Archives Record Center, Seattle.

Campbell, Robert. "A Narrative of Col. Robert Campbell's Experiences in the Rocky Mountains Fur Trade from 1825 to 1835." MS. Missouri Historical Society, St. Louis.

Denman, C. "Culture Change among the Blackfoot Indians of Montana." Ph.D. diss., University of California, 1968.

Great Britain. Parliament. "Report on the Select Committee on Hudson's Bay Company." *Parliamentary Papers.* 15 (1857). Appendix 2 (D1). SEE 15.394.

Harriot, John Edward. "Memoirs of Life and Adventure in Hudson's Bay Company Territories, 1819–1825." Coe Collection. Yale University Library, New Haven.

Hudson's Bay Company Archives. Post Journals; Post Correspondence Books; London Correspondence Books. Provincial Archives of Manitoba, Winnepeg.

Mayfield, Barbara J. "The North-west Mounted Police and the Blackfoot Peoples, 1874–1884," Master's thesis, University of Victoria, 1979.

McDonald, Archibald. Correspondence. Donald Ross Collection. British Columbia Provincial Archives, Victoria.

McLeod, John. Journals and Correspondence. Donald Ross Collection. British Columbia Provincial Archives, Victoria.

Raynolds, W. F. *Report on the Exploration of the Yellowstone River.* 40th Cong., 1st sess., 1868, H. Doc. 77.

Stevens, Isaac I. *Report of Exploration of a Route for the Pacific Railroad near the 47th and 49th Parallels, from St. Paul to Puget Sound.* Vol. 12. 33d Cong, 1st sess., 1860. S. Doc. 129.

Stuart, John. Letterbook 4. Microfilm. Oregon Historical Society, Portland.

Teit, James. "Salishan Tribes of the Western Plateau." *Forty-fifth Annual Report of the United States Bureau of Ethnology.* Washington, D.C.: GPO, 1930.

Thompson, David. "Rocky Mountain House Journal." Notebook 18, microfilm reel no. 2. Archives of Ontario, Toronto.

Wissler, Clark. "The Blackfoot Indians." *Annual Archaeological Report, Appendix to the Report of the Minister of Education of Ontario,* 1905.

Index

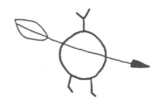

About the Author

A native Oregonian, John C. Jackson traces his Indian ancestry to a band of Kitchesipirini Algonkin who lived on an island in the Ottawa River and were among the first North Americans to experience the tragedy of dispossession. As a boy, listening to the pioneer stories of his grandmother gave Jackson a special appreciation of his Métis heritage, which he later confirmed and further explored through research.

After twenty years as an advertising designer in Portland, Jackson left his career in 1982 to become an independent scholar and author, focusing on the North American fur trade and its impact on native peoples. His first book, *Shadow on the Tetons*, is the only book-length biography of fur trader David Jackson, for whom Jackson Hole is named. *Children of the Fur Trade*, Jackson's second book, examines the Métis of the Pacific Northwest. He is also the author of *A Little War of Destiny* and numerous journal articles.

A member of several historical associations, Jackson is also a board member and active participant in the Kitchen Garden Project, which develops vegetable gardens for low-income people in the lower Puget Sound area. He lives in Olympia, Washington.